Find Your Career With Springer Publishing Company

To learn more and order, visit www.springerpub.com

101 Careers in Social Work

Jessica A. Ritter, BSW, MSSW, PhD, is associate professor and director of the BSW program at Pacific University in Forest Grove, Oregon. Jessica has 20 years of experience as a social worker. She earned a BSW, MSSW, and PhD in social work at the University of Texas at Austin. Her career as a social worker and academic has been dedicated to political advocacy, child welfare, and children's rights. Over the course of her career, she has held a variety of positions at both the micro and macro levels—from working as a caseworker at Children's Protective Services, to working in an administrative capacity in child welfare, to conducting research. Today, her passion includes teaching policy and macro level social work courses with the goal of getting undergraduate social work students excited about social policy, demystifying the political process, increasing students' levels of political efficacy, and inspiring students to be engaged politically. She is a Fulbright scholar and serves on the board of directors of Children First for Oregon.

Halaevalu F. Ofahengaue Vakalahi, BS, MSW, MEd, PhD, is professor and associate dean in the School of Social Work at Morgan State University in Baltimore, Maryland. She is a Pacific Islander, born in Tonga and raised in Hawaii. Her areas of teaching include human behavior and the social environment and social policy. Her research interests include Pacific Islander culture and community, and the experiences of women of color in academia. She received a PhD in social work from the University of Utah, an MSW from the University of Hawaii, a master's in educational administration from the University of Utah, and a BS in business management from Brigham Young University–Hawaii. Prior to Morgan State University, she was an accreditation specialist at the Council on Social Work Education and served on the faculty at San Francisco State University, Brigham Young University–Hawaii, George Mason University, and New Mexico State University.

101 Careers in Social Work

Second Edition

JESSICA A. RITTER, BSW, MSSW, PhD
**HALAEVALU F. OFAHENGAUE VAKALAHI,
BS, MSW, MEd, PhD**

SPRINGER PUBLISHING COMPANY
NEW YORK

Springer Publishing Company, LLC
11 West 42nd Street
New York, NY 10036
www.springerpub.com

Acquisitions Editor: Stephanie Drew
Composition: Amnet

ISBN: 978-0-8261-2905-5
e-book ISBN: 978-0-8261-2906-2

17 18 19 / 9 8 7

The author and the publisher of this Work have made every effort to use sources believed to be reliable to provide information that is accurate and compatible with the standards generally accepted at the time of publication. The author and publisher shall not be liable for any special, consequential, or exemplary damages resulting, in whole or in part, from the readers' use of, or reliance on, the information contained in this book. The publisher has no responsibility for the persistence or accuracy of URLs for external or third-party Internet websites referred to in this publication and does not guarantee that any content on such websites is, or will remain, accurate or appropriate.

Library of Congress Cataloging-in-Publication Data

Ritter, Jessica A.
 101 careers in social work / Jessica A. Ritter, BSW, MSSW, PhD, Halaevalu F. Ofahengaue Vakalahi, BS, MSW, MEd, PhD. — Second Edition.
  pages cm
 Includes bibliographical references.
 ISBN 978-0-8261-2905-5 (print : alk. paper) — ISBN 978-0-8261-2906-2 (e-book)
 1. Social service—Vocational guidance—United States. 2. Vocational guidance—United States. 3. Job hunting—United States. I. Vakalahi, Halaevalu F. Ofahengaue. II. Title. III. Title: One hundred one careers in social work.
 HV10.5.R58 2015
 361.3023'73—dc23

                                                                              2014029367

Printed in the United States of America by McNaughton & Gunn.

This book is dedicated to my wonderful and amazing family who never stop believing in me: my mother, Christina Ritter, for teaching me the meaning of love and compassion and the art of listening; my father, Clinton Ritter, for inspiring my love of politics and the fight for the underdog; and my sister, Alissa Ritter, for being my best friend in this life.

—JAR

To my son Tuihakavalu, the light of my life; and my parents Moana and Faleola Ofahengaue, who inspired me to think and live outside the box in order to achieve my passion in social work.

—HFOV

CONTENTS

Contents

Contents

PREFACE

We were extremely motivated to write this book because there has never been a greater need for smart, competent, and compassionate social workers than right now. There are many pressing social problems at home and around the world. In recent years, we have witnessed the wars in Iraq and Afghanistan, the home mortgage crisis, rising income inequality, Hurricane Sandy and other natural disasters around the world, mass shootings, and a heated political debate surrounding illegal immigration. We know that social workers will continue to be in demand as the aging population grows and as we grapple with the millions of Americans who are unemployed and/or struggling financially while the cost of food, gasoline, and higher education continues to rise. Social workers will also be needed to aid returning American soldiers and their families, many of whom will need medical and mental health services for years to come.

However, despite these challenges, there is hope; many Americans have been galvanized by these issues and want to have their voices heard. The wars in Iraq and Afghanistan are winding down, the Patient Protection and Affordable Care Act is being implemented, and the issue of growing income inequality has found its way into the national discourse. These are exciting times—especially for social workers!

After reading this book, we hope that readers will understand the mission and values of the social work profession and will use this book as a guide to help them assess which field(s) of social work practice might be a good fit for them. We hope they will be inspired by the real stories of social workers from all across the country who are doing exciting and interesting things (see the "Social Worker Spotlights" in Chapters 4 through 17).

Finally, we wrote this book because we are troubled by the idea that very few people "get" the social work profession. The general public has a fairly limited view of what social workers do across this country every day. Many people are familiar with the clinical or direct services work carried out by social workers, but have no idea that there is a "big picture" side to the social work profession and that the mission of the social work profession includes a commitment to social justice. Most do not realize that social workers work with organizations and communities, and in the political and international arenas.

They do not know that social workers are filmmakers and artists and politicians and community activists. We want to educate people about the countless array of options out there for social workers with an earned bachelor's, master's, or doctorate in social work, and inspire them to be very creative in designing their career based on their own unique skills and passions. We hope that after reading this book, you will realize that there is no "typical" social worker—and no "typical" social work career.

ACKNOWLEDGMENTS

We would like to acknowledge the following social workers who shared their inspiring stories with us for the "Social Worker Spotlight" sections of this book:

Elizabeth Alex, MSW

Joel T. Andrade, MSW, LICSW, PhD

Marilyn Peterson Armour, MSW, PhD

Marleine Bastien, BSW, MSW, LCSW

Sheryl Bruno, MSW

Alison Cusick, MSW candidate

Lori Delagrammatikas, MSW/PhD candidate

Odis Dolton, MSSW

Anne Driscoll, LCSW

Johnnie Fielding, MSW

Magda Flores, MSSW

Jacqueline Frausto, BSW, MSSW

Tracy Harris, BSW, MSW, LGSW

Richard B. Joelson, DSW, LCSW

April Kerwin, LCSW, MSW

Mary Kiernan-Stern, MSW, LCSW

Robert Klekar, LCSW, LCDC

Amy Krings-Barnes, BSW, MSW

Kristin Noel Ludwig, MSW

Brandy Macaluso, BSW, CVP

Purnima Mane, MSW, PhD

Sue Matorin, MS, ACSW

Murali D. Nair, PhD

Elliott Naishtat, MSSW, JD

Mary Jane O'Rourke, MSW

Simon Paquette, LCSW, RC

Elaine Charpentier Philippi, BSW, MSW

Juliane Ramic, MSW

Brian Rivers, BSW, LSW

Trina Scordo, MSW candidate

Shana Seidenberg, MSW, LSW

Greg Shufeldt, BSW, MSW

Lyn K. Slater, MA, MSW, PhD

Laura Elmore Smith, LMSW

Erica Solway, MSW, MPH

Cindy Southworth, MSW

Susan Kosche Vallem, EdD, LISW

Agnes Zarcaro, LCSW

I ■ THE PROFESSION OF SOCIAL WORK

1 ■ WHAT IS SOCIAL WORK?

In these times of difficulty, we Americans everywhere must and shall choose the path of social justice, the path of faith, the path of hope, and the path of love toward our fellow man.
—Franklin Delano Roosevelt, October 2, 1932

Congratulations! By picking up this book, you are taking an important step in exploring a career in social work. Perhaps we're a little biased, but we believe that social work is a career for an extraordinary life. This book will help you assess whether social work is for you or, if you have already decided to be a professional social worker, help you decide which specific fields of social work practice are a good fit for your interests, skills, preferences, personality, and—of course—passions! In fact, this book profiles more than 101 different career options for social workers—including classic or traditional social work vocations as well as emerging ones and a few that are somewhat unconventional.

People find their way to social work in many different ways. Some have a close friend or family member who is a social worker and so are somewhat familiar with the kinds of things social workers do. Many have probably seen social workers portrayed in movies, such as *I Am Sam* or *White Oleander*, or in television shows, such as *Grey's Anatomy* or *Judging Amy*. (Unfortunately, many portrayals of social workers in the media are not always accurate or do not give very positive depictions of the profession.) Others find their way to social work because they know that they want to help others or improve society but are not sure what path to go down—perhaps teaching, counseling, psychology, nursing, law, or public policy? Maybe social work? In social work programs, you will find a wide range of students, from young, traditional-aged college students to those who are not so traditional, such as career-changers who want to do something completely different from what they were originally trained to do.

The variety of options available to those who have a social work degree is extremely impressive and is one of the many reasons students choose to pursue a social work degree. If you are looking for a career that is meaningful and challenging—and never boring—social work might be for you. A degree in social work will help you create your own unique career path—one full of exciting possibilities.

SEPARATING THE FACTS FROM THE FICTION

Some say social work is a science, and some say it is an art. We argue that it's both. But after you become a practicing social worker, you quickly learn that most people have a fairly narrow conception of what social workers do and the kinds of jobs they hold. There are also a number of myths about the social work profession. If you want to try an interesting experiment, ask people the following question: "What do social workers do?" The following responses are fairly typical: Social workers "help people"; they "work with abused children and their families"; they "work with poor people who are receiving government benefits." Although these answers aren't wrong, they barely skim the surface when it comes to the options available to those interested in a career in social work, let alone the knowledge and skills required to be a professional social worker.

According to the *Code of Ethics* of the National Association of Social Workers (NASW, 2008), the primary mission of the social work profession is

> [T]o enhance human well-being and help meet the basic human needs of all people, with particular attention to the needs and empowerment of people who are vulnerable, oppressed, and living in poverty. A historic and defining feature of social work is the profession's focus on individual wellbeing in a social context and the wellbeing of society. Fundamental to social work is attention to the environmental forces that create, contribute to, and address problems in living.

One very simple definition of social work is that it is the study of social problems and human behavior. Thus social workers address any number of important social problems in this country and around the world, including, but not limited to

- Poverty and homelessness
- Child abuse, neglect, and exploitation
- Disabilities
- Teen pregnancy, suicide, and other problems facing youth
- Family problems such as poor communication, divorce, and family violence
- Sexual violence
- Depression, anxiety, and other mental health disorders
- Community problems such as crime, substandard schools, violence, and lack of jobs and community resources
- Supporting older adults
- Assisting immigrants and refugees
- Working with individuals diagnosed with chronic or terminal illnesses
- Discrimination against individuals who have been oppressed in U.S. society, such as those living in poverty, women, racial/ethnic minorities, sexual minorities, and those with disabilities
- Substance abuse/addictions
- Crisis intervention (e.g., natural disasters; mass shootings)

Top 7 Myths About the Social Work Profession

Myth #1: Most social workers are employed by the government.

Fact: The majority of social workers work in the private sector for nonprofit organizations, in for-profit settings, and for faith-based organizations. Many are self-employed.

Myth #2: All social workers are poorly paid.

Fact: Although some social workers do receive salaries that are lower than they should be, many social workers are well paid, particularly those who move into administrative or supervisory positions (see individual career chapters for more information about specific salary ranges). Some social work fields, such as medical social work and mental health, pay salaries that are quite competitive. (See Table 1.1 in this chapter, for specific salary information.)

Myth #3: All social workers have stressful jobs.

Fact: Though some social workers, such as child protection caseworkers, have very stressful jobs, many social workers jobs' rate low on the stress scale. However, an important skill for a social worker is self-care to avoid burnout.

Myth #4: Anyone who has a job that involves helping others can be called a "social worker."

Fact: Only those who have earned a degree in social work can call themselves a social worker. In some states, you must also be licensed to use this title.

Myth #5: To do therapy or counseling, you need a degree in psychology or counseling.

Fact: Actually, the majority of mental health practitioners in the United States have a MSW degree and are licensed clinical social workers. Some choose to have a private practice; others work for the government or in a nonprofit or for-profit organization.

Myth #6: Social workers "enable" their clients by solving their problems for them.

Fact: Social workers empower others by providing them with the skills and resources they need to resolve challenging situations and problems.

Myth #7: Social work is "easy," because it deals with "touchy-feely" stuff.

Fact: Though social workers are caring and compassionate individuals, they also need to be intelligent and have strong critical thinking skills to understand research, policy, and the various theories guiding social work practice.

TABLE 1.1 Employment and Median Salary by Type of Social Worker, 2012

	NUMBER OF JOBS	MEDIAN SALARY
Child, family, and school social workers	285,700	$41,530
Health care social workers	185,500	$49,830
Mental health and substance abuse social workers	114,200	$39,980
All other	61,200	$54,560

Source: U.S. Department of Labor, Bureau of Labor Statistics (2014).

Social workers are change agents who work with a wide variety of client populations in a vast array of settings. They work in schools; family violence shelters; adoption agencies; the court system; hospitals and clinics; substance abuse treatment centers; advocacy organizations; government agencies; for-profit, nonprofit, and faith-based organizations; community centers; assisted living and long-term care facilities; homeless shelters; international organizations; and the military. To be able to use the title of social worker, in most states you must have a degree in social work (BSW or MSW) and be licensed by the state. However, after you have met these requirements, your job title may vary depending on your job setting. Common social work job titles include community organizer, mental health clinician or therapist, caseworker/case manager, activist, researcher, professor, program manager/supervisor, and executive director. Social workers also work in the political arena as lobbyists, advocates, and legislative aides. And the best part is that social workers can work with one client population for a number of years, then decide to switch to another field of practice for an exciting new challenge. Have we hooked you yet?

HOW IS SOCIAL WORK DIFFERENT FROM OTHER RELATED PROFESSIONS/DISCIPLINES?

Many are confused about how social work is different from other related professions, such as sociology and psychology, or various degrees in counseling, so we'll help sort this out for you. A number of unique features define the social work profession, setting it apart from other disciplines. One of the most important distinctions is that social workers engage in both *micro- and macropractice*. This means that we work directly with individuals and families but are also concerned with social and political change and working to address pressing social problems at the local, national, and international levels. We are concerned about addressing problems such as discrimination, oppression, and human rights violations, and we work to achieve *social and economic justice*. This means that social workers work toward creating a more just and fair society in which everyone has access to equal opportunity. We care about the problems of poverty and economic inequality and the fact that millions of

Americans do not have access to quality health care and mental health services. In sum, social workers not only help individuals function better within their environment (microsocial work), but also work on changing the environment so that it works better for individuals and families (macrosocial work). This is what we call social work's *person-in-environment* perspective. When social workers are doing an assessment of an individual or family, they must examine the client in the context of the client's social environment. Doing this helps provide a holistic assessment that includes various challenges and opportunities in the client's larger social environment (e.g., family, community).

Table 1.2 shows some of the differences in educational requirements, course work, and focus between social work and related disciplines.

The social work profession has a number of core values that help define and guide our practice. These core values are outlined in the NASW's (2008) *Code of Ethics:* service, social justice, dignity and worth of the person, importance of human relationships, integrity, and competence. You can read the entire Social Worker's *Code of Ethics* at the NASW website, www.socialworkers.org. It outlines the importance of *client confidentiality,* meaning that you cannot share anything a client shares with you without the client's express permission. You also cannot treat someone without his or her *informed consent.* Before agreeing to treatment, clients have the right to be informed about many things, including what the treatment will involve as well as its benefits and risks.

Social workers value *diversity* and are trained to be *culturally competent.* In social work, diversity is broadly defined and encompasses race, culture, religion, gender, age, sexual orientation, and socioeconomic status. When we work with individuals, families, groups, and communities, we operate from a *strengths perspective.* We use interventions that *empower* others to face challenges of daily living. We respect an individual's *right to determine his or her own course of treatment* and to make his or her own decisions, except in cases when he or she is at risk of hurting self or others. We believe that people are *resilient* and *can change* when they have the will and the necessary knowledge and resources.

Social workers who earn their bachelor's degree in social work (BSW) are trained to be generalist social work practitioners, which means they have the skills required to work with individuals, families, groups, communities, and organizations in a variety of social work and host settings. A host setting is a work setting in which social work is not the primary role or function of the organization, such as a school or hospital. Earning a master's degree in social work (MSW) allows social workers to develop advanced skills and to concentrate or specialize in a specific area of practice (e.g., health/mental health, community practice, aging, children and families). Social workers who earn their doctorate (PhD) pursue careers in research or work as university professors. Anyone interested in pursuing a BSW or MSW degree should ensure that the program he or she attends is accredited by the Council on Social Work Education (CSWE). For more information on social work education and licensure, please see Chapter 3.

TABLE 1.2 Social Work and Related Fields

	SOCIAL WORK	PSYCHOLOGY	SOCIOLOGY	COUNSELING PROGRAMS
Education	Can practice with a bachelor's degree, but many employers prefer a master's degree	Although some jobs are available to those with a master's degree, the PhD is strongly preferred and is required for many jobs as a psychologist	A PhD is required to work as a researcher or university professor, but there are a variety of potential settings for those with a master's degree in sociology	A master's degree is needed; some programs have a special focus such as school counseling, substance abuse, marriage and family, pastoral counseling, etc.
Course Work	Liberal arts perspective; required course work will include policy, human behavior and the social environment, research, practice courses, and elective courses	Specialty areas: clinical psychology, school psychology, cognitive, developmental, neuroscience, social, and personality Heavy focus on research	Courses may include deviance, medical sociology, race, gender, religion, social stratification, organizations, research, social statistics, and the family	Education and training focused on assessment, counseling theory, and individual/group interventions
Primary Focus	Micro- and macropractice; help people with problems of daily living that may require direct intervention or referral; also concerned with social justice and helping clients who are oppressed and living in poverty	Heavy focus on psychological testing, diagnosing client disorders, and providing psychotherapy	Study of human behavior and interactions at the group level and also of the social structure and institutions that humans create Tends to be more of an academic, rather than an applied, profession	Helping people through individual, couples, family, or group therapy

HOW DID SOCIAL WORK BEGIN?

Social work has a rich and colorful history. In 1898, Columbia University became the first school of social work in the United States, marking the beginning of the social work profession. However, many individuals did what we now identify as "social work" before social work was professionalized. Perhaps the most famous example of one of these early social workers is that of Jane Addams, a remarkable woman who founded Hull House in Chicago, a settlement house that provided a wide range of services to recent immigrants in Chicago who were facing serious problems, including exploitation on the job, life in unsafe and overcrowded tenement buildings, poor health, discrimination, child labor, juvenile delinquency, insufficient sanitation, and poverty. The women who worked at Hull House lived in the community where they worked instead of returning to their middle-class communities as was more typical at the time. They also advocated for those that they served, pressuring city leaders to improve the living and working conditions in industrial, urban areas.

The philosophy behind the settlement house movement included many of the hallmarks of the social work profession, including respect for ethnic diversity and customs, valuing community members' taking care of each other, belief in the inherent *dignity and worth of all individuals*, political advocacy, and recognition that poverty and lack of opportunity are often the greatest barriers to success—but are not flaws of one's character.

The social work profession was greatly expanded and legitimized by the presidencies of Franklin Delano Roosevelt (New Deal) and Lyndon Johnson (Great Society) when they significantly expanded the role of the federal government in providing for the social welfare of its citizens. Frances Perkins, a social worker, was the first woman to be appointed to the cabinet of a U.S. president. As President Franklin D. Roosevelt's secretary of labor, Perkins drafted much of the New Deal legislation in the 1940s. In 1955, the NASW was founded, and in 1998, the social work profession celebrated its hundredth birthday!

WHAT IS THE FUTURE OUTLOOK FOR SOCIAL WORKERS?

The job outlook for professional social workers is very good. Unfortunately, because individuals and families will continue to face personal problems and challenges, and because social problems such as poverty, illness, substance abuse, and family violence continue to persist, social workers will be needed. In fact, certain demographic trends—such as the growing number of older Americans (the "graying of America) and the continuing influx of immigrant populations, many of whom will need social services and support—mean that social workers will be in higher demand than ever. The areas of practice that will be most in demand for social workers in the coming years will be working with children and families in a variety of settings, working with individuals who suffer from substance abuse and mental health disorders, and working in the medical field with a variety of populations, including aging adults. Social workers will also be needed to work in advocacy organizations to be a voice for those populations (e.g., children; older adults; lesbian, gay, bisexual, and transgender [LGBT] individuals; low-income individuals) who need advocates in the

A Brief History of the Social Work Profession in the United States

1877 American Charity Organization: First organized attempt to help people with severe social problems.

1886 Settlement House movement begins, the most famous being Hull House in Chicago led by Jane Addams. These settlement houses provide a wide range of services to immigrants and those living in poverty.

1898 Columbia University becomes the first school of social work in the United States.

1916 Social worker Jeannette Rankin becomes the first woman elected to Congress.

1931 Social work pioneer Jane Addams receives the Nobel Peace Prize.

1935 Franklin D. Roosevelt's New Deal: Social Security Act passed, creating a number of important federal social welfare programs (e.g., Social Security, unemployment compensation, public assistance) and a safety net for those below the poverty line. Social worker Frances Perkins serves as FDR's Secretary of Labor.

1952 Council on Social Work Education (CSWE) is formed.

1955 National Association of Social Workers (NASW) is formed.

1965 Lyndon B. Johnson's Great Society and War on Poverty: Many social programs created, including Head Start, food stamp program, VISTA program, Medicare, and Medicaid.

1998 Social work profession celebrates its centennial!

political and legislative arena so that our local, state, and federal legislators will be responsive to their needs.

According to the U.S. Department of Labor (2014), the employment of social workers is expected to increase faster than the average for all occupations in the coming years. The employment of social workers is projected to increase 19% between 2012 and 2022, particularly for those working with older adults, with children and families, and in substance abuse and medical/mental health settings. The growth of health care social workers is expected to be 27%, whereas mental health/substance abuse social workers will grow by 23%, much more quickly than the average. According to the U.S. Department of Labor, social workers held about 607,300 jobs in 2012. Table 1.1 provides a breakdown of social workers by type.

Individuals who have an earned degree in social work are very marketable—employers know that they are trained to be excellent communicators, to be skilled in crisis intervention, to be creative problem solvers, to have good "people skills," and to have a valuable skill set transferable to many work settings.

Social work is a dynamic profession, constantly evolving and growing. The profession has a colorful history and continues to be relevant and vital to many individuals, families, and communities across the country and the globe. It is a noble profession, dedicated to service and social justice. Social workers have a unique mission and value system to help them serve people in need, many of whom are forgotten or invisible to the general public.

One of the most appealing features of the social work profession is that there are so many diverse career options. The possibilities are endless when you consider the variety of roles held by social workers, the diverse range of client populations they work with, and the various work settings open to those who have a BSW or MSW. One of the most distinctive features of social work is how incredibly broad the profession is. This book will profile more than 101 career paths for professional social workers, including a checklist in each career chapter to help you assess which ones might be a good fit for you. Social work is a wonderful career, but it is not for everyone. Chapter 2 will help you assess whether it might be for you. Good luck!

REFERENCES

Code of Ethics of the National Association of Social Workers. (2008). Approved by the 1996 NASW Delegate Assembly and revised by the 2008 NASW Delegate Assembly. Retrieved from www.socialworkers.org/pubs/code/code.asp

U.S. Department of Labor, Bureau of Labor Statistics. (2014). *Occupational outlook handbook, 2014–15: Social workers*. Retrieved from www.bls.gov/ooh/community-and-social-service/social-workers.htm

2 ■ GOT SOCIAL WORK?

Social work is an extraordinary profession, but it is not for everyone. One of the goals of this book is to help you figure out whether a career in social work is a good fit for you. A part of the self-assessment process (discussed in the following section) is determining whether you have the values, ethics, personal characteristics, knowledge, and practice skills necessary for a successful career in social work. For a start, completing a degree in social work will provide you with a foundation of knowledge and practice skills.

IS SOCIAL WORK FOR YOU?

Social work is a demanding but highly rewarding field for those who are willing to accept the call to restore, maintain, and enhance the social functioning of individuals, families, groups, and communities from diverse cultural and economic backgrounds. Grounded in a collective and inclusive paradigm, social workers focus on both the person and environment. This focus on multidimensional individuals and their physical and social environments has increased salience in light of current globally prevailing social and economic crises and injustices.

In assessing your interest in and suitability for social work, consider the following general issues and questions (Morales, Sheafor, & Scott, 2012):

- Commitment to humanity despite challenging social and economic conditions: Are you passionate about social change and social and economic justice? Are you concerned about social problems such as poverty, racism, and inequality? Are you committed to working with people from diverse backgrounds to enhance their social functioning and thus contribute to the betterment of humanity as a whole? Are you resilient and committed to cultivating resilience in others? Do you possess empathy for others? Do you genuinely care about people? Are you willing to advocate for the most vulnerable members of our society and connect them to resources necessary for a better life?
- Self-awareness: Are you able or willing to acknowledge and examine your own biases as well as other hindering personal issues, maintaining an open mind toward working with people from diverse backgrounds?
- Adherence to professional values and ethics: Are you willing to adhere to the National Association of Social Worker's (NASW) *Code of Ethics*

and demonstrate commitment to these values and ethics in working with individuals, families, groups, organizations, and communities from diverse backgrounds? Do you possess, or are you willing to develop, the quality of professionalism, being nonjudgmental and accepting of others? Do you believe in the worth and dignity of every human being? Are you willing to grapple with and resolve ethical dilemmas?

■ Commitment to diversity in all its forms: Are you accepting of differences and diversity by race/ethnicity, family background, social economic status, sexual orientation, national origin, immigration status, age, class, disability, gender, and religion?

■ Collaborative working style: In addressing the issue at hand, are you willing to share power and work in partnership with those you serve? Do you acknowledge and engage the experience and expertise of service recipients and providers as crucial in your problem solving processes?

■ Commitment to confidentiality: Are you committed to confidentiality and showing respect for other's rights to privacy? Are you committed to building relationships of trust with others?

■ Superior interpersonal skills: Do you employ, or are you willing to develop, problem-solving and decision-making skills? Are you willing to make hard decisions and follow through with them? Do you have, or are you willing to develop, superior leadership, networking, and teamwork skills that are necessary for effective social work?

■ Excellent analytical and communication skills: Are you willing to develop excellent analytical, organizational, and communications skills to use in your practice with individuals, families, groups, organizations, and communities? Do you have, or are you willing to develop, strong listening and interviewing skills, as well as other skills such as confrontation, support, limit setting, and self-disclosure? Do you have strong problem-solving skills?

■ Flexibility and balance: Can you willingly work unorthodox hours while maintaining a healthy balance between your professional and personal lives? Are you able and willing to undertake multiple tasks and assume awe-inspiring responsibilities?

■ Lifelong learning: Are you committed to lifelong learning, keeping abreast of current literature, evaluating your own practice, and contributing knowledge to the profession? Are you willing to accept criticism and use it for self-improvement and continuous professional growth?

BENEFITS OF A CAREER IN SOCIAL WORK

In 2014, four social work careers were listed in *U.S. News and World Report*'s Best Jobs of 2014: substance abuse counselor, clinical social worker, child and family services social worker, and mental health counselor (*U.S. News and World Report*, 2014); and between 2012 and 2022, the Bureau of Labor Statistics predicts a 19% increase in social work employment growth (U.S. Department of Labor, 2014). One of the greatest benefits is the extensiveness of the profession in terms of career paths and opportunities. One of the most exciting features of social work is that social workers get to work with a wide variety of client populations in a vast array of settings, both public and private, such as schools, criminal justice, health care, child welfare, nonprofit organizations, advocacy organizations, the political arena, international organizations, and mental health facilities, to name just a few.

Unlike other careers, social work provides endless opportunities to advocate for social change and build individual, family, and community capacities. Some social workers are drawn toward working at the micro level with individuals and families; others find it exciting to work on the macro level, engaging with organizations, large systems of care, and communities or working for social or political change. Fundamental to the profession is working toward greater social justice and equality.

In addition, a career in social work provides opportunities for personal and professional growth. Becoming a social worker means having the opportunity to learn about yourself as you grow into your career. You cannot be a competent social worker without engaging in constant self-reflection and personal growth. Because they work with vulnerable populations, social workers must constantly evaluate their work to ensure that they are operating in the best interests of their clients, not serving their own needs. Social workers must have clear boundaries and a strong ethical foundation.

A career in social work is an opportunity to engage in important and meaningful work that is always exciting, interesting, and challenging and never boring. Social work offers the opportunity to work in a community of committed and inspired social workers; experience feelings of gratification in helping others; engage in lifelong learning, including learning to critically think about human behavior and complex social problems; use one's creativity in solving problems; build rewarding relationships with clients and other professionals from diverse backgrounds; and experience career advancement, including supervisory and administrative positions.

CHALLENGES OF A CAREER IN SOCIAL WORK

However, the characteristics that reflect the benefits of social work can also be its greatest challenges. For example, the very nature of the work and interaction with human beings and multiple systems can make a career in this profession challenging. Whether a social worker is working with individuals, families, groups, or communities, helping people with complex psychological, health, social, or financial problems is part of a social worker's normal workday.

This investment in helping people, at the same time dealing with the system in which they work, can be emotionally draining and sometimes result in disappointments with self or clients. The stressful nature of the job emphasizes the absolute necessity of self-care and living a balanced personal and professional life. Likewise, working with people who are troubled or unstable also speaks to safety as a critical issue. Dealing with ethical dilemmas associated with helping people can also be particularly difficult.

Social work is often affected by larger external factors, such as the social, political, and economic climate. In recent years, the United States has experienced an economic crisis, increasing poverty, and high rates of unemployment. The wars in Iraq and Afghanistan have resulted in returning veterans who have a wide range of needs. The rising number of school shootings and other mass shootings brings grief, fear, and uncertainty to many communities. Politically, the country is very divided over the role of government and a host of social issues such as immigration and lesbian, gay, bisexual, and transgender (LGBT) rights. These challenges all affect front-line social workers and must be confronted by the social work profession at large.

Moreover, the ever-changing nature of social work demands that social workers stay effective by keeping abreast of the existing research literature to stay current on the latest knowledge in our field. This requires additional time and effort in education, training, and other professional development endeavors. However, you must be careful not to be trapped in the "perfect social worker" syndrome. There is no perfect social worker—we all make mistakes, and from these mistakes we learn to do our jobs better.

As in other helping professions, such as teaching and nursing, social work continues to advocate for respect as a profession and equity in compensation. The broadness of the profession can present a challenge in unifying social workers who work in increasingly specialized work settings. This makes it tough for social workers to organize as a collective group to advocate for better pay and working conditions. Because such changes are slow at times, it is necessary to be patient and continue to press forward.

THE SOCIAL WORK OATH

Social work is a profession built on professional education, accreditation of social work schools, licensure, ethics, and competencies. This combination contributes rigor to the development and training of new, as well as seasoned, social workers. To this end, social workers adhere to the NASW *Code of Ethics* (National Association of Social Workers, 2008) and the Standards for Cultural Competence in Social Work Practice (National Association of Social Workers, 2001), among other core documents guiding the profession.

The NASW *Code of Ethics* provides the core values, ethical principles, and ethical standards that guide the conduct of social workers. The core values upon which the social work profession is grounded include service, social justice, dignity and worth of the person, importance of human relationships, integrity, and competence. From these core values are ethical principles, which state that social workers help people address social problems, challenge social injustice, promote respect for the inherent dignity and worth of the person, recognize the centrality of human relations, behave in a trustworthy manner, practice within their areas of competence, and continue developing their expertise. Based on these core values and ethics are the standards that guide the professional activities of all social workers. These standards articulate all social workers' ethical responsibilities in practice settings to clients and colleagues, ethical responsibilities as professionals, and ethical responsibilities to the social work profession as well as the broader society.

In addition, to meet the constant changes in demographics in the United States and affirm the ethical responsibility of social workers to be culturally competent in serving diverse populations, the NASW also issued the Standards for Cultural Competence in Social Work Practice (National Association of Social Workers, 2001). These standards define the meaning of cultural competence in social work practice and provide indicators for achievement of such standards through the articulation of social workers' ethics and values, self-awareness, cross-cultural knowledge, cross-cultural skills, service delivery methods, empowerment and advocacy, promotion of diverse workforce, professional education, importance of language diversity, and cross-cultural leadership.

AN INVITATION TO YOU

Because life is complex and complicated, yet precious, there is always a need for dedicated and effective social workers. Social workers are needed by individuals, families, and communities from diverse walks of life. In the words of Lynch and Vernon (2001):

> You'll need a Social Worker . . . when you come into the world too soon; when you can't find anyone to play with; when you are left home alone; when you hate the new baby; when you don't think your teacher likes you; when you are bullied; when you don't want mommy and daddy to divorce; when you miss your big brother; when you don't like how the neighbor touches you; when you get into fights at school; when you don't make the team; when your best friend moves away; when you get poor grades; when you always fight with your siblings; when your friends pressure you to get high; when you can't adjust to the move; when you can't talk to your parents; when you want to quit school; when your friends don't like you anymore; when you didn't want this baby; when you feel like running away; when your friend swallows an overdose; when you are the only one that thinks you're fat; when you can't find someone who speaks your language; when you can't forget the assault; when you can't decide on a career; when your family pressures you to marry; when your boss is hitting on you; when you can't stick to a budget; when you

want to adopt; when you wonder if you are drinking too much; when you think you are neglecting your kids; when you are hated because of who you are; when you lose your baby; when your community has gang problems; when your kids want to live with your ex; when your partner is unfaithful; when you want to meet your birthparent; when your disabled child needs friends; when your step-kids hate you; when your mother won't speak to you; when you just can't face moving again; when your spouse wants a divorce; when you want to be a foster parent; when your city officials don't respond; when your best friend has panic attacks; when you find drugs in your son's room; when your job is eliminated; when your mother-in-law wants to move in; when your neighborhood needs a community center; when you find there is no joy in your life; when your car accident destroys your career; when you sponsor a refugee family; when your legislature passes a bad law; when your brother won't help care for dad; when your partner has a midlife crisis; when you are stressed by menopause; when you are caring for parents and children; when you want to change careers; when you lose your home in a fire; when you are angry all the time; when your nest really empties; when your partner insists you retire; when you can't afford respite care; when you can't find a job and you're sixty; when your kids demand you move in with them; when your daughter suddenly dies; when you are scared about living alone; when you can't drive anymore; when your children ignore your medical decisions; when your retirement check won't pay the bills; when you learn you have a terminal illness; when you need a nursing home.

If you are ready for a challenging and extraordinary professional life, we invite you to consider a career in social work. For most of us, it is a passion—we have never looked back!

REFERENCES

Case Western Reserve University, Mandel School. (2012). *Want to be a social worker? It's one of the best jobs in 2012.* Retrieved from http://blog.case.edu/msass/2012/03/09/want_to_be_a_social_worker_its_one_of_the_best_jobs_in_2012.html

Lynch, D., & Vernon, R. (2001). *Life's challenges—Social workers are there for you.* Retrieved from http://www.ollusa.edu/s/1190/images/editor_documents/You_Need_A_Social_Worker.pdf

Morales, A. T., Sheafor, B. W., & Scott, M. E. (2012). *Social work: A profession of many faces* (12th ed.). Needham Heights, MA: Allyn & Bacon.

National Association of Social Workers. (2008). *Code of ethics.* Washington, DC: Author.

National Association of Social Workers, National Committee on Racial and Ethnic Diversity. (2001). *Standards for cultural competence in social work practice.* Washington, DC: Author.

U.S. Department of Labor, Bureau of Labor Statistics. (2014). *Occupational outlook handbook, 2014-15 edition: Social workers.* Retrieved from http://www.bls.gov/ooh/community-and-social-service/social-workers.htm

U.S. News and World Report. (2014). The best 100 jobs. Retrieved from http://money.usnews.com/careers/best-jobs/rankings/the-100-best-jobs

3 ■ FOLLOW THE YELLOW BRICK ROAD: EDUCATION AND LICENSURE FOR SOCIAL WORKERS

One thing is certain in pursuing a career in social work—you will be taking a clear path of adventure and challenge in completing your professional education toward this goal. In reviewing your educational options, you will realize that there is more than one entry point into the social work profession. For example, some social workers discover early on that they want to be a social worker and major in social work as an undergraduate and then graduate student. Others discover social work after they have pursued a different career path: After working in one career field for a number of years, they decide to apply to graduate school to earn their master's degree in social work (MSW). To give you a clearer picture of what we mean, let us share with you how we came to be social workers.

- Valu began her career by studying business administration as an undergraduate. After working for a while with this degree, she decided to pursue a master's degree in education (MEd). Valu loved working in the educational system and found her business background very helpful in her administrative role. Yet somehow the work wasn't focused enough on Valu's real passion—helping others in more direct ways. So it wasn't too long before Valu returned to graduate school to earn an MSW. Employed as a professional social worker as well as as an educator, Valu later made a career decision to earn a doctorate in social work (PhD) so that she could teach and conduct research in university settings. This way, she would be able to use all her practical experience to contribute to the development of knowledge and skills in the social work profession.
- Jessica always knew she wanted to be a social worker. As an undergraduate, Jessica's college offered a bachelor's degree in social work (BSW), and she was able to begin working in Child Protective Services (micro practice) shortly after graduation. Jessica soon realized she wanted to learn the skills needed to make changes within larger child welfare systems at the macro level. She returned to graduate school and completed her MSW very quickly as an advanced standing student: Having a BSW allowed her to skip the first year of the 2-year master's program. After working in the field with her MSW for a

number of years, she decided to return to school to earn her PhD in social work because she had a new passion for educating students in university social work programs.

WHAT STEPS ARE INVOLVED IN BECOMING A PROFESSIONAL SOCIAL WORKER?

A number of steps are involved before you can become a practicing social worker, but they are very doable. Because social workers often work with vulnerable populations, those who enter the profession must demonstrate the knowledge, skills, values, and ethics necessary to qualify as a practitioner. Clients deserve to have a social worker who is ethical, compassionate, and competent. The following steps are necessary to practice social work in the United States and to use the title "social worker":

■ Earn a BSW or MSW in social work from an accredited social work program.
■ Obtain your state license (not required for all social work jobs; see more on licensing later in this chapter).
■ Get continuing education and training to stay up to date on the latest research and knowledge in your field.

WHAT DEGREE DO I NEED TO BECOME A SOCIAL WORKER?

A BSW prepares an individual to go out into the workforce as a professional with the general knowledge and skills to assist individuals, families, groups, and communities in coping with basic day-to-day problems in living. Thus, those with a BSW are referred to as "generalists." Most BSW undergraduate programs have a liberal arts foundation and offer a number of required courses in beginning-level social work. Accredited BSW programs require students to complete 400 field hours as part of their social work education. This means that students are placed in a social service organization for their "field practicum" and are supervised by a practicing social worker. This is a crucial part of social work education, because students learn a lot in the classroom but they also need to learn through experience. As of June 2014, there were 500 accredited BSW programs in the United States.

Earning an MSW provides you with more advanced and specialized knowledge and skills. Although an MSW is not required for you to be a social worker, most decide to pursue their MSW to acquire a higher level of knowledge and training, and because those who have an MSW are much more desirable to employers. Many social work positions do require an MSW, and these jobs generally pay higher salaries than those only requiring a BSW. Most MSW programs are 2-year programs, and some offer part-time options for working professionals, with online and distance education programs becoming more popular nowadays. However, applicants who have earned their BSW can apply to an advanced standing MSW program that can be completed in only 1 year. Such students can opt out of the first year of the MSW program, already having learned the material in their BSW program. Several universities also offer dual-degree programs that allow you to receive the benefit of earning two graduate degrees—one in social work and the other in a related area, such as law, public health, or public policy. As of June 2014, there were 233 accredited MSW programs in the United States.

Most frequently, a person who pursues a doctoral degree in social work has worked in the field for a number of years. A career path toward the PhD will provide opportunities as a researcher to investigate the causes and solutions of various social problems, as well as the option of teaching in higher education. After becoming experienced as a practicing social worker, a select few will decide to pursue the PhD to become a college professor, driven by their passion for teaching and preparing future social workers. Careers in academia include teaching college classes, producing scholarship, and providing service to the university and community. A doctoral program can take anywhere from 3 to 10 years to complete, depending on the person and other factors. The required course work typically takes 2 years, but the time to complete and write the dissertation study can vary widely. Obtaining a doctorate is a huge commitment, but it can be a wonderful career option for social workers.

As an example, a BSW-prepared worker in a family services agency would be able to help clients find housing or health insurance, make referrals to appropriate community resources, or facilitate a support group for persons returning to employment. An MSW might be the mental health provider to which clients of this agency are referred, or even the supervisor or executive director of the agency. A person who has a PhD could be a college professor researching the causes of homelessness or poor health outcomes for foster youth while also teaching courses to social work students.

WHAT ARE THE PREREQUISITES FOR BEING ACCEPTED TO A SOCIAL WORK PROGRAM?

The Council on Social Work Education (CSWE) website (www.cswe.org) can help you search all accredited colleges and universities that have undergraduate (BSW) and graduate (MSW, advanced standing, and PhD) programs. It is critical that you attend a program that is accredited by CSWE, or you may be limited when it comes to future employment, licensure, and higher education. The Baccalaureate Program Directors website (www.bpdonline.org) includes many links regarding social work educational programs, student resources, and professional issues. The Group for the Advancement of Doctoral Education in Social Work (www.gadephd.org) includes links to doctoral programs and information regarding social work research.

When applying to a specific BSW or MSW program, it is important that you check the website for the specific requirements for admission, which vary from program to program. However, the following are fairly common admission requirements:

- GPA requirement (evidence of academic success)
- GRE (for some MSW programs)
- Experience in, or exposure to, the human services field (employment or volunteer work)
- Alignment with the mission and values of the social work profession
- Sensitivity to issues of human diversity
- Strong personal statement
- Strong letters of recommendation from professors and work/volunteer supervisors
- Certain course work (e.g., human biology, liberal arts foundation)

WHO QUALIFIES AS A SOCIAL WORKER?

Our profession defines a professional social worker as a person who holds a BSW or an MSW from a college or university program that has been accredited by the CSWE. The CSWE sets the educational standards that all educational social work programs must meet to be accredited. In 2008, the CSWE began requiring that accredited social work programs prepare their students to achieve the following 10 competencies:

- Identify as a professional social worker and conduct oneself accordingly.
- Apply social work ethical principles to guide professional practice.
- Apply critical thinking to inform and communicate professional judgments.
- Engage diversity and difference in practice.
- Advance human rights and social and economic justice.
- Engage in research-informed practice and practice-informed research.
- Apply knowledge of human behavior and the social environment.
- Engage in policy practice to advance social and economic well-being and to deliver effective social work services.
- Respond to contexts that shape practice.
- Engage, assess, intervene, and evaluate with individuals, families, groups, organizations, and communities.

The National Association of Social Workers (NASW) is the professional membership organization for social workers in the United States, and the NASW *Code of Ethics* is the universally accepted standard of professional social work behavior. Many states and professional social work organizations have used the NASW *Code of Ethics* as their guide in writing their licensing requirements. According to the U.S. Department of Labor, all states, including the District of Columbia, have some form of licensing or certification requirement for social workers. However, not every state agrees on the definition or requirements for the occupational job title "social worker." The regulation and establishment of licensing standards for many professional occupations is the responsibility of state governments.

WHAT IS THE PURPOSE OF LICENSING?

You may be wondering, "Why it is not enough to earn my degree in social work? Why do I also have to become licensed to practice?" Social work professionals are not alone in being required to obtain a license from the state before they are allowed to practice. Other professions that require licensure include nursing and other medical practice, psychology, law, and still other professions that involve working with people. The primary purpose of licensure is to have a mechanism for protecting clients from unethical or incompetent practitioners.

If a social worker is accused of unethical behavior, for example, an investigation can be completed by the state authorities. If the allegations are true, the social worker's license can be taken away, thereby preventing him or her from continuing in practice. Licensure typically involves passing an exam, paying licensing fees, and undergoing continuing education (earning CEUs). The state has a fundamental interest in protecting the consumer. Having licensed professional social workers at all levels of practice enhances the public's trust in the social work profession and commensurately raises the profession's value to society.

WHAT DO I NEED TO KNOW ABOUT SOCIAL WORK LICENSING?

The Association of Social Work Boards (ASWB) is the professional organization that sets the national standards for licensing examinations. All licensing boards only recognize BSW and MSW degrees from accredited CSWE programs. The ASWB has written a Model Law that many states have adopted as the "best practice" guide in determining the minimum standards to set in protecting the consumer from incompetent practitioners. The licensing exams created by the ASWB ask questions in all areas of social work practice in direct service, administration, social policy, and research. The exams set the minimum competency standards every social worker should meet regarding social work knowledge and skills, as well as values and ethics. The ASWB offers, for a fee, a practice study guide with sample questions for each examination level (see www.aswb.org).

It is important to understand that each state has its own regulatory board for licensing social workers; thus, the licensure process and regulations vary from state to state. There are four categories of practice that states may regulate:

- Bachelor-level exam: To qualify to take this exam, you must have a BSW; in some cases, you may also need post-BSW work experience.
- Master-level exam: An MSW is required to apply for this examination, and you are eligible to take this exam right after graduation.
- Advanced generalist-level exam: An MSW is required, as are 2 years of post-master's work experience. Your work experience only qualifies if you have been supervised by a social work professional licensed at this level or higher.
- Clinical-level exam: An MSW is required, with 2 years' post-master's work experience in direct clinical social work providing assessment, diagnosis, and treatment of mental, emotional, and behavioral disorders, conditions, and addictions. You must have been supervised by a licensed clinical social worker for your work experience to qualify.

IS LICENSING REALLY NECESSARY FOR THE SOCIAL WORK PROFESSION?

Many NASW state chapters support the licensing of all social workers to protect the title of "social worker" as meaning a person who has graduated with a BSW or MSW from an accredited program. This is to ensure that state and local governments and human service agencies cannot hire nonprofessional social workers without our specialized training. One of the benefits of licensure laws is that they often include title protection for social workers. This means that only those who have a degree in social work can call themselves a social worker. One thing that is frustrating to social workers is when the media does a negative story about a "caseworker" who works for the state and refers to him or her as a "social worker" when in reality he or she did not have a degree in social work.

DO ALL SOCIAL WORK JOBS REQUIRE GETTING A LICENSE?

Not all social work positions require a license. In many states, there are "exempted from licensure" settings such as community mental health centers and state agencies. However, many social work professional organizations, including the ASWB, are advocating that all social work positions have some level of licensure. Under the ASWB's Model Law, there are no exempted job settings: The ASWB believes that no consumer should be less protected than another.

Your employer will know what regulations to follow and will be able to tell you whether you need a license, and at what level. A clinical license is always required in any state if you decide to treat people for a mental health condition through the use of psychotherapy as an intervention.

IF I AM LICENSED IN ONE STATE, WILL I BE ABLE TO USE THIS LICENSE IN A DIFFERENT STATE IF I RELOCATE FOR A JOB?

Currently, there is no "reciprocity" between state jurisdictions. If your new job in another state requires a license, you will need to apply to the state board of health or state board of professional occupations. The state board will have all information you require.

If you would like to research the requirements in a particular state before you relocate, the ASWB has complete contact information and a hyperlink to every state licensing board's website where you can find what you need. The ASWB also has a national registry that, for a small fee, will allow you to register all your professional information for each license you hold, making it very convenient for you to apply for a license in a new jurisdiction. See www.aswb.org/licensees/social-work-registry for more information.

WHAT ARE THE DIFFERENCES BETWEEN A LICENSE, A CERTIFICATION, AND A CREDENTIAL?

- A license is the legal authority to practice an occupation or to operate a business.
- Certification typically means that a person has received approved training required for a particular occupation.
- To be licensed as a professional, you must have a credential such as a BSW or MSW. Having additional credentials beyond the BSW or MSW is not required in any state to be licensed as a professional social worker.

AFTER GRADUATION FROM MY UNIVERSITY'S SOCIAL WORK PROGRAM, WILL I BE ABLE TO OBTAIN A LICENSE?

In most regional jurisdictions, graduates from accredited MSW programs will have satisfied the basic academic requirements for a license. In addition to your degree, you may need to meet other requirements, such as work experience providing direct services to individuals, families, and groups. After graduation, you will need to check with the licensing board of the jurisdiction or state in which you are employed to see whether a license is required.

WHERE CAN I LEARN MORE ABOUT THE REQUIREMENTS FOR SOCIAL WORK EDUCATION, SUPERVISION, AND LICENSING?

The following organizations can provide you with specific guidance for their jurisdiction. If the information you obtain from their website is not clear, please contact the licensing board and request assistance from a social work licensing specialist.

Association of Social Work Boards (www.aswb.org)

Council on Social Work Education (www.cswe.org)

National Association of Social Workers (www.socialworkers.org)

POSTSCRIPT

Information and regulations are always subject to change, so ultimately it is each person's responsibility to obtain the information needed for his or her specific circumstance.

II ■ CAREERS IN SOCIAL WORK

4 ■ CAREERS IN CHILD WELFARE

When you ask social work students what they want to do after they graduate, one of the most popular replies is, "I want to work with children and families." According to the U.S. Department of Labor, Bureau of Labor Statistics (2014), almost half of all social workers (47%) are child, family, and school social workers. Most of these social workers will choose to work in programs and agencies that are dedicated to ensuring that families have their basic needs met and that they have access to crucial medical and mental health services. Working in the field of child welfare also includes ensuring that children are safe and protected, helping them thrive at school and at home, and helping families through a crisis.

If you are interested in working with children and families, the good news is that you will have a wide range of options. You can work as a counselor or therapist, a case manager or caseworker, an advocate, or as a program manager or administrator. One thing to keep in mind when working with families as a social worker is that there is no "typical" family structure—you will work with many types of families, including single-parent households, two-parent households, homes with foster or adoptive children, families headed by gay or lesbian parents, children raised by grandparents or other family members, blended families, immigrant families, and families of diverse racial, cultural, and religious backgrounds.

This chapter highlights a number of popular fields of practice for social workers who want to work with children, including child protection, social work in private or nonprofit agencies, child welfare research, careers with the government, child advocacy, adoption, and foster care. However, many other chapters in this book include careers that involve working with children and families (e.g., mental health, medical social work, social work with older adults, criminal justice, school social work), so read on!

CHILD PROTECTION CASEWORKER

Child Protective Services (CPS) caseworkers usually come to mind when people think about various jobs performed by social workers. For obvious reasons, this job is not for everyone. CPS work has a reputation for high rates of burnout due to the intensity of the job and the high caseloads carried by many caseworkers. Nonetheless, it is an extremely important and rewarding career for a social worker. Many dedicated child advocates spend their entire careers working in this system that assists families and protects vulnerable children.

CPS caseworkers, who are employed by the state or local government, are charged with protecting children and making decisions that are in the best interest of the child. It is important to note that CPS workers will not only work with children but they also work with parents or caregivers of the child who may be the source of abuse or neglect. CPS agencies have a dual mission: focusing on protecting children and child safety and at the same time focusing on family preservation and reunifying children with their parents whenever possible. With the passage of the 1997 Adoption and Safe Families Act, there is a much stronger focus on child safety and quickly finding safe, permanent homes for children to prevent them from languishing in the foster care system. As a result, caregivers have a much shorter time frame (typically 12 to 18 months) to work toward having their child(ren) returned to their care and custody.

The CPS investigator, who comes knocking on the door and has the authority to intervene and take someone's child away in very serious cases of abuse and neglect, is the most commonly cited type of CPS caseworker. However, in most CPS offices around the country (with the exception of rural areas), caseworker positions are very specialized, as there are a range of responses that may take place before and after removing children from their home. Examples of CPS caseworker positions are as follows.

Social Worker Spotlight
JESSICA A. RITTER, BSW, MSSW, PhD
Children's Protective Services, Austin, Texas

After graduating with my BSW from the University of Texas at Austin, I accepted a position as a caseworker at CPS. In my first position as a practicing social worker, I worked with the most severe cases of child abuse and neglect, since cases were transferred to me after a child was removed from the home by a CPS investigator. It was my job to work with the family and to make attempts to reunify the family if possible. I set up services for the parents, such as parenting classes, substance abuse treatment, and individual counseling. It was also my job to find a temporary placement for the child, usually with a foster family or relative. I also arranged therapeutic services, if they were needed, for children. I supervised visits between the child and the parents and would get to know everyone in the family very well. I went to court frequently to update the judge on how the case was progressing. When children were not able to be returned home to their parents, I was charged with finding another permanent home for them. The best option was that the child would be adopted by a relative or a new loving family.

What I really loved about my job at CPS as a substitute care caseworker was spending time with the kids on my caseload—trips to McDonald's for ice cream, driving them to appointments, and visiting them in their foster homes. I realized right away how important I was in their lives. I was their link to their families, and I would have major input into deciding where they would end up living permanently. This was a heavy responsibility, and I took it very seriously. I built special relationships with a number of children on my caseload, and I still think about them today and wonder how they are doing. This job was very stressful at times, but I will never regret starting my career at CPS. I learned and grew so much in those years. Not only did I learn about the dynamics of child abuse, I also learned about domestic violence, severe mental illness, poverty, substance abuse, the challenges of parenting, and how the court system works. I could go on and on. What an amazing experience for a beginning social worker!

INTAKE WORKER

Intake workers are charged with taking reports of the abuse, neglect, and exploitation of children, as well as determining if a report meets the legal criteria for child abuse and whether it warrants investigation by a caseworker. In some areas, the intake department is set up in a large room, like a hotline, and caseworkers take calls from individuals around the state who are reporting the abuse, neglect, or exploitation of a child. Calls to report child abuse and neglect are typically routed through the state agency's 1-800 telephone number.

CPS INVESTIGATOR

Investigators talk with the child, parents, and anyone else who may have information about the family to make an informed assessment about the family's functioning, the risk to the child, and to determine whether the child was abused or neglected. It is important to note that children are only removed when there is a reasonable cause to believe there is an immediate danger to their physical health or safety and there is no other way to ensure their safety. CPS investigators often work with families, referring them to community services. They may also refer the case to the family preservation unit at CPS if they are eligible.

FAMILY PRESERVATION CASEWORKER

Family preservation caseworkers provide needed child abuse prevention services to a family to prevent a child from being removed from the home. The services may include counseling for parents and/or the children, parent education, home visits, financial planning, substance abuse treatment, and referrals to other community resources. The relationship with the family is less adversarial, and the family often views the family-preservation caseworker as helpful and supportive, instead of "the bad guy" who wants to take their child away. Some critics of the CPS system believe that CPS should offer more prevention services to families to keep families together and prevent children from entering the custody of the state.

SUBSTITUTE CARE CASEWORKER

Substitute care caseworkers work with families when a child has been removed from the home. After the child is removed by the CPS investigator, the case is transferred to a substitute care caseworker. These caseworkers attempt to reunify the family by providing parents with needed services in the hope that they can be rehabilitated. They are also charged with finding a temporary placement for the child (e.g., foster home, relative, group home, residential treatment center) and ensuring that the educational, medical, recreational, and therapeutic needs of the child are met. If family reunification is not possible, the caseworker will find another permanent home for the child. This plan for permanency may include permanent placement with a relative or family friend or terminating parental rights and placing the child for legal adoption.

FOSTER CARE AND ADOPTION CASEWORKER

Foster care and adoption caseworkers are charged with recruiting, training, and supporting individuals who foster and adopt children. This is an important job because fostering and/or adopting a child who has been abused or neglected can be quite challenging. Depending on how the responsibilities are defined, they may also be responsible for matching children with families and preparing children for adoption. A recent trend is that an increasing number of relatives are adopting children or becoming their legal guardian, thus new programs have been developed to serve these "kinship care" families. Witnessing a happy ending for a child to be wanted and placed in a home for adoption is certainly an upside of this work.

As you can see from these descriptions, career planning and development is possible as caseworkers are able to transition from one position to another using their skills and knowledge base. Some common duties of all CPS caseworkers include case assessment and documentation, supervising visits between parents and children, arranging needed services for children and parents, examining children for abuse and neglect, making home visits, transporting children and parents to needed services and appointments, attending court hearings, working with other professionals on a case (e.g., service providers, psychologists, therapists, attorneys, community volunteers, foster parents), keeping supervisors informed of case progress, and case planning for children and parents.

CAREERS WITH PRIVATE OR NONPROFIT AGENCIES

There are a number of child welfare–related jobs that are located outside of the formal child welfare system. Many of these jobs are with private or nonprofit agencies that contract with CPS to provide services to children and families. Some social workers work in children's advocacy centers, which are charged with conducting forensic interviews of children who have been sexually or physically abused. Social workers are also employed by Court Appointed Special Advocates (CASA), a national organization (with many state and local chapters) that trains members of the community to be advocates for children in CPS custody. Furthermore, social workers are employed in emergency shelters, residential treatment centers, or private foster care agencies where children are placed after they have been taken into custody by CPS. Social workers can also be found in organizations that provide transitional housing or other independent living programs to youth who will "age out" of the foster care system after they reach a certain age or graduate from high school.

CAREERS IN CHILD WELFARE RESEARCH

Some social workers with a strong interest in child welfare choose to work at the macro level by conducting research. They enjoy doing research so that we can better understand the root causes of child abuse and the best way to intervene with children and families. This is how we ensure that the interventions that we use with clients are evidence based. A few of the many questions that can be answered through research include the following: Why do people abuse/neglect their children? What types of children and families are most vulnerable to experiencing child abuse? What types of interventions are most effective when treating abusive parents? Why are children of color overrepresented in the foster care system? How many children experience adoption disruptions? What are the long-term outcomes for youth who emancipate from the foster care system in the United States?

Social workers interested in conducting research typically work for universities, the government, or nonprofit research organizations. Prominent organizations that conduct research in child welfare include the Children's Bureau/Administration for Children and Families, the Child Welfare League of America, Casey Family Programs, Chapin Hall Center for Children (at the University of Chicago), Prevent Child Abuse America, and the American Humane Association.

CAREERS WITH THE GOVERNMENT

Some child welfare social workers who become recognized as experts in their field find themselves working for the government (city, county, state, or federal) after having many years of direct experience in the field. Many states have a Department of Children and Family Services that employs social workers to engage in the important administrative work required to run successful child protection programs. For those interested in working at the federal level, there is the Administration for Children and Families; the Administration on Children, Youth, and Families; and the Children's Bureau; Early Childhood Development, Family and Youth Services Bureau; and Office of Child Care, all under the auspices of the U.S. Department of Health and Human Services. Most of these jobs include working in policy, program planning, or program evaluation. The upside of working in a high-level government job is that it includes good benefits, regular working hours, and often higher salaries because you are recognized as an expert in your field.

CHILD WELFARE ADVOCATE

After gaining a number of years of experience at the micro level, some child welfare social workers choose to move into an advocacy or policy-making role. Social workers interested in advocacy educate the public about children's issues and influence legislators to pass legislation at the local and national level that would benefit children and families. In recent years, child welfare advocates have been successful in getting funding for grandparents raising grandchildren, children who emancipate from the child welfare system, and adoption subsidies for parents who adopt children with special needs. They also urge lawmakers to appropriate more funding to state child welfare systems that tend to be understaffed and underfunded. Social workers interested in this type of work might work for a legislator or an advocacy organization such as the National CASA, the Child Welfare League of America (CWLA), Every Child Matters, Prevent Child Abuse America, or the Children's Defense Fund.

Core Competencies and Skills

- Passion for helping children and families overcome obstacles and thrive
- Excellent risk assessment and decision-making skills
- Sensitive to parents needs as well as children's needs
- Strong interviewing skills and ability to ask sensitive questions
- Assertiveness/firmness/ability to confront others when necessary
- Strong writing skills (e.g., court reports, case documentation, case plans)
- Comfort dealing with conflict and working in an adversarial environment
- Strong rapport with youth of all ages
- Ability to prioritize and multitask
- Strong crisis management and problem-solving skills
- Ability to maintain a balance of objectivity and empathic understanding in dealing with families living in stressful and crisis situations
- Self-care, as this job can be emotionally draining
- Strong verbal communication skills (e.g., meetings with clients, court testimony)
- High degree of cultural sensitivity; can respect various cultural practices of diverse families

Educational and Licensing Requirements

Social workers can be employed at CPS with a bachelor's degree in social work (BSW) or a master's degree in social work (MSW). Many social work education programs across the country receive federal funding to place BSW and MSW students in CPS field placements. This varies by university, but students are usually provided with a generous stipend as well as reimbursement for tuition and fees. In return, students sign an agreement to work at CPS for a certain time period after graduation (at full pay). Likewise, some social work programs receive federal funding that allows current CPS employees to earn their MSW while being employed full time. Again, they will sign an agreement to return to work at CPS for a certain time period after graduation (at full pay).

Unfortunately, because CPS workers around the country are in such high demand, many caseworkers are hired without social work degrees. Because this job requires a high degree of knowledge, skill, and training, candidates with a social work degree or related degree are preferred, and many efforts are being made to increase the number of caseworkers with social work degrees. Having a professional degree ensures that you will be well qualified upon graduation for the demands of such work.

Best Aspects of This Job

- Working with children of all ages from infants to young adults
- Learning about the dynamics of child abuse and neglect as well as a range of other social problems that often contribute to the abuse/neglect of a child (e.g., poverty and homelessness, domestic violence, juvenile justice, substance abuse, mental health issues, severe mental illness)
- Opportunity to work with many types of professionals (e.g., judges, attorneys, therapists, psychologists) and the community resources available to help solve problems
- Extensive learning about children and families; a wonderful job to launch a career in social work. One can do anything after this job!
- Playing an important role in the lives of the children on your caseload
- Being a significant influence on the outcomes of your cases and working in the area of prevention
- Being a witness to many happy endings (e.g., seeing parents make enough progress so that reunification can occur or watching a child get adopted into a wonderful new family)
- Every single day is different; never a boring moment in this job!

Challenging Aspects of This Job

- Seeing the effects of abuse and neglect on children is not easy
- Being caught in a catch 22—CPS divisions are often criticized in the media for either intruding into the lives of families too much or for not intervening promptly enough
- Dealing with criticism and conflict; every day can be stressful
- The heavy burden of being responsible for making decisions that affect the safety of children
- Working with involuntary clients can be challenging
- Because CPS cases often involve volatile or crisis-driven situations in which the child may be taken away, caseworkers must be careful

to assess and guard their own safety. Safety precautions include bringing another caseworker or a police officer with you when you visit someone's home and having your cell phone with you at all times.

- Some CPS agencies are understaffed (though this varies by location). Because CPS agencies are funded by the government, they are at the mercy of legislators who decide how much funding they will receive.
- Working in a system that often does not operate from a strengths perspective and does not allow clients much in the way of self-determination
- The work is stressful and can be emotionally draining. Self-care and having a balanced life is imperative.

Compensation and Employment Outlook

Because CPS workers are employed by local or state governments, they tend to earn higher starting salaries than many other social workers (though this certainly varies by region) and typically receive good benefits. Social workers who have a master's degree usually start at a higher level on the pay scale. Because child abuse and neglect will unfortunately continue to be a problem in this country, there will always be a demand for social workers to work in child protection. As shown in Table 4.1, there are a wide range of salaries depending on the state or region of the country in which a social worker resides, years of previous experience, and type of degree (undergraduate or graduate degree). Moving into a supervisory or program administrator role means a nice raise in your salary (see Connecticut section in Table 4.1).

Self-Assessment Checklist: Is This Job for Me?

- Do you have a passion for protecting children of all ages from diverse backgrounds and making sure they are safe?
- Are you able to work with parents from diverse backgrounds who have abused, neglected, or exploited their children?
- Do you enjoy having a job where your workday is often unpredictable and crisis driven?
- Would you enjoy having a job where an important aspect of your work is to participate in court hearings within the family court system?
- Would you enjoy the challenge of working with involuntary clients who are not happy to have you in their lives?
- Would you be able to see and hear details of how a child has been abused and/or neglected, including physical abuse, sexual abuse, emotional abuse, and various forms of child neglect and exploitation?
- Would you be comfortable having a job with unpredictable work hours?

TABLE 4.1 Salary Ranges for CPS Caseworkers in Selected States, 2013

STATE	QUALIFICATIONS	SALARY RANGE FOR CPS CASEWORKERS (2013)
Texas	Bachelor's degree in social work not required	$2,644.08 to $2,970.91 per month
		Investigators get a $416.00 monthly stipend as well
Oregon	Bachelor's in social work, human services, or closely related field, or bachelor's degree in a field not closely related and 1 year of human services–related experience	$3,382 to $4,929 per month
Illinois	Requires a bachelor's degree in social work with 1 year of directly related professional experience, or a bachelor's degree in a related human service field with 2 years of directly related professional experience. MSW preferred.	$4,291 to $6,452 per month
Connecticut	Prefer social work degrees:	
	1. Social Work Trainee (2-year training period)—need BSW or related field	1. $45,700 to $52,872 per year
	2. Social Worker—undergraduate degree and 2 years of experience or MSW; must pass exam	2. $59,633 to $75,897 per year
	3. Social Work Supervisor—MSW in social work or closely related field required; must pass supervisor exam	3. $65,626 to $83,186 per year
	4. Program Supervisor	4. $72,741 to $93,304 per year

Source: www.dfps.state.tx.us/Jobs/cpsinv.asp; http://www.oregon.gov/jobs/Pages/index.aspx; http://www.state.il.us/dcfs/docs/BW_Are_You_Interested.pdf; http://www.ct.gov/dcf/lib/dcf/employment_services/pdf/career_series_social_work.pdf.

- Would you be comfortable visiting with clients in their homes (e.g., parents, relatives, foster parents)?
- Do you have an assertive personality, and are you comfortable dealing with conflict?
- Would you be comfortable working for a government agency that is somewhat bureaucratic and has many rules, regulations, policies, and procedures to follow?

If you answered "yes" to seven or more of the preceding questions, then working in child protection might be for you!

RECOMMENDED READINGS/WEBSITES TO LEARN MORE

Child Welfare League of America: www.cwla.org

Court Appointed Special Advocates (CASA): www.casaforchildren.org

Crosson-Tower, C. (2002). *From the eye of the storm: The experiences of a child welfare worker.* Boston, MA: Allyn & Bacon.

Crosson-Tower, C. (2012). *Exploring child welfare: A practice perspective, 6th edition.* Boston, MA: Allyn & Bacon. Great chapter on child protection.

Crosson-Tower, C. (2013). *Understanding child abuse and neglect* (9th ed.). Boston, MA: Allyn & Bacon.

Prevent Child Abuse America: www.preventchildabuse.org

"The Case of Marie and Her Sons" (2006, July 23). A moving profile of a Connecticut CPS caseworker. *New York Times Magazine.*

Most states have a website for their department of children and families. For example, in Texas, visit www.dfps.state.tx.us. Just Google "Department of Children and Families" or "Children Protective Services" along with the state where you reside.

Child Protection Caseworker Exercise Test Your Knowledge

1. CPS investigates the following allegations within families:
   a. Physical abuse
   b. Medical or physical neglect
   c. Sexual abuse or exploitation
   d. Abandonment
   e. Emotional or psychological abuse
   f. Inadequate parental supervision of a child
   g. All of the above
2. True or False
   Child *abuse* cases are more prevalent than child *neglect* cases.
3. Which of the following famous writers was an early advocate for children's rights and child protection?
   a. Jane Austen
   b. Charles Dickens
   c. Herman Melville
   d. Ernest Hemingway
4. True or False
   The Society for the Prevention of Cruelty of Animals (SPCA) was founded before the Society for the Prevention of Cruelty to Children (SPCC).
5. When CPS removes a child from their parent(s) or caregiver(s), the case gets heard in a _____ court.
   a. Criminal
   b. Civil or Juvenile

6. Which of the following is an example of a permanency plan for a child who has been removed from his or her home?
   a. Return home to parents/caregiver
   b. Permanent placement with a relative
   c. Adoption
   d. All of the above

7. True or False
   CPS agencies are typically funded by a combination of monies from the state and federal governments.

8. When a child is being abused by a caregiver or family member, _____ investigates, but if a child is abused by a stranger, or someone who is not a family member, the _____ investigate.
   a. Police
   b. Child Protective Services

9. In any given year, there are usually approximately _____ children in the custody of CPS in the United States.
   a. 25,000
   b. 100,000
   c. 400,000
   d. million

10. True or False
    There is an abundance of foster and adoptive homes available for children in the child welfare system.

Answers: 1. g;   2. false;   3. b;   4. true;   5. b;   6. d;
   7. true;   8. b, a;   9. c;   10. false.

ADOPTION SOCIAL WORKER

Many social workers who are interested in child welfare find themselves working in the fascinating field of adoption. This is a more positive side of child welfare because you get to witness the joyful experience of a child being placed into a new "forever" family. The job of the adoption social worker is to prepare the biological parents, the child, and the adoptive parents for the adoption. As you can imagine, it is a very exciting and emotional time for the child who needs a "forever home" and the families who want a child to love and parent. Many families who decide to adopt a child have not been able to conceive a child on their own.

It is important to know that adoption has changed in recent years. Due to the increased acceptance of abortion and birth control, as well as the trend toward teen mothers keeping their babies, there are fewer healthy infants available for adoption. Children available for adoption today are more likely to be older, nonwhite, and have special needs (medical or emotional problems). Social workers need to be skilled and creative to find the right homes for these children because many adoptive parents are seeking healthy infants.

Another major change is the increasing number of "open adoptions," adoptions that allow some continued contact between the biological parents, the child, and the adoptive parents. Sometimes, letters and pictures are exchanged, while in other cases, children may have periodic visits with their biological parents. Social workers assist parties in coming to an agreement that is in the best interests of all who are involved in the adoption triad.

New federal laws have been passed in recent years that emphasize the idea that children in foster care have the right to be in a permanent home as soon as possible. There is a strong emphasis on finding adoptive homes for these children, as soon as possible, so they do not grow up in the foster care system. Finally, it is important to know that adoption is a lifelong process, and the social worker's job often does not end when the child is placed with their new adoptive home. Many families will continue to need support and postadoption services to help with adjustment and ongoing issues.

Once families decide they want to adopt a child, they have a number of options: Do they want an international adoption? Do they prefer adopting through the child welfare system in the United States? Do they feel more comfortable going through a private adoption agency? Thus, you will find adoption social workers in each of these settings (e.g., state child welfare agency or private agencies that specialize in domestic or international adoptions). A growing number of "kinship adoptions" are also taking place (e.g., family member, typically a grandparent or aunt and uncle, adopts a child related to them because the biological parent is unable to parent the child, in many cases due to incarceration or substance abuse). These families also need help and support, and there are a growing number of programs to meet this need. The following tasks are routinely performed by adoption social workers:

1. **Preparing children for adoption.** Before older children can be placed for adoption, they must be adequately prepared. In some cases, they may need counseling. Sometimes social workers help the child prepare a "Life Book," which helps them document their life before the adoption and to process why they could not continue to live with their birth parents. If children are not sufficiently prepared, there is a risk that the adoption process will be disrupted and the child will not be able to stay in the adoptive home.

2. **Counseling the birth parents.** As you can imagine, the decision to place a child for adoption is not easy. The parent(s) will need counseling and support to grieve the loss of the child and to help guide them through the adoption process. Some parents place their child for adoption voluntarily, whereas those involved in the child welfare system sometimes have their parental rights terminated by the court against their will.

3. **Recruiting prospective adoptive parents.** It is unfortunate that there are not enough adoptive homes for all of the children who are available for adoption in this country. Recruitment is especially important for special needs children. Social workers may use a variety of strategies, such as community presentations, public service announcements on radio and television, and the Internet, to find homes for these children.

4. **Training and approving prospective adoptive parents.** Many adoption agencies require parents to complete training (typically 10 to 12 weeks) to learn the adoption process, all of the requirements, and also to prepare them for the challenges and benefits of adopting a child. An important part of this process is conducting a very thorough home study to assess the suitability of those who wish to adopt a child. Parents will be assessed on their motivation for adopting a child, the stability of their relationship (if married), their physical and emotional health, and their financial stability. The agency will also perform a criminal background and child abuse check. Some social workers perform home studies on a contract basis with a state or private agency.

5. **Matching children and parents.** This is an art as much as it is a science. It takes experience and good assessment skills to match a child with the right family. Social workers must know the child and the prospective adoptive parents very well in order to make a good match. In some cases, the birth mother is allowed to select, or at least have input into selecting, the adoptive parents.

6. **Supporting families after the adoption placement.** Many agencies recognize that adoption is a lifelong process and that families may need short- or long-term services, such as counseling, support groups, in-home support by caseworkers, and referrals to other community resources, as needed.

7. **The legal work required to finalize an adoption.** Social workers need to become well versed on the legal process for finalizing an adoption. Adoption social workers will spend some of their time doing legal paperwork and appearing in court.

8. **Helping adoptees and birth parents with the search.** When a child or a birth parent decides that they would like to search and meet each other, they will often need to seek the help of a social worker to guide them through this process so that it can be as successful as possible. This is an emotional journey for everyone involved.

Core Competencies and Skills

■ Ability to do thorough assessments of children and families (home studies and matching children with adoptive parents)

- Strong counseling skills and understanding of the grieving process (birth parents who are losing a child or adoptive parents who were not able to conceive a child)
- Thorough understanding of the adoption process and how it affects each member of the adoption triad (i.e., child, biological parents, adoptive parents)
- Strong presentation and training skills (e.g., community presentations, training of adoptive parents)
- Understand the importance of cultural identity (this is especially important in transracial adoptions)
- Ability to mediate between biological parents and adoptive parents
- Media and marketing skills (recruiting adoptive families)
- Good legal skills and knowledge of the laws surrounding domestic and intercountry adoption

Educational and Licensing Requirements

You may be able to get a job as an adoption social worker with a BSW, but many employers prefer those with a master's degree and previous experience in the child welfare field. Agencies may also require a social work license, depending on the state where you reside.

Best Aspects of This Job

- Playing a role in creating a new family can be very rewarding.
- Finding a wonderful forever family for children, some of whom may have experienced abuse and/or neglect or a turbulent or uncertain beginning in life
- Helping biological parents make peace with the decision that it would be in their child's best interest to be placed for adoption
- Placing a child into an adoptive home, and helping adoptive parents realize their dream of having a child
- Facilitating a successful open adoption so that a child can stay connected with their biological family and community of origin
- Helping adoptive parents understand the importance of keeping a child connected to their culture or country of origin, especially when there are cultural differences between the child and the adoptive parents
- Facilitating a successful reunion between an adopted child and a biological parent when the child reaches adulthood
- Working in a field that is extremely fascinating and complex—the emotional rewards are great.
- Finding a loving home for an older child or a child with special needs is awesome.

Challenging Aspects of This Job

- Dealing with the stereotypes and myths surrounding adoption.
- It can be tough to balance the needs of the adoptive triad.
- Adoption often has happy endings, and yet it also involves grief and loss. Many families, children, and professionals have a hard time dealing with this concept.
- As with all social work, it is not an exact science and can be a roller coaster of emotions as you work with adoptive parents, children, and birth parents.
- Adoptive parents who are anxiously awaiting an addition to their family are looking for a sense of fulfillment; they want to "get from" the child and to feel the return love of a child. This doesn't always happen, especially not immediately.
- Working with children who have a difficult time attaching to their new family.
- Helping adoptive parents deal with not having the perfect, idealized child they have always dreamed of having.
- Convincing families that adoption is a lifelong process and will present new challenges at different life stages.
- Seeing some children wait for long periods of time for their "forever home," and others who will not be placed due to having significant physical, behavioral, or emotional needs.
- Working with children who have experienced abuse, neglect, and termination of parental rights can be challenging to deal with emotionally.
- When an adoption disrupts or does not work out, putting the pieces back together is very difficult. (The child and the adoptive parents are hurt and grieving. The child has experienced a rejection.)

Social Worker Spotlight
AGNES ZARCARO, LCSW
Spaulding for Children, Houston, Texas

I received my MSW in 1971 from the University of Houston. Today, I am a licensed clinical social worker (LCSW). I have worked in the field of adoption for 36 years.

My present position is manager of the South Texas Adoption and Family Support Programs of Spaulding for Children; these programs are located in Corpus Christi, McAllen, and Laredo, Texas. The Adoption Program centers on the adoption of older children who are in the Texas state foster care system—those who have had parental rights terminated and are awaiting a permanent adoptive home. The Family Support Program offers an array of services to the families as they await an adoptive placement. Once the adoptive placement occurs, the families and children are offered services through the finalization of the adoption and the postlegal adoption period. These programs include marriage communication; family, parent, and children's support groups; family retreats; and therapy.

The field of adoption has changed dramatically since I began in November 1971 as a birth-parent counselor, assisting "unwed mothers" (as they were called at that time) with making a decision about their "unplanned" pregnancy. Most birth mothers at this time did choose adoption for their babies. In the late '70s and '80s, birth mothers began parenting their children more and more, so the "homes for unwed mothers" began to change and began offering many more services to teens who decided to parent their children. In the '90s, infant adoptions were few and far between. International adoptions increased in numbers as U.S. families continued to want infants and found adopting domestically to be too expensive and complicated. The majority of children available today in the United States are older children or children with various special needs.

Within the field of adoption, there are many different areas where a social worker might concentrate. One can work with all triad members, or only one member of the triad. One can work in the preadoption, placement, or postadoption phase. One can work solely as a recruiter of adoptive families, or one can work in the clinical arena assisting families and children as they move through the phases and issues of the adoption. One can work in the legal system as a liaison with the courts on terminations and adoptions. Another area is postadoption, including the search and reunions of adoptees and birth parents. One can work for the state CPS agency or a private adoption agency that specializes in either domestic or international adoptions. Research is always an option as well. Our program is funded through

(continued)

AGNES ZARCARO   *(continued)*

two large federal grants, and we are obliged to have a research component, which will help to advance the field as well as help in the evaluation and efficacy of the work.

The best part of working in adoption is that it is such a diverse field and it is very challenging. Families are made! Children will have a family in which they belong. When a teen who has been in the foster care system since age 2 is adopted at age 15, this is such a wonderful thing to happen for that child.

Compensation and Employment Outlook

Social workers who work in adoption are typically employed by either the state CPS agency or a private, nonprofit organization. For information on salaries for CPS caseworkers, please refer to the beginning of this chapter. Salaries for social workers working in a private adoption agency will vary greatly from agency to agency and by state. Due to the knowledge and skills required for this job, many social workers apply and get hired after gaining experience in other jobs within the child welfare system (e.g., CPS). In the state child welfare agency, jobs in the adoption unit are competitive and are reserved for experienced child welfare caseworkers. Seasoned caseworkers can enjoy a career transition to this division, which comes with the reward of finding children their "forever home."

Self-Assessment Checklist: Is This Job for Me?

- Do you have a passion for finding homes for children available for adoption?
- Can you work with and support birth parents who are placing their child for adoption?
- Do you believe there is a home for every child if you can just find it?
- Would you enjoy working with children, some of whom have experienced child abuse and have abandonment issues?
- Can you work with and support adoptive parents who long to have a child and have a history of infertility?
- Would you be comfortable making home visits?
- Are you comfortable asking people very sensitive questions to determine their suitability to be adoptive parents?
- Are you able to balance the needs of the child, the biological parents, and the adoptive parents?

- Would you enjoy the challenge of working with adoptive families after the child has been placed to support that placement?
- Would you be able to hear details of how a child has been abused and/or neglected including physical abuse, sexual abuse, emotional abuse, and various forms of child neglect and exploitation?

If you answered "yes" to seven or more of the preceding questions, then working in the field of adoption might be for you!

RECOMMENDED READINGS/WEBSITES TO LEARN MORE

AdoptUSKids: www.adoptuskids.org

Center for Adoption Support and Education (CASE): www.adoptionsupport.org

Child Welfare Information Gateway: www.childwelfare.gov

Child Welfare League of America: www.cwla.org

Crosson-Tower, C. (2012). *Exploring child welfare: A practice perspective* (6th ed.). Boston, MA: Allyn & Bacon. Excellent chapter on adoption.

The Donaldson Adoption Institute: www.adoptioninstitute.org

National Adoption Day: www.nationaladoptionday.org

National Resource Center for Special Needs Adoption: www.spaulding.org

North American Council on Adoptable Children: www.nacac.org

FOSTER CARE SOCIAL WORKER

Though many child welfare social workers have a passion for adoption, others love the challenge of foster care. Because this field of practice has much overlap with adoption, we advise you to read the previous section. According to data reported by the U.S. Children's Bureau, there were almost 400,000 children in foster care in September 2012 (Child Welfare Information Gateway, 2013). Here we will highlight some of the distinct aspects of working in foster care as a social worker.

At least initially, foster care is somewhat of a different experience from adoption because it is meant to be a temporary placement for the child while efforts are made to reunify the child with his or her parents. Foster parents must learn to deal with feelings of grief and disappointment when a child leaves their home to be reunified with their parents or is placed permanently with a relative, or when the child is exhibiting dangerous behaviors and needs to be placed in a more structured environment, such as a residential treatment center. A growing trend is the increasing number of relative foster homes in the United States. In September 2012, 47% of children were placed in nonrelative foster homes and 28% were in relative foster homes; 15% of foster youth with higher needs were in institutions or group home settings (Child Welfare Information Gateway, 2013).

Unfortunately, foster parents are often perceived in a negative light due to the small number of high-profile media cases where foster parents have been found to be abusive to children in their care. However, many foster parents are generous, caring people who are willing to take children into their home who have suffered serious abuse and/or neglect at the hands of their caregivers. Foster parents come from all walks of life. They may be childless young couples hoping to adopt, single parents, gay couples, relatives, older couples who have already raised their children, or families who already have biological children but want to add to their family.

Social workers who wish to work in foster care are typically employed by the state child welfare agency or by private foster care agencies that contract with the state to provide this service. The following tasks are very commonly carried out by foster care case managers:

- Recruiting members of the community to be foster parents—this is crucial since there is a severe shortage of foster parents in most states.
- Training and certifying individuals to be foster parents. Foster care agencies require prospective foster parents to complete training (typically 10 to 12 weeks) to learn about the process, all of the requirements, and to prepare them for parenting abused children who often have a range of emotional problems and challenging behaviors. An important part of this process is conducting a very thorough home study to assess the suitability of these parents to foster a child. The agency will also perform background checks on all adults in the home.
- Supporting foster parents after the child has been placed. The child typically has their own caseworker, so the social worker's job is to offer the foster parents guidance and support and ensure that they have the resources they need (e.g., counseling, clothing vouchers, adequate financial compensation).
- Advocating for the foster parents on your caseload and ensuring that they are treated as a respected member of the team by the state child welfare agency and judicial system.
- Making frequent home visits and monitoring the placement to evaluate whether the child is safe and is receiving good care. Ensuring that the foster parents are continuing to meet licensing requirements (e.g., ongoing foster parent training, fire inspection, CPR certification).
- Helping the family through the legal process of adopting the child if he or she becomes available for adoption, or providing emotional support if the child later leaves the home.

Core Competencies and Skills

Many of the same competencies and skills that are required for adoption social workers are needed for foster care social workers as well (see previous section).

In addition, foster care social workers must have the ability to work with abused and special needs children. Foster care social workers, in some cases, need to have the ability to support the child and foster families if and when the child leaves the foster home for a permanent home. In September 2012, 51% of the children who exited foster care were reunited with their parents or primary caregiver.

Best Aspects of This Job

- Seeing children who are dealing with the trauma of being removed from their home being placed in a safe, loving foster home—one that you were responsible for recruiting and training
- The joy of finding the perfect foster home for a large sibling group so the children do not have to be separated
- Witnessing the happy ending of a foster home placement that turns into a permanent adoption for a child in need of a "forever home"
- Working with amazingly giving foster parents who take "special needs" children into their home, some with serious physical and mental disabilities
- Seeing children thrive in a foster home, with love and structure, and heal from the abuse and/or neglect they suffered

Challenging Aspects of This Job

- Dealing with the shortage of foster homes in most communities can be very frustrating
- Witnessing the devastation of foster parents who lose a child they have become extremely attached to. Helping foster parents accept the decision when it is in a child's best interest to go back home
- Working with a foster family when a child has to leave the foster home due to escalating problems, or when a child is unable to attach to their new caregivers
- Dealing with a child abuse allegation in a foster home
- Balancing the needs of the child, the foster parents, and the biological parents

RECOMMENDED READINGS/WEBSITES TO LEARN MORE

Casey Family Programs: www.casey.org
Child Welfare League of America: www.cwla.org
Crosson-Tower, C. (2012). *Exploring child welfare: A practice perspective* (6th ed.). Boston, MA: Allyn & Bacon. Great chapter on foster care.
Fisher, A., & Rivas, M. (2001). *Finding fish: A memoir.* New York, NY: HarperCollins.

National Foster Care Coalition: www.nationalfostercare.org
National Foster Parent Association: www.nfpainc.org
Pew Commission on Children in Foster Care: www.pewfostercare.org

Foster Care and Adoption Exercise Case Study

You are a caseworker in the adoption unit at the child welfare agency in your state, and your supervisor has just assigned a new case to you. Her name is Sarah, she is 10 years old, of Latina origin (she speaks Spanish and English), and she is available for adoption. You begin reading her file and see right away that this will not be an easy case. Sarah was sexually abused by her stepfather for a number of years before she was removed from her home. As a result, she does not trust men. She has had a difficult time talking about this in therapy, as she is embarrassed and ashamed. She is still very angry and hurt that her mother did not protect her from this abuse.

Her adjustment to foster care has not been an easy one. She has been in a foster home for 2 years and has been able to maintain a stable placement, but her foster parents report that she will not let them get close to her. She has not been able to talk with them much about her life prior to foster care. On the positive side, she does well in school, gets along well with other children, and makes good grades. She is on the soccer team at school and plays the piano. She loves animals and would like to be a veterinarian one day. So far, she has expressed that she does not want to be adopted, even though her biological parents' rights have been terminated. She harbors fantasies of being reunited with her mother someday.

Questions

1. What thoughts and feelings do you have as you read this case scenario?
2. What do you think Sarah's chances are of being placed into an adoptive home?
3. How would you build a relationship with Sarah? Plan your first meeting with her.
4. How would you work with Sarah to help her become more open to the idea of being adopted?
5. Do you think Sarah is ready for adoption yet? If not, what kinds of services does she need to help her move forward?
6. What kind of family would be ideal for Sarah? List a few family characteristics that you feel would be important.
7. Do you think her current foster home might be an option for her? Why or why not?
8. Does Sarah have the right to decide whether she will be adopted?

EMERGING FIELD OF PRACTICE:
HOME VISITING PROGRAMS

One of the criticisms of the child welfare field is that professionals do not intervene with families in need until a crisis has occurred and the problems have been occurring for a long period of time. Child advocates have argued that more prevention or "early intervention" programs are needed to help prevent child abuse and neglect from occurring in the first place. Home visiting programs have received increased attention in recent years and research has shown them to be effective with regard to child abuse prevention. In these programs, nurses, social workers, or other trained professionals make frequent home visits to families with young children, from birth to age 5, since these early years are the most critical in terms of healthy child development. Goals include reducing parental stress and depression and promoting positive parenting skills, health and child development, and school readiness. There are a number of home visiting programs around the country including Parents as Teachers, Nurse–Family Partnership, Early Head Start, Home Instruction for Parents of Preschool Youngsters, and Healthy Families America. This is an exciting new development in the child welfare field!

REFERENCES

Child Welfare Information Gateway. (2013). *Foster care statistics 2012*. Washington, DC: U.S. Department of Health and Human Services, Children's Bureau. Retrieved from https://www. childwelfare.gov/pubs/factsheets/foster.pdf

U.S. Department of Labor, Bureau of Labor Statistics. (2014). *Occupational outlook handbook, 2014–15 edition, Social workers*. Retrieved from http://www.bls.gov/ooh/community-and-social-service/social-workers.htm

5 ■ SCHOOL-BASED AND SCHOOL-LINKED SERVICES

The U.S. education system has been under attack in recent years as the U.S. government continues to grapple with our lowered rankings on the international stage compared to our peer countries. Some blame the teachers and school administrators, others the families and communities of students or wider social problems, such as poverty. Meanwhile, many schools are being asked to do more with fewer investments from the state and federal governments while experts point out troubling problems in our schools, such as racial segregation and wide economic disparities between wealthy and resource-strapped school systems. Historically, equity and equal access have been a challenge, particularly for ethnic minorities (U.S. Department of Education, Office of Vocational and Adult Education, 2014). This is an important social justice issue because many Americans feel that education should be "the great equalizer." This idea was very prevalent during the 1960s, when President Lyndon Johnson made federal education funding a significant priority of his Great Society legislation.

The United States has a long history of providing health and social services for children and youth in school settings. According to Tyack (1992), the history of school social work can be traced to the early 1900s. Because educators are not trained to provide social work services, school systems often appreciate the skillset that a social worker can bring to an educational setting. However, when school budgets are tight, it can be difficult for schools to find the resources to employ social workers, and thus schools sometimes prioritize the hiring of school counselors and school psychologists (who play different roles, also important). The climate for school social workers varies widely from state to state, although in some states school social work continues to be an established career option. According to the School Social Work Association of America (SSWAA), the Midwest is currently the strongest area for school social work, whereas a few other states make only very limited use of school social workers.

When a social worker chooses to become a school social worker, he or she is making a decision to work in a "host setting," which means that social services are not the primary service being offered. In essence, you are considered an invited guest into this work setting but you have been invited because the professionals in that setting value the services that a social worker can bring to their organization. Social workers can be invaluable employees in a school setting, being trained to assist students who are falling through the cracks and experiencing a range of problems that may be hindering their ability to succeed in school. They are trained to provide a range of services to students and their families and to be advocates for students who need access to resources. Social workers are often the link between the school and the home.

School-based and school-linked health and social services use a systems approach that emphasizes the interconnection of health, welfare, and education and the need for immediate and comprehensive services and collaborative problem-solving methods. The evolution of school-based and school-linked services has been influenced not only by the political climate, economic conditions, and demographic portrait of the time, but also by the citizens' sense of responsibility and obligation to provide a wholesome environment to all children from across cultures everyday, to act in their best interest, and to assist in their developmental adjustments in school settings (Kronick, 2000; Perry, Steele, & Hilliard III, 2004).

School-based and school-linked services are designed to be immediate and comprehensive. These services include individual, group, and family counseling and therapy; adolescent group work; tutoring; mentoring; recreation; the National Head Start Association; and so forth. Many schools also offer free or reduced breakfast and lunch programs to qualifying students. Likewise, other schools' programs focus on college preparation for high school students. School-based and school-linked services may be provided by social workers employed by community organizations as well. Examples of community organizations in which social workers are employed and that commonly provide services in school settings include Americorps, Big Brothers Big Sisters, Boys and Girls Clubs of America, Communities in Schools, Teach for America, local nonprofit organizations, and so forth.

Although each state differs in their definitions and requirements of workers providing school-based and school-linked services, the following are commonly cited job descriptions as well as educational and licensing requirements for those with social work education, training, and work experience.

SCHOOL SOCIAL WORKER

As members of a specialized area of practice within the profession of social work, school social workers bring unique knowledge and skills to the school system and the educational team. They are committed to enhancing the educational experience of students, their families, and their community by providing social, emotional, behavioral, and adaptive functioning support. They serve as the bridge between the school, home, and community, on behalf of students.

In any given day, school social workers provide assessment for students with problems such as abuse, neglect, self-injury, substance abuse, grief and loss, and other issues. They plan and implement developmentally appropriate prevention programs, including educational groups on healthy self-image, prevention of adolescent pregnancy and sexually transmitted diseases, substance abuse, bullying, and violence prevention. When necessary, these social workers also provide interventions, such as individual and group counseling for students and family counseling. They are key players in crisis intervention plans, both proactively creating them and offering support in the event of a critical incident (e.g., the 9/11 attacks, school shootings).

Essentially, school social workers provide services to students in special education and work with at-risk students, particularly relating to school dropout prevention, violence prevention, mental disorders, body image, teenage pregnancy, substance abuse, truancy, and other misconduct. They are valuable resources for students and teachers in terms of dealing with problem behaviors of students and in providing support during times of adjustments and transitions (School Social Work Association of America, 2014). They are often tasked with supporting students who are facing serious challenges such as the loss of a parent, children who are in foster care, or children who recently immigrated to the United States. And they are often in the position of making reports to child welfare authorities when they receive information that a student may be experiencing child abuse and/or neglect.

Social Worker Spotlight
MAGDA FLORES, MSSW
School Social Worker, Communities in Schools, Austin, Texas

I received my MSW at the University of Texas at Austin. After years of working in child welfare (residential treatment and Child Protective Services), I found myself wanting to do something dealing more with prevention. My job search led me to school social work through a nonprofit agency called Communities in Schools (CIS), where I have worked for over 10 years now at both the elementary and junior high school level. What initially drew me to school social work was the agency's mission, which basically states that we help children prepare for a successful life by helping them stay in school. The longer I worked at CIS, the more I realized just how many things get in the way of a child's academic success and how many social problems could be alleviated when children are able to complete their education and acquire viable job skills.

In my work as a school social worker, I am able to address a wide variety of issues, and my client is always there, meaning I don't have to concern myself with missed appointments or an inability to pay. School social work often includes individual and group counseling, which covers topics such as domestic violence, substance abuse, self-esteem, social skills, self-harm, divorce, grief issues, empowerment, and a variety of other issues that may present themselves. Because of the flexibility and independent nature of my work, I am able to address these topics in whatever manner is most effective. I can use the school district's ropes course, or I can do art activities, or I can do traditional talk therapy. In true social work fashion, my work also involves linking children and families with community resources, advocacy (within the complex and sometimes intimidating educational system), and assistance with basic needs. Recognizing that so many children lack exposure to many experiences, I am able to take students on field trips to universities, cultural events, overnight camping trips, and other activities. Furthermore, my job often includes planning and implementation of school-wide family events, sponsorship of school activities (e.g., chess club), and tutoring.

Topics and events often change from year to year, just as the student population changes. Part of a school social worker's job is to work in conjunction with school personnel and administration to provide the most pertinent and effective programming in order to adapt to the changing needs of students. Because the work is so flexible and dynamic, and because I can truly see and feel the positive impact that my work has on children's lives, I go to work each day with a smile on my face, anticipating what the day's challenges (and rewards) will bring.

If I Want to Work With Youth in a School Setting, Should I Get a Degree in Social Work or School Counseling or School Psychology?

This is a tough question, and one that students frequently ask their social work professors. Our best advice is to decide whether you want to have a broad degree that gives you the knowledge and skills to work with many different populations in many different settings (social work) or whether you want to spend your entire career in a school setting *and* want to get very specialized training in this field. Also, the role of a school counselor tends to be much more focused on the educational success of students, and the role of the school psychologist focuses heavily on psychological testing and working with children in special education. School social workers focus more on the emotional, behavioral, and family challenges of students in a more general and holistic manner. To help you decide, you should interview each of these professionals—even job shadow them, if possible—to determine the best fit for you. You also want to know the degree that will make you most marketable in the area in which you want to work and live.

AFTER-SCHOOL PROGRAM COUNSELOR

After-school program counselors may be members of a school's educational team or a community organization who provide services, such as after-school tutoring; study hall; music, dance, and art groups; and recreational programs, to students in need of additional support. These counselors are committed to providing support for a student's academic progress, including tutoring on specific subjects and a study hall to complete homework. They are committed to strengthening the student, family, community, and school relationship. They are vital to keeping students supervised, occupied, and engaged in positive activities that help keep them out of trouble.

DAY-CARE OR SCHOOL READINESS PROGRAM WORKER

Day-care and school readiness program workers provide child development, mental health supervision and management, and head start services to children up to age 12. They plan and implement daily programs and services that help children develop educationally and personally. For instance, development of self-esteem, imagination, speech, physical skills, health, and nutrition are daily tasks of these workers. They provide parent conferences, home visits, socialization groups, psychosocial and developmental assessments, crisis intervention, and community collaborations to improve children's educational experience. It is the oath of these day-care and school readiness program workers to maintain a professional image and treat all children with dignity and respect (National Association for the Education of Young Children, 2007, 2014).

ADULT LITERACY PROGRAM WORKER

Adult literacy program workers provide literacy, remedial, and self-enrichment education to out-of-school youths and adults. They work with individuals from a variety of cultures, languages, education levels, and economic backgrounds to meet their needs in reading, writing, and speaking English; basic mathematics; and other subjects. These workers help youths and adults who did not make it through the mainstream educational system develop the knowledge and skills necessary to participate in their communities, hold a job, complete the GED exam, or pursue higher education. With the changing demography of the United States, it is commonplace for these workers to assist immigrants whose native language is not English (U.S. Department of Labor, Bureau of Labor Statistics, 2014).

SPECIAL EDUCATION SOCIAL SERVICE WORKER

In the school system and organizations that provide services to the school, certain social workers specialize in offering services to children and youth in special education. These workers are involved in the creation and implementation of the Individualized Educational Program (IEP) for each student who uses the school's special education services. They conduct assessments of the student's physical and mental disabilities and family situations, which help in creating the IEP. As part of a team that acts in the best interest of the student, a special education social service provider facilitates the involvement of the family, community, and other organizations in the development of a sound educational program for the student. Several of the specific services provided to the student and family include individual and family counseling, social skills classes, tutoring, parenting classes, and other services to help students and families cope with the disability. In addition to providing micro-level services, these social workers are also involved in policy development and advocacy for students with disabilities.

As shown by the aforementioned descriptions, there are many career opportunities for social work in school settings. As providers of school-based and school-linked services, these social workers promote educational and personal development and growth of all students in their families and communities.

SOCIAL WORKER ON A COLLEGE CAMPUS

When we think about school social work, we usually think about social work in a K–12 public school. However, another exciting career option for social workers includes working for a university. Today's college students experience a range of challenges and stressors such as balancing work and school; financial stressors due to the increased cost of a college education; mental health problems; and dating violence. The issue of sexual assault on college campuses has been raised recently since President Obama made this an area of focus for his administration. Colleges are being asked to review how well they are respond-ing to issues of sexual violence on their campuses. Some social workers work in the university counseling center where they provide therapeutic services to college students who are experiencing a variety of problems, both personal and academic. Problems might include anything from dealing with a sexual assault, to depression, to coping with the stress of working and going to school full time. These positions require an earned master's degree in social work (MSW) as well as licensure.

Social workers are also hired to work in various university programs, some-times referred to as student services. They might be in charge of educational programming on issues such as sexual assault, violent dating relationships, and substance abuse. They might also run support groups on campus for gay/lesbian college students or other groups of students in need of this type of service. Some of these positions are more specialized and are termed *wellness coordi-nators* or *sexual assault advocates*. More and more universities are recogniz-ing the value of having social workers and other mental health professionals on campus to help support students and address the wide array of problems and needs they often experience in today's college environment. Finally, social workers are sometimes hired as internship coordinators to support students in various types of student internships.

Core Competencies and Skills

- Passion for working with students, including those at risk and in special education
- Ability to contextualize practice relative to issues in urban and rural communities in which the school system exists and interacts
- Cutting-edge, ongoing knowledge and skills in campus safety, especially in light of recent prevalence in campus shootings and violence
- Advanced skills in grief and loss services to children and their families who have been affected by school violence
- Comfortable working in a bureaucratic yet fast-paced environment and maintaining cooperative relationships with multiple parties, including students, families, community, politicians, and so forth
- Comfortable working with a diverse population of students, particularly in urban schools
- Excellent knowledge of child and adult growth, development, and behavior characteristics
- Excellent knowledge of methods for supervising, managing, motivating, and remediating students
- Excellent verbal and written communication skills for meetings, documentation, court reports, and so forth

- Strong educational and career counseling, crisis management, and problem-solving skills
- High degree of cultural sensitivity toward bicultural students, their families, and community; ability to work respectfully with children, families, and communities regardless of age, gender, sexual orientation, race/ethnicity, national origin, immigration status, disabilities, and socioeconomic status
- Ability to work with bilingual students and their families (e.g., provide access to information in the appropriate language as well as provide translators)
- Excellent assessment and decision-making skills
- Excellent skills in prevention and intervention, particularly related to school dropout, teenage pregnancy, substance abuse, truancy, gangs, and youth violence (e.g., parent conference, home visit, socialization group, psychosocial and developmental assessment, crisis intervention, community collaborations)
- Self-care (school settings are demanding and multifaceted)

Educational and Licensing Requirements

School social workers can be employed in school settings with a bachelor's, master's, or PhD degree in social work, depending on the policies of the particular school system. In the United States and its territories, many MSW education programs have concentrations or specializations in school social work that prepare students specifically for this career. Licensure in school social work requires an individual to meet both the Standards for School Services Professionals and the Standards for School Social Work Professionals (School Social Work Association of America, 2014).

Qualifications of after-school program counselors vary tremendously by state and program. However, the emphases of these counselors are on knowledge, skills, and experiences such as the ability to work with children, communicate effectively, time management and organization, analytical abilities, sound judgment, and being a good role model. Although there is no specific licensure for after-school program counselors, licensing is required at the agency/organizational level according to specific fields (e.g., child day-care licensing, social work).

The educational requirements for day-care and school readiness program workers range from high school diploma, knowledge of child development, and on-the-job training to courses in education, nutrition, psychology, and speech or an associate's degree in early childhood education. For workers interested in administrative positions, a bachelor's degree and sometimes a state teacher certificate/license or master's degree is required.

Educational and licensing qualifications for adult literacy program workers vary by state and program. For example, most states require at least a bachelor's degree and preferably a master's degree. Others require the state teacher certificate/license and a certificate in English as a second language or adult education (U.S. Department of Education, Office of Vocational and Adult Education, 2014).

As discussed thus far, school-based and school-linked service providers have a very delicate and precious population for whom they are responsible, including children and disenfranchised adults who were unable to successfully progress through a traditional educational system. Because of the length of time children spend in school as well as the intensity of the demand and responsibility for the care of children and disenfranchised adults, a high degree of knowledge, skills, and training are required to successfully and effectively meet their needs. Consequently, workers with a social work degree or related field are needed in school settings.

Best Aspects of This Job

- Working with students, their families, and their communities
- Contributing to the lives of adults who are more than likely vulnerable to social problems because of their limited education or undereducation
- Expanding knowledge about diverse cultures, including those of immigrants, and developing cultural competency skills
- Expanding knowledge about languages and skills to mobilize resources to ameliorate the negative effects of language barriers
- Expanding knowledge about risk and protective factors (e.g., personal, family, peer, school, community-based) that contribute to or hinder the educational achievements and aspirations of students
- Opportunity to work with schools, families, and communities to mobilize resources that will help students, both children and disenfranchised adults, with their families and community
- Opportunity to be a part of an educational team with teachers, counselors, coaches, and the like for the best interest of the student
- Being important in the lives of the students whose care has been entrusted to you
- Being a significant influence on students, both children and disenfranchised adults
- Being a witness to achievements such as change to appropriate behavior, increased classroom performance, self-enrichment, and graduation
- Working with motivated, self-directed, and confident adults who are seeking self-enrichment opportunities
- Every single day in the school system is unique and exciting.

Challenging Aspects of This Job

- Competition with school counselors and school psychologists for limited school budget resources
- Constantly changing schools in communities that present competing demands for scarce resources
- Dealing with systemic barriers to equity and equal access, particularly for students of color
- Possible difficulty engaging parents as team members
- Occasionally, difficulty working with education professionals who do not have social work education or experience
- Knowledge of problems in the home that negatively affect innocent students (in some cases, notification of child protection authorities)
- Knowing that sometimes problems stem from the traditional educational system (e.g., inaccessibility to needed resources and information)
- The heavy burden of being responsible for appropriate assessments and making decisions that affect children and disenfranchised adults
- Sometimes working with at-risk students who are unwilling or unable to collaborate on a solution
- Threats to personal safety in some situations
- Caring for oneself and having a balanced life amid an extremely high-demand setting
- Having a successful program eliminated from the school due to lack of funding

Compensation and Employment Outlook

School-based and school-linked service providers are employed by both public and private entities, so compensation varies by setting, program, state, and region. Those working for a school system or government typically receive good salaries and benefits. School social workers with master's degrees usually start at a higher level on the pay scale. For instance, in 2012, school social workers' median annual income was $41,530 and ranging from $27,000 to $72,000. The median annual income for social workers in elementary and secondary schools was $54,500 (U.S. Department of Labor, Bureau of Labor Statistics, 2014).

Depending on the program, geographical location, and qualifications of the individual, after-school program counselors may be paid hourly wages ranging from as little as $7 to as much as $25, or even higher. Some such counselors are hired by the school; others are hired by agencies and organizations in the community who are stakeholders with students in the school.

Day-care and school readiness program workers tend to be low-paid compared to those who hold other school-based and school-linked positions.

Depending on geographical location, program, and qualifications of the individual, day-care and school readiness program workers may have earned about $15,000 annually in Virginia to about $25,000 annually in Hawaii in 2013 (PayScale Inc., 2014).

Among adult literacy program workers, in 2012, the median hourly earning was $23, ranging from $9 to $28. Part-time adult literacy workers are paid hourly or per class and receive no benefits, whereas full-time teachers are paid a salary and receive good benefits if they work for a school system or government (Bureau of Labor Statistics, U.S. Department of Labor, 2014). As indicated earlier, there is a wide range of salaries for school-based and school-linked service providers depending on position, employer, program, state or region, years of previous experience, and type of degree (e.g., undergraduate or graduate degree).

In terms of outlook, employment of school social workers is not only expected to grow, but also be competitive thanks to increases in student enrollments, in in-school diversity, and in the academic, personal, social, and mental health needs of students in both general school population and special education. Nonetheless, the greatest determining factor in this growth within the schools remains to be funding available from the federal, state, and local governments (U.S. Department of Labor, Bureau of Labor Statistics, 2014).

After-school programs have been a resource for working parents for decades. The employment outlook for after-school program counselors may be positively affected by the increase in school enrollments, student needs for social and behavioral prevention and intervention, and the demand for after-school programs by women and men with children who are working outside of the home.

The job outlook for day-care and school readiness program workers is very good through 2022 thanks to high turnover rates and increases in the number of children needing day care because mothers are entering or returning to the labor force (National Association for the Education of Young Children, 2014). In terms of adult literacy program workers, opportunities are expected to be very good through 2022, especially for teachers of English as a second language, owing to large increases in immigrant populations and self-enrichment courses because of the current trend of embracing lifelong learning. The large number of people retiring and the constant high demands for teachers will also create jobs. Like other employment opportunities, the demand for literacy education fluctuates with the economy (U.S. Department of Education, Office of Vocational and Adult Education, 2014).

Self-Assessment Checklist: Is This Job for Me?

- Do you have a passion for working with children from diverse backgrounds and ensuring their educational, personal, social, and mental health needs are met?

- Do you think that you are able to work with parents from diverse backgrounds, both culturally and linguistically as well as with their communities?
- Do you enjoy having a job in which your workday is spent working with multiple systems, including students, teachers, families, communities, and courts, to mobilize resources for the best interest of the child?
- Would you enjoy having a job in which you are able to contribute to the betterment of the lives of disenfranchised adults who otherwise have no opportunity to succeed in a traditional educational system?
- Would you enjoy the challenge of working with a range of individuals from at-risk children to motivated adults?
- Would you enjoy advocating for access to resources and information for children, their families, and communities?
- Would you be comfortable visiting children in their homes (e.g., parents, relatives, foster parents)?
- Do you have an assertive personality? Are you comfortable dealing with conflict?
- Would you be comfortable working for a somewhat bureaucratic system with many rules, regulations, policies, and procedures to follow?

If you answered "yes" to seven or more of the preceding questions, then working at a school setting might be the place for you!

RECOMMENDED READINGS/WEBSITES TO LEARN MORE

Education Encyclopedia: http://education.stateuniversity.com/pages/2000/FullService-Schools.html

Frances, A. (2013). *Saving normal: An insider's revolt against out-of-control psychiatric diagnosis, DSM-5, big pharma, and the medicalization of ordinary life*. San Francisco, CA: William Morrow/Harper Collins.

Johnson, J., Uline, C., & Perez, L. (2012). *Teaching practices from America's best urban schools: A guide for school and classroom leaders*. New York, NY: Routledge.

Klein, J. (2013). *The bully society: School shootings and the crisis of bullying in America's schools*. New York, NY: New York University Press.

Kozol, J. (2005). *The shame of the nation: The restoration of apartheid schooling in America*. New York, NY: Three Rivers Press.

Massat, C. R., Constable, R., McDonald, S., & Flynn, J. P. (2008). *School social work: Practice, policy, and research* (7th ed.). Chicago, IL: Lyceum.

National Association for the Education of Young Children: www.naeyc.org

School Social Work Association of America: www.sswaa.org

School Social Work Exercise

Birat Rahim is a 6-year-old boy in the first grade. His parents emigrated from Pakistan when he was 3, and the family speaks both Urdu and English at home. Birat's teacher has noticed that for the 2 weeks after report cards went home for the second quarter, he has been very withdrawn in class. Birat has not been playing with his usual friends, nor has he been eating his school lunch. At least three times a week, Birat asks to visit the school nurse at the clinic, telling the nurse he has a stomach ache. The teacher contacts the school social worker for assistance.

QUESTIONS

1. As the school social worker for this referral, what is the first step you would take in assessing this child?
2. What could be the possible areas of concern causing such a change in Birat's behavior?
3. Before you work with this family, what kinds of things would be important to learn about the family's native culture and language?

REFERENCES

Kronick, R. F. (2000). *Human services and the full service school.* Springfield, IL: Charles C Thomas.

National Association for the Education of Young Children. (2007). *Promoting excellence in early childhood education.* Retrieved from www.naeyc.org/about

National Association for the Education of Young Children. (2014). *Our mission.* Retrieved from www.naeyc.org/about/mission

PayScale, Inc. (2014). *Salary survey report for industry: Child care/day care (2000–2007).* Retrieved from www.payscale.com

Perry, T., Steele, C., & Hilliard III, A. (2004). *Young, gifted, and black: Promoting high achievement among African-American students.* Boston, MA: Beacon Press.

School Social Work Association of America. (2014). *About School Social Work Association of America.* Retrieved from www.sswaa.org

Tyack, D. (1992). Health and social services in public schools: Historical perspectives. *Future of Children, 2,* 19–31.

U.S. Department of Education, Office of Vocational and Adult Education. (2014). *Strategic plan for fiscal years 2014–18.* Retrieved from www2.ed.gov/about/reports/strat/plan2014-18/draft-strategic-plan.pdf

U.S. Department of Labor, Bureau of Labor Statistics. (2014). *Occupational outlook handbook: 2014–2015.* Retrieved from www.bls.gov/ooh

6 ■ SOCIAL WORK WITH OLDER ADULTS

Though many social workers choose to work with children, others enjoy working with individuals at the other end of the age spectrum. In the coming years, there will be an increasing demand for social workers (and other health and helping professionals) who work with older adults. The proportion of Americans aged 65 and older is rapidly growing, a phenomenon that has been called the "graying of America." The U.S. Census Bureau estimates that by 2020 one in five Americans will be classified as an older adult. The demographic shift has begun, and the large population of urban-dwelling older Americans in particular are experiencing both the positive and negative outcomes of such a shift (Yancey, Baldwin, Saran, & Vakalahi, 2014). This has created a number of important challenges and opportunities for the social work profession as we strive to meet the needs of older Americans from different backgrounds and cultures.

Most of us can identify with this, because we have parents and grandparents, and we want them to be able to live independently and experience a high-quality life for as long as they can. We look to federal government programs, such as Medicare, Social Security, and subsidized housing, to help ensure that older adults have access to medical care and enough money to meet their basic needs when they retire. Other services, such as Meals on Wheels and community senior centers, are important programs for older adults at the local level.

Social workers who work with older adults are concerned with a variety of issues and problems, including elder abuse, Alzheimer's disease and dementia, assisting grandparents who are raising grandchildren, age discrimination, and end-of-life care. Older adults with physical or mental impairments, or who are suffering from a chronic disease, may need assistance at home or in a long-term care residence. Some older adults suffer from depression or substance abuse and require the care of a mental health professional.

Increased attention is needed on the collective experience of aging across cultures defined through race/ethnicity, gender, sexual orientation, class, national origin, and other experiences. Focused responses are needed on the effects of the recent economic recession, technology use and literacy, and issues around sex, sexuality, and STD prevention, with regard to the aging population (Vakalahi, Simpson, & Giunta, 2014). Social workers with the appropriate social work education and skills are urgently needed to provide services, education, and advocacy for and with older adults. Working with older adults requires a high degree of knowledge and skills and can be a very rewarding career. This chapter profiles a number of important work settings for social workers who want to work with older adults.

Gerontology, the study of the biological, psychological, and social aspects of aging, is a relatively new field in social work; it became an established field of social work practice in the 1980s. According to Segal, Gerdes, and Steiner (2004), "The goal of gerontological social workers is to promote and advance older clients' social, emotional, and physical well being so that they can live more independent and satisfying lives" (p. 173).

ADULT PROTECTIVE SERVICES CASEWORKER

Most people are familiar with the role of child protective services (CPS) within their state. However, many are less familiar with the concept of elder abuse and do not realize that many states employ adult protective services (APS) caseworkers who investigate allegations that an older adult, or disabled adult, is being abused or neglected by a family member or caregiver. According to the National Center on Elder Abuse (2014), the best available estimates suggest that about 4 million Americans, or 1 in 10 aged 65 or older, have been subject to some form of elder abuse, and the majority of abusers are family members, typically an adult child or a spouse (Acierno et al., 2010).

Elder abuse may take the following forms: physical abuse, sexual abuse, emotional abuse, neglect, financial exploitation, and abandonment. APS workers perform many of the same tasks as CPS workers: They investigate reports of abuse and neglect, interview the victim and the alleged perpetrator(s), work within the court system, arrange needed services for the family, and sometimes arrange an alternate placement for the victim to keep them safe. (Please read the description of the CPS caseworker in Chapter 4: The skills and competencies needed for APS casework are very similar to the casework performed by CPS caseworkers.)

However, there are also a few differences between CPS and APS work. The major difference is that the APS victim, being an adult, has a choice of whether to receive help and assistance from APS. This is very different from how things work in the CPS system, in which laws mandate that caseworkers protect the child, and sometimes remove him or her from the home, even against the child's wishes. Anecdotally, many APS caseworkers report that their jobs are less stressful than that of CPS caseworkers and that the caseloads are more manageable. In some states, APS caseworkers also investigate allegations of abuse and neglect occurring in nursing homes and other residential care facilities.

Social Worker Spotlight
LORI DELAGRAMMATIKAS, MSW/PhD CANDIDATE
Program Coordinator, Project MASTER, Academy for Professional Excellence, San Diego State University School of Social Work, San Diego, California

I didn't get involved with social work until I was in my forties. My first social work job was determining the amount of home care needed by impoverished, disabled seniors through California's In-Home Supportive Services program. I loved the job, because I was able to provide the kind of help that truly makes a difference in clients' lives. I met some fascinating individuals, like the wheelchair-bound woman who, despite insufferable pain, went to a nursing home every morning to read to the blind, or the elderly Dutch woman who had hidden Jewish families during World War II and now hid food throughout her home.

My next job was as a program specialist for APS. Although this was an administrative job, without direct client contact, I liked the wide variety of duties and experiences. APS social workers investigate abuse of elders living in the community (as opposed to abuse of elders living in nursing homes). The types of abuse range from financial scams to physical/sexual abuse and include self-neglect situations. My job included working with both social workers and management to develop policies and procedures about how workers conducted investigations, delivered services, and managed cases. I met with other community agencies (e.g., law enforcement and mental health) to determine how our agencies could work together. My duties included developing materials to teach the public about elder abuse and reviewing new legislation to determine how it would affect practice. In the process, I became very passionate about elder abuse. I eventually got involved at the state level by volunteering to sit on a statewide APS committee. I helped write the California elder abuse regulations, and I chaired the committee when it published a study of all the elder abuse reports received in California on a specific day.

During the time I worked in APS, I came to realize that we know very little about the dynamics of elder abuse, the size of the problem, and the best ways to intervene. The baby boomers are aging, and we are facing a tidal wave of abuse. We need to be ready! So I recently retired from my government job to return to school and earn my PhD in social research. I am also working part time developing an APS Training Academy, in association with the National APS Association, to provide standardized training to new APS social workers (http://theacademy.sdsu.edu/programs/Project_Master/projectmaster-1.htm).

I invite new social workers to consider a career in APS. The field is growing. It's never boring. And there are very few jobs as rewarding!

SOCIAL WORK IN ADULT DAY CENTERS

Adult day centers are daytime programs that serve older adults who are living at home. By providing older adults with a supervised place to stay during the day, they offer needed respite for caregivers, particularly caregivers who are caring for someone with Alzheimer's or other cognitive impairments. This is an extremely valued service for caregivers who need a break to re-energize from the daily grind of caring for someone who needs full-time care. This gives caregivers the opportunity to run errands or just have some time for self-care. However, adult day centers also provide a valuable service to the older adults and help to meet their health and mental health needs, as well as reduce their social isolation.

Adult day centers usually provide a range of services, including educational, recreational (e.g., water aerobics, dancing), and self-help. Some might also have a health or wellness component. They often serve meals and offer transportation to and from the center.

There are a number of roles individuals can play in adult day centers if they have received a bachelor's degree in social work (BSW) or a master's degree in social work (MSW). They can act in an administrative capacity and may have the title of director or program manager in one of these programs. In this role, the social worker would be charged with developing programs, working with the community, and managing the funds of the organization. Social workers can also act in the role of care coordinator or case manager. In this role, they will assess the client's needs to determine eligibility and appropriateness of services and provide information and referrals, thereby linking them to other programs in the community.

RESIDENTIAL CARE CASE MANAGER

There are a number of residential settings for older adults, depending on the level of care and support required. Adults who are healthy and are able to live independently may choose to live in a retirement community for seniors. Those who need more care may reside in a skilled nursing or assisted living facility. Those with the highest level of care may need to reside in a long-term care rehabilitation facility or nursing home. Social workers can be found working in these various residential settings for older adults. Social workers often perform a case management role to ensure that clients receive services appropriate to their needs, and they work with family members by providing support and information. Psychosocial supportive and educational counseling is often a component of working with adults to help them plan for and cope with life changes.

CAREERS IN PSYCHOGERIATRICS

Some social workers work with older adults who are suffering from depression or other emotional or psychiatric conditions. According to the Centers for Disease Control and Prevention (2013):

- More than 20% of Americans age 55 and older experience specific mental disorders that are not part of "normal" aging, including depression, anxiety disorders, and dementia (including Alzheimer's disease).
- Between 8% and 20% of older adults in the community, and up to 37% in primary care settings, suffer from depressive symptoms as the most prevalent mental health problem.
- Among Americans 65 years and older, approximately 6% to 10% have dementia—and two thirds of people with dementia also have Alzheimer's disease.

Recent research, on the other hand, has focused on "healthy aging" and on various activities that can help older adults maintain their mental and emotional health.

This is a burgeoning field and a good fit for those interested in the behavioral and biological aspects of geriatric mental health. Some social work clinicians in private practice specialize in bereavement and loss. There are a growing number of hospitals around the country that have specialized psychiatric programs for older adults. For more information on social work in the field of mental health, please refer to Chapter 8.

SOCIAL WORK IN HOSPITALS AND OTHER HEALTH CARE SETTINGS

Older adults suffer from a wide range of illnesses, for which they need medical, social, and emotional support. According to the Centers for Disease Control and Prevention (2013), 80% of those older than 65 years of age have at least one chronic health condition (e.g., heart disease, cancer, stroke, diabetes), and 50% have at least two.

Gerontological social workers in this setting provide a range of services, including psychosocial assessments, family support services, home health care, hospice, discharge planning, and counseling and support. For more information on social work in the medical field, please refer to Chapter 7. Here, we will focus on two popular settings when working with older adults in a medical setting: hospice and home health care.

Social Worker Spotlight
SHERYL BRUNO, MSW
Social Work Supervisor, Providence ElderPlace, Portland, Oregon

My family always "told" me that I'd be a nurse. However, in college, I realized that I hated bodily fluids, science, and math, so I switched to other aspects of the human spirit and mind. In 1984, I graduated from the University of Hawaii, having received a bachelor's degree in human development. For the most part, I decided to pursue my MSW for two reasons: I wasn't quite ready to leave college, and I wasn't sure what reaction I would get from potential employers to a degree called "human development." So, by December 1986, I graduated and considered myself ready. For what, I had no idea.

I've always had a strong affinity for older adults, and I was continually exposed to this population with my work in acute care settings as a discharge planner for numerous hospitals in Hawaii and Washington (Seattle and Bellevue). My work took on a different focus while at Harborview Medical Center, however, when I worked as a case manager for the AIDS clinic, then later as a therapist for women and children who were sexually abused. Throughout these experiences, I continued to have a "calling" to go back to geriatrics. With my relocation to Portland, Oregon, I was hired as a social work case manager for Providence ElderPlace, and I have been here for the past 12+ years. My professional growth continued with Providence, from being a direct line staff member to that of supervisor and manager.

Providence ElderPlace is a comprehensive care program that offers a range of services to older adults and their families—medical and mental health services, housing assistance, social services, recreational therapy, end-of-life care, care coordination, and more—all in one program! (To learn more about this model of care, please visit www.providence.org/oregon/Programs_and_Services/ElderPlace/default.htm.)

Social workers at Providence ElderPlace provide case management; relocation planning of patients to appropriate housing settings such as adult foster homes, residential care facilities, and assisted living facilities; financial planning; family conferencing; strong interdisciplinary teamwork; home visits; detailed psychosocial assessments; crisis management; discharge planning; and mental health counseling.

The running theme for my professional career is the desire to help those who are vulnerable and in extreme need. This theme worked well at all of my jobs, but particularly with my job within the Providence Health System because of its strong mission and values of justice, stewardship, compassion, respect, and excellence. Perhaps this explains why I have been with

(continued)

SHERYL BRUNO   (*continued*)

Providence Health System for over 12 years and have no intentions of leaving soon. I've also stayed in social work because the field allows me to explore many areas in helping others, such as by being a direct case manager, a therapist, and, most recently in my professional career, a supervisor and manager. Although it can be stressful, as most jobs in the health care field can be, I continue to see the value of the social work role every day thanks to my staff's commitment to the people we serve every day.

HOSPICE SOCIAL WORKER

Generally speaking, hospice agencies provide services for people with terminal illnesses who are expected to die within 6 months, either in the patient's home or in an inpatient hospice facility. In response to the growing number of older Americans, usage of hospice services is rising and will continue to do so. According to the National Hospice and Palliative Care Organization (2013), an estimated 1.3 million patients received services from hospice in 2006, a 162% increase in 10 years; and an estimated 1.5 to 1.6 million received hospice services in 2012.

The role of the hospice social worker includes helping the dying patient and his or her loved ones prepare for the end of his or her life, assisting the patient and the family with bereavement, providing relief from pain (e.g., palliative and supportive care), improving the patient's quality of life, assisting with difficult decision making, and mediating between the patient and the medical professionals involved in the patient's care. Because the focus of this work is on death and dying, there is often a spiritual or religious component to this work as well. Hospice social workers work with a team of professionals, including hospice nurses, physicians, and chaplains. Doing hospice work also involves knowing the laws that govern end-of-life decision making. For example, a few states such as Oregon and Washington have made it legal for some terminal patients to end their life with the aid of a physician.

Social Worker Spotlight
MARY JANE O'ROURKE, MSW
Hospice and Palliative Care of Washington County, Hillsboro, Oregon

I have an MSW from Eastern Washington University. As a medical social worker at Hospice and Palliative Care of Washington County (HWC) in Hillsboro, Oregon, I assume a variety of social work roles. For the past 2½ years, I have provided direct social work services to hospice patients and families as part of HWC's in-home hospice, designed to meet terminally ill patients'—and their families'—physical, social, psychological, and spiritual needs. I serve as a resource coordinator, counselor, and educator for patients and families. When a patient's physician refers him or her to hospice, an MSW and RN meet with the patient and family to educate them about hospice, assess individual needs, and gather the various resources needed for particular patients.

Hospice is a concept of care designed to provide support and care for patients with incurable diseases, so they may maintain quality of life and comfort as they journey through the dying process. Hospice social workers are required to have a BSW; HWC prefers an MSW as well.

Working with people at the end of their lives is a privilege and an honor. The end of life can be a vulnerable yet meaningful time for hospice patients and families. The gift lies in the invitation to enter one's home and life at such a vulnerable time. Respecting each person for who he or she is, how he or she has lived his or her life, and how he or she wants to leave the world is the main task of a hospice social worker. I am constantly learning valuable lessons about the human spirit and the beauty of life and death.

HOME HEALTH SOCIAL WORKER

Private home health agencies have proliferated in recent years as the number of adults who need care but want to remain in their home continues to grow. This service will continue to be in demand in the coming years. Social workers employed in home health agencies primarily play a case-management role. They refer families to needed services and programs; "trouble-shoot" problematic situations between the caregiver and the care receiver; arrange alternative care options; facilitate communication between family members, medical professionals, and service providers; and counsel families dealing with illness and end-of-life issues.

GERIATRIC CASE MANAGER

This growing field of social work practice will continue to expand in the coming years as more and more families need assistance from a professional in managing the needs of their loved ones. Any family member who has been faced with the daunting decision to move an older family member to a care facility knows how overwhelming it can be. In a very short period of time, the family must sort through where the parent should live, whether the parent will be eligible, how to pay for it, and how to access various government programs such as Medicare and Medicaid. And on top of all of this, they want to ensure that their loved one will be in a place where he or she will be safe and cared for.

Geriatric case managers may work in a private, for-profit agency or have their own private practices. Social workers in this role commonly perform the following tasks: conduct care planning assessment and link the client with appropriate resources and providers; assist with arranging in-home services or moving an older adult to a retirement community, assisted living facility, or nursing home; provide counseling and support, including crisis counseling; assist with medical, legal, and financial issues; provide case management and facilitate communication between family members, medical professionals, and service providers; monitor service delivery to ensure that the patient is receiving high-quality care that is timely; and provide advocacy when necessary. This job has the potential to be quite lucrative, because many case managers are in business for themselves and the number of families in need of this type of service will continue to grow.

Social Worker Spotlight
SIMON PAQUETTE, LCSW, RC
Medical Social Worker, Independent Case Management, Camas, Washington

In 1992, I received my MSW from Springfield College in Springfield, Massachusetts. I had many years of experience as a practicing social worker before going back to graduate school at age 40. In graduate training, as part of my hospice career path, I became sensitized to the issues and family dynamics when a family member is dying from an illness. I found myself gaining tremendous experience in the medical management of terminal illness and supportive interventions to family members. I gained knowledge about poor medical practice, social work interventions, and evidence-proven pathways. I remained in this field for 9 years. I began a transition process of immersing myself back into mental health, chronic disease management, pain management practice reform, regulating long-term care, nursing home social service, and home health, ultimately dissatisfied with each choice. I found my knowledge of medical management useful but not contributing enough to improving the lives of others.

The role I evolved into was independent case management of the total care of persons with guardians, conservators, and trust officers. I found an outlet for my skills in situations in which a client requires comprehensive care solutions. I took on several difficult cases with clients involving families at odds with the legal system, each other, and the guardianship community. I became valued for my skills and knowledge base by those who were contracting with me. My clients achieved more independence, quality of life, and consistent care. I also found the recognition of other medical disciplines because I could deal with the total care need. I had found a niche—and, more important, excitement—finding solutions resulting in the kind of care outcomes I had been frustrated in achieving in the past. This time, however, I was able to continue to facilitate and coordinate care over time, resulting in increased quality of life, reduction of medical needs, and stable health/mental health disease process. My many years of work experience involving mental/medical health, disease process management, funding streams, legal, ethical, and values issues had all come together. I feel a sense of greater value as a professional in contributing to the well-being of others, as well as personal satisfaction with the outcomes of my work.

I have experienced successful outcomes with clients that had required immense resources being reduced to routine care management. A lifetime of gained experience has translated into the most satisfaction I could have ever imagined in the practice of social work. I am independent, valued, and

(continued)

SIMON PAQUETTE   (*continued*)

growing as a professional in the later stages of my career. Having gained the knowledge base to understand funding, care management systems, medical culture, and the politics involved, from macro to the micro levels, I have discovered a new career area for myself and colleagues that is quite remarkable for providing all the support, tools, and teamwork to fulfill all aspects of social work practice. The impact of aging in our society has yet to be fully understood. The challenges it poses are ideal for the advanced social work practitioner.

CAREERS IN RESEARCH AND POLICY

Some social workers choose to work as lobbyists or in advocacy organizations, such as the AARP, to try to pass legislation that improves conditions for older adults. Areas of focus might include making improvements to the Medicare and Social Security programs, making prescription drugs more affordable, providing financial and other benefits to grandparents who are raising grandchildren, and obtaining affordable housing for seniors. Social workers also work as researchers in the field of aging/gerontology. They typically work for universities, the government, or nonprofit research organizations. Social work researchers strive to conduct research to evaluate the efficacy of various interventions that may be used with aging adults, their caregivers, and other family members.

CAREERS WITH THE GOVERNMENT

Social workers all across the country begin working for the government (city, county, state, or federal) after having some direct experience in gerontology. Many states and localities have an office or department of aging. For those interested in working at the federal level there is the Administration on Aging, under the auspices of the Department of Health and Human Services. Most related jobs include working in policy or program planning. They may also involve applying for a grant to start a new outreach program, or other needed program, for older adults in your community. The upside of working in a high-level government job is that it typically includes good benefits, regular working hours, and a higher salary because you are recognized as an expert in your field.

Core Competencies and Skills

■ Knowledge of the aging process, chronic illnesses and mental impairments associated with aging, and commonly used medications and medical interventions

- Knowledge of the stressors that can occur as one adjusts to older adulthood, such as retirement, widowhood, physical decline, loss of loved ones, and approaching end of life
- Strong advocacy and mediation skills to ensure that older adults are receiving the professional care and services to which they are entitled
- Awareness of cultural and religious/spiritual differences when it comes to attitudes and beliefs on aging and death and dying
- Awareness of the dynamics of urban and rural contexts on aging and gerontology service availability and accessibility
- Sensitivity to aging and gerontology issues across cultural groups, including lesbian, gay, bisexual, transgender, and queer (LGBTQ); immigrants; homeless and economically deprived older adults; and so forth
- Advanced knowledge and skills in addressing issues of technology use, sex and sexuality, health and disease, and the like
- Working knowledge of financial literacy and technology to assist the aged in accessing services and resources
- Knowledge and skills in responding to the increase in HIV/AIDS and substance abuse, particularly prescription medication abuse, among the aging population
- Effective working with large systems of care, such as medical and mental health systems
- Knowledge of and sensitivity to dynamics and risk factors related to elder abuse and neglect
- Strong knowledge of the latest research on loss, bereavement, and death and dying
- Strong assessment and counseling skills with a life-course perspective
- Knowledge of the major government programs, laws, regulations, and public policies pertaining to older adults, such as Medicare, Social Security, Social Security Supplemental Income (SSI), guardianship, living wills, power of attorney, and end-of-life care

Educational and Licensing Requirements

It is a good idea to attend continuing education workshops in your community that pertain to social work with older adults, many of which will emphasize end-of-life care, mental health, or medical issues. There are BSW-level positions available in gerontology if you are interested in working in residential settings, such as independent and assisted living centers, rehabilitation centers, community senior centers, or APS.

Many social work jobs that involve working with older adults require a master's degree and specialized training, particularly if you are interested in working in the fields of health care, mental health, or hospice. Some jobs may also require licensure. There are a number of ways to get experience and specialized training if you are interested in working in this field. It would be advisable to choose field internships in this area when you are completing your undergraduate or MSW. Additionally, there are some MSW programs that offer concentrations in gerontology or certificate programs that allow for advanced training in the field. You may also look for social work programs that offer elective courses on aging, grief, or death and dying. The Council on Social Work Education's (CSWE) Gero-Ed Center website maintains a list of accredited programs that feature gerontology (http://depts.washington.edu/geroctr/Resources4/sub4_4J5GeroSWPrograms.html).

Best Aspects of This Job

- Working in a multidisciplinary setting with other professionals (e.g., physicians, nurses, dietitians, occupational and physical therapists, mental health professionals, chaplains) makes for an interesting and diverse work environment.
- Working with older adults enables you to work with individuals from diverse backgrounds who have lived varied and interesting lives.
- Many social workers who work with patients who are dying feel it an honor to be able to provide comfort to patients and their families in their final days.
- Hearing the stories of older adults as they share their wisdom and life experiences with you is a privilege.
- Working with persons as they grow older helps you keep your own priorities in perspective.
- Protecting older adults from abuse and neglect and helping them achieve a high-quality life can be very rewarding.

Challenging Aspects of This Job

- Seeing patients who are dying or in pain takes an emotional toll; self-care is very important.
- It is difficult to watch an older adult give up his or her independence and to see his or her quality of life decline when support and resources are not available.
- Assisting families with making end-of-life decisions for their loved one (e.g., when to remove the feeding tube) can be challenging.
- Setting clear boundaries with patients and families can be a sensitive area.
- Understanding and working with your own grief can be challenging.
- Dealing with societal views around issues of grief, death, and aging can be frustrating.
- You must be flexible and willing to change course when patients and families are in crisis.

Compensation and Employment Outlook

One of the biggest growth areas for helping professionals, including social workers, in the coming years will be working with older adults. According to the Bureau of Labor Statistics (U.S. Department of Labor, 2014), as baby boomers age, they and their families will require help from social workers to find care, increasing the need for health care social workers. Thus, social workers interested in working with older adults exclusively or as part of the general clientele will be in great demand in the coming years as a result of these changing demographics.

Salaries for APS caseworkers are comparable to the salaries of CPS caseworkers in each respective state. Salaries for those jobs requiring an MSW (e.g., hospice, mental health settings, medical settings) will be significantly higher than for those jobs requiring a BSW (e.g., community senior centers or residential settings, such as nursing homes and assisted living facilities). Administrative and supervisory positions in agencies and organizations serving older adults will also pay higher salaries.

Self-Assessment Checklist: Is This Job for Me?

- Do you have a healthy respect and admiration for older adults and the rich life experience they bring to the table?
- Would you enjoy working with and supporting the family members of older adults?
- Would you find it interesting and exciting to work with an interdisciplinary team of medical and mental health professionals?
- Are you comfortable seeing adults who are ill and working with issues of death and dying?
- Do you enjoy the company and companionship of older adults?
- Would you be able to see and hear details of how an older adult has been abused or neglected by one of their family members or in a residential facility?
- Are you creative in planning social and recreational activities for older adults?
- Are you able to refrain from forcing your own religious and spiritual beliefs about death and dying onto the patients you will be working with?
- Are you good at taking care of yourself to allow yourself to deal with the emotional toll of working with issues of death and dying?
- Would you be comfortable working in a host setting with other professionals who were educated differently and who may have different views and values than those of social workers?

If you answered "yes" to seven or more of the preceding questions, then working with older adults might be for you!

RECOMMENDED READINGS/WEBSITES TO LEARN MORE

General Information on Aging

Administration on Aging, U.S. Department of Health and Human Services: www.aoa.dhhs.gov

AARP: www.aarp.org

American Society on Aging: www.asaging.org/about.cfm

Berkman, B. (2006). *Handbook of social work in health and aging*. New York, NY: Oxford University Press.

Council on Social Work Education Gero-Ed Center: http://depts.washington .edu/geroctr

Grobman, L. M., & Bourassa, D. B. (2007). *Days in the lives of gerontological social workers: 44 professionals tell stories from "real-life" social work practice with older adults*. Harrisburg, PA: White Hat Communications.

Hooyman, N., & Kiyak, H. A. (2010). *Social gerontology: A multidisciplinary perspective*. New York, NY: Pearson.

Institute on Aging and Social Work: www.css.edu/Academics/Centers-and-Institutes/AgingSocial-Work-Institute.html

National Association of Professional Geriatric Care Managers: www.caremanager.org/index.cfm

Elder Abuse

Clearinghouse on Abuse and Neglect of the Elderly: http://db.rdms.udel .edu:8080/CANE/index.jsp

Mellor, J., & Brownell, P. (2006). *Elder abuse and mistreatment: Policy, practice, and research*. Philadelphia, PA: Haworth Press.

National Center on Elder Abuse: www.ncea.aoa.gov/NCEAroot/Main_Site/ Library/CANE/CANE.aspx

National Committee for the Prevention of Elder Abuse: www.preventelderabuse.org

Woolf, L. (1998). *Elder abuse and neglect*. www.webster.edu/~woolflm/abuse.html

Visit the following website to watch a video about a real APS case in Texas: www.dfps.state.tx.us/Adult_Protection/video/default.asp

Hospice/Death and Dying

Albom, M. *Tuesdays with Morrie*. New York, NY: Doubleday. (A beautiful true story of a man suffering from Lou Gehrig's disease who lived and died with great dignity.)

Kübler-Ross, E. (1989). *On death and dying*. London, UK: Routledge.

National Hospice and Palliative Care Organization: www.nhpco.org

Alzheimer's Disease

Alzheimer's Association: www.alz.org

Social Work With Older Adults Exercise Case Study

You are an APS caseworker and have been given the following case to investigate: Mr. Harris is 77 years old and lives with his 52-year-old son. The caller reports that the son hits his father and constantly calls him names and threatens to throw him out of the house when the son has had too much to drink. The caller has seen bruises on the face and arms of the victim on numerous occasions. The caller also alleges that the son is taking his father's Social Security money each month. He uses the money to finance his hunting trips with friends and to purchase alcohol and other expensive gifts for himself. His father often goes without needed medication for his high blood pressure and diabetes. The caller is very worried about the victim and believes he should be living in a safer environment, one in which he is cared for and loved. The caller believes that Mr. Harris is scared of his son and, though he would like to be living elsewhere, believes he has nowhere else to go.

Questions

1. What are your thoughts and feelings as you read this case?
2. If you were the APS caseworkers assigned to investigate this case, what would your next steps be?
3. Who would you talk to, and what questions would you ask?
4. What would you do if Mr. Harris denies the allegations even though other close family members report that he is being abused?
5. What would you do if Mr. Harris confirms the allegations but refuses your help and services and says he will deal with this on his own?
6. How would you deal with the son if he is hostile or if he angrily denies that he harms his father in any way?
7. If these allegations are true, what kinds of services could be provided to help this family?

REFERENCES

Acierno, R., Hernandez, M. A., Amstadter, A. B., Resnick, H. S., Steve, K., Muzzy, W., & Kilpatrick, D. G. (2010). Prevalence and correlates of emotional, physical, sexual, and financial abuse and potential neglect in the United States: The National Elder Mistreatment Study. *American Journal of Public Health, 100*(2), 292–297.

Centers for Disease Control and Prevention. (2013). *Health information for older adults.* Retrieved from www.cdc.gov/aging/pdf/mental_health.pdf

National Center on Elder Abuse. (2014). *Elder abuse: The size of the problem*. Retrieved from www.ncea.aoa.gov/Library/Data/#problem

National Hospice and Palliative Care Organization. (2013). *NHPCO facts and figures: Hospice care in America*. Retrieved from www.nhpco.org/files/public/Statistics_Research/NHPCO_facts-and-figures_Nov2007.pdf

Segal, E. A., Gerdes, K. E., & Steiner, S. (2004). *Social work: An introduction to the profession*. Belmont, CA: Brooks/Cole.

U.S. Department of Labor, Bureau of Labor Statistics. (2014). *Occupational outlook handbook, 2014–15 edition: Social workers*. Retrieved from http://www.bls.gov/ooh/community-and-social-service/social-workers.htm

Vakalahi, H. F. O., Simpson, G. M., & Giunta, N. (Eds.). (2014). *The collective spirit of aging across cultures*. New York, NY: Springer Science and Business Media.

Yancey, K., Baldwin, T., Saran, A., & Vakalahi, H. F. O. (2014). City life—What a wonderful way of life: Aging in the urban environment. In H. F. O. Vakalahi, G. Simpson, & N. Giunta (Eds.), *The collective spirit of aging across cultures*. New York, NY: Springer Science and Business Media.

7 ■ SOCIAL WORK IN HEALTH CARE

Kissing the boo-boo doesn't help the pain . . . It helps the loneliness.
—Rachel Naomi Remen (1996)

When we examine the mission of social work, a case may be made that all social work involves the practice of healing. This is no more evident than when considering the diverse roles of social workers in the field of health care.

The health care delivery system in America is complex and varied. At the turn of the 20th century, the focus on medical care began to shift from individual patient disease and pathology to a broader understanding of public or community health, with an emphasis on prevention. This was most notable during the devastating flu epidemic of 1918 that killed thousands of people in America and abroad. The first public health recommendation in the wake of this human disaster resulted in a public education campaign to promote the value of frequent handwashing as the primary prevention measure in combating the transmission of deadly communicable diseases. Social workers had a major role in this campaign and were known as "community workers" in densely populated urban centers, which appeared to be the focus of several communicable diseases. The public health system is where the role of the medical social worker was born (Fort Cowles, 2003).

Health care in the United States has certainly undergone many transformations over the past 100 years—and with it, so has the role of social work. The United States is an outlier among Western industrialized nations for not having universal health care, a system of care that guarantees everyone health care coverage. Americans continue to debate whether health care is a privilege or a right. In 2012, more than 48 million people in the United States had no health insurance coverage (U.S. Census Bureau, 2013). The National Association of Social Workers views health care as a right and supports a national health care system that provides individuals with universal access to a full range of health and mental health care throughout all stages of life.

Unequal access to comprehensive care is a major barrier in the treatment and prevention of illness in populations of people who are the most vulnerable, particularly children, women, ethnic minorities, and persons living in poverty. Grave disparities in receiving medical care persist as a result of chronic poverty and/or membership in a particular minority or ethnic group. This has created an area of research for those interested in studying health disparities in the United States.

The rapid development and growing availability of medical technology have created more options for care and improved quality of life. However, this growth has also contributed to exorbitant costs in providing health care and to introducing social, legal, and ethical dilemmas for individuals, families, communities, and health care providers. A major role for social workers in health care is to help people navigate the system and manage the psychosocial stressors of entering the system and making health care decisions (Darnell, 2007).

> Social workers look at the person-in-environment, including all of the factors that influence the total health care experience. Social workers practice at the macro and micro level of health care and thus have the ability to influence policy change and development at local, state, and federal levels and within systems of care. (National Association of Social Workers, 2005, p. 8)

Social workers who choose to work in the health care field must become experts of the U.S. health care system, which is quite complex, to help patients navigate the vast array of programs and health care coverage options: private health care coverage; Medicaid; Medicare; CHIP program; the VA system; and the new state-based, health care exchanges that were created by the Patient Protection and Affordable Care Act. Social workers are found in many areas of the health care system (both public and private) and help to ensure that patients receive the appropriate level of care they need as they move throughout the system.

Social workers practice in the public health system, acute and chronic inpatient hospitals, rehabilitation and residential care settings, home health agencies, hospice centers, doctor's offices, outpatient clinics, and ambulatory care centers. They provide an array of services, including health education, psychosocial support through counseling and group work, crisis intervention, and case management. In today's world, health care social workers are increasingly relied upon to respond to regional, national, and global critical incidents, providing intervention for traumatic events and disasters. The common thread throughout the various social work settings and functions in health care is the value and importance of the role of patient advocacy.

THE PATIENT PROTECTION AND AFFORDABLE CARE ACT, OR "OBAMACARE"

In 2010, the Patient Protection and Affordable Care Act was signed into law by President Obama, causing the biggest change to the U.S. health care system since the Medicaid and Medicare programs were created during the Lyndon B. Johnson presidential administration during the 1960s. The law was passed after a bitter, partisan 15-month battle that political conservatives fought every step of the way. The intent of the new law was to reform the health insurance system so that more Americans would be able to afford health care coverage. This new law has also created new career opportunities for social workers (see "Patient Navigators" at the end of this chapter). The main features of the new law are as follows:

■ The health reform legislation requires that all individuals have health insurance or else pay a tax penalty (some exemptions included).

■ The poorest Americans are covered under a Medicaid expansion.

■ Young adults will now have the option of being covered under their parents' plan, up to age 26.

■ Those with low and middle incomes who do not have access to affordable coverage through their jobs will be able to purchase coverage (with federal subsidies) through newly created state-based health insurance exchanges. There are four benefit categories: bronze, silver, gold, and platinum.

■ Employers are not mandated to provide health benefits, but businesses employing more than 50 employees will pay penalties if their employees receive insurance subsidies. Small businesses will be able to access more plans through a separate exchange. Tax credits will be provided to small employers that purchase health insurance for employees.

■ Health plans will not be allowed to deny coverage to people for any reason, including preexisting conditions.

■ Outlines the minimum "essential health benefits" that must be included on all health insurance plans in the marketplace, including the requirement that plans include coverage of preventive services and immunizations.

■ Investments in community health centers, school-based health centers, and various strategies to improve the health care workforce, including social workers, are included.

The Patient Protection and Affordable Care Act is new and is still unfolding, so the jury is still out in terms of how well the new law will affect Americans' health and access to health care coverage. The new law made some significant changes to the U.S. health care system but left many Americans disappointed. It was too radical for many conservatives and Tea Party activists who feared that this was just the first step toward a "government takeover of health care," and it was not radical enough for many liberals and single-payer activists who were stunned to hear the Congressional Budget Office estimate that the bill would provide coverage to 32 million uninsured people yet leave 23 million uninsured in 2019, thus falling short of the goal of ensuring that all Americans have health insurance coverage. However, there is no doubt that the new ObamaCare law is a very significant change in U.S. health care policy.

SOCIAL WORK IN HOSPITALS AND OTHER MEDICAL SETTINGS

Social workers who work in hospital settings help patients and their families cope with a new diagnosis, injury, or chronic illness by providing direct services to meet their needs in assisting them to return to independent functioning within the community. Medical social workers provide psychosocial support to people, families, or vulnerable populations so they can better cope with their diagnosis and treatment.

As part of a multidisciplinary team, medical social workers have many functions. Social workers provide a valuable resource to doctors and nurses by providing them with critical information for the treatment and recovery process of patients by obtaining in-depth social histories and assessments. The following scenario provides an example of a medical social worker in action.

Mr. Fuller was admitted to the hospital for severe and chronic back pain. His doctor decided to hospitalize him because Mr. Fuller required increasingly higher dosages of pain medication, which prevented him from returning to work, and he still was not feeling any better. A social worker was given the referral for an assessment of Mr. Fuller, and through the course of their conversation, the social worker learned that Mr. Fuller's only son had died 6 months earlier. It was shortly after his son's death that Mr. Fuller's back pain severely increased. The social worker understood that the mental health condition of depression often intensifies the physical experience of pain for persons with a pre-existing condition. She provided the doctor with her information and assessment of Mr. Fuller's present condition. The doctor was unaware of the extreme grief the patient was experiencing, and she promptly contacted her colleague, a psychiatrist, to evaluate Mr. Fuller for depression. The psychiatrist met with Mr. Fuller and subsequently prescribed an antidepressant. Mr. Fuller was discharged to home, and the social worker followed up with him a week later by telephone. She learned that Mr. Fuller was sleeping better and felt less pain. The social worker suggested attending a bereavement group close to where he lived, and Mr. Fuller agreed to participate. During a 6-week follow-up phone call, Mr. Fuller reported that he was using less pain medication and had been able to return to his job.

Other functions that medical social workers may provide include the following:

- Facilitating psychosocial support groups for persons newly diagnosed with a condition or recovering from treatment
- Finding help for caregivers
- Educating patients and families by helping them understand the treatment plan and adhere to the doctors' recommendations
- Promoting wellness by helping people change unhealthy behaviors
- Helping people access insurance and financial benefits and understand their rights as patients

- Communicating with doctors and medical teams
- Screening and assessment for neglect and abuse, psychosocial high-risk factors, and other needs

Many medical social workers are able to specialize in an area of medicine by population (e.g., pediatrics or gerontology) or by specific illnesses or conditions (e.g., renal disease, diabetes, cancer, obstetrics and gynecology, HIV/AIDS, pain management).

Social Worker Spotlight
JACQUELINE FRAUSTO, BSW, MSSW
Medical Social Worker
Dell Children's Medical Center of Central Texas, Austin, Texas

My social work education began at the University of Texas at Austin, where I received my bachelor of social work (BSW) and master of science in social work (MSSW) degrees.

I began my social work career in child welfare, but for the past 7 years I have worked in the health care field. Today, I work as a medical social worker at the Dell Children's Medical Center of Central Texas. For the first 5 years, my job involved working with chronically ill children in an outpatient setting. Many of these children required a tracheostomy/ventilator to breathe; others had spasticity issues that affected their movement. I helped the children and their families cope with their diagnosis and worked with the families to resolve issues preventing them from focusing on caring for their child. Typically, resolving these issues involved advocating on the patient's behalf to ensure that the child had stable living accommodations, was provided appropriate academic services, and, if the patient was insured, was being provided needed equipment and support by the insurance provider.

For the past 2 years, I have been part of an interdisciplinary medical team at the Craniofacial and Reconstructive Plastic Surgery Center. The team consists of several plastic surgeons, an orthodontist, a dentist, an otolaryngologist, a speech therapist, a pediatrician, and a social worker. Our team's goal is to provide comprehensive care to children and adolescents with congenital malformations or traumatic injury that require lengthy treatment. We work in a collaborative manner to provide family-centered and culturally competent care to our patients and their families. My role is to provide the rest of the team a glimpse of the patient's life outside of the clinic and to identify the patient's strengths and possible barriers to effective treatment. For the patients, I offer guidance and counseling to help them navigate the social and emotional aspects of their condition, identify helpful community resources, and make referrals to appropriate agencies and organizations.

We serve as many as 800 patients each month. Each patient is seen in one of our weekly clinics. It is difficult to describe the day-to-day nature of my job, because every day I am called upon to address a highly varied range of needs for patients with vastly different backgrounds. For example, on a recent workday, I was asked to consult with a single mother of a 9-year-old child with special needs. This mother felt overwhelmed by her son's behaviors, was homeless, and was unable to maintain steady employment due to

(continued)

JACQUELINE FRAUSTO   (continued)

her son's many medical appointments. She desperately wanted counseling to deal with the ending of her marriage. She also needed help understanding her immigration status, as both she and her son were undocumented, which presents a large barrier to accessing resources.

After speaking with her, my next consult was a newborn with a cleft. The child's mother was single, very young, and legally blind. She needed assistance accessing parenting support services for herself so that she could care for her child as independently as possible. Next, the team asked me to meet with a 17-year-old female who was undergoing a nasal reconstruction procedure and who had expressed suicidal ideation. A hospital psychiatrist provided the initial intervention, and it was determined that ongoing therapy was required. However, the patient lives in a part of southwest Texas where counseling options are very limited.

My last two patients were a brother and sister who both suffer from a syndrome that is manifested by orthopedic and cranial anomalies. Their mother has been living on her own for 3 years and has been successful in making certain her children's medical needs are met. This visit, however, she reported that her husband, who has been incarcerated on domestic violence charges, is being released from jail and will be returning home in a month.

During each of these encounters, I have to be fully present, offer encouraging support, and working with the patient or family to develop a plan to make certain that everyone's concerns are addressed, that the patients are safe, and that the team's treatment goals are met. After I meet with the patients, I make a list of tasks to accomplish as swiftly and as efficiently as possible to further assist the patient and their family. Often I have only a few hours to accomplish these tasks for each patient that I consult with before a new day begins and I am greeted with new patients and their families, who also need a social worker to listen to them and to assist them on their journey to wellness.

At the beginning of my career, I never saw myself working in the health care field. My interests were child protection, foster care, and adoption. What I like most about working in the health care field is that every day it gives me the opportunity to help children and their families cope and, hopefully thrive, during a stressful time in their life. It is especially rewarding to be part of a team that genuinely appreciates the value that a social worker adds to the team, and that appreciates the social worker's perspective, especially in those instances when the team is at odds over what the best course of action for a patient may be.

The health care field is complex and quite difficult to navigate. I believe that the experience I have gained while working in various settings, along

(continued)

JACQUELINE FRAUSTO   (*continued*)

with the relationships I have developed with medical providers, enables me to effectively guide patients and their families toward adequately meeting their or their child's medical needs, and leave them with a positive impression of our facility. Almost 20 years after obtaining my social work education, I find myself thankful to be working at a premiere pediatric health care facility with an amazing, compassionate, and talented group of medical providers who perform truly miraculous acts each day.

EMERGENCY ROOM SOCIAL WORKER

This is a specialized area of medical social work that requires skills in crisis intervention, critical incident debriefing (CID), helping people cope with acute trauma and loss, preparation for public health emergencies, and providing victim assistance. Emergency room (ER) social workers work in an extremely fast-paced environment and usually do not have a 9-to-5 schedule. They often work different shifts much as doctors and nurses do.

ER social workers are essentially in a "liaison" role to the medical team and patient's families when patients need to be transferred for further treatment in an appropriate intensive care unit (ICU) within the hospital or another facility (e.g., large community hospital with a burn unit).

In many instances, ER social workers provide "psychological first-aid" (PFA) to patients, victims, families, and communities. Emergency room social workers are on the forefront of helping people cope with and recover from crisis and trauma, from the children injured in a school bus accident, to helping a "lost" loved one with Alzheimer's disease. The ability to translate critical information, navigate complex service delivery systems, and advocate for the best interests of patients and families are the primary functions of social work practice in the ER.

HOSPICE SOCIAL WORKER

See Chapter 6 for a description of this career option.

DIRECTOR OF SOCIAL WORK

Because of their expertise, it is not surprising to find medical social workers employed as part of the administrative team in health care delivery systems. As directors of social work departments, case management, or quality assurance departments, social workers in these managerial roles play a vital part in the day-to-day functioning of providing care to patients and families, in addition to providing professional support to social work staff, other health care employees, and the community.

Social work managers are responsible for the supervision, professional development, and continuing education of social service staff to maintain the highest standards in service delivery as required by accreditation standards of hospitals and clinics, in addition to the National Association of Social Workers *Code of Ethics* (2008). Improving patient care, in the context of managing available financial resources, is part of the daily routine for social work administrators.

Social workers in this role examine and address issues such as the following:

- The types of patients staying too long in the hospital because they are homeless or there is no one to take care of them if they are discharged
- The increased number of ER referrals for persons with mental health issues because of a lack of treatment providers in the community
- The large number of uninsured women who are being discharged too quickly after delivering a baby, only to return with complications and be readmitted

Social work directors are often part of multidisciplinary bioethics review teams and quality improvement committees in hospital settings. Social work directors are members of these teams and committees because of their professional knowledge of human behavior and the social environment, as well as the leadership and facilitation skills they bring to the problem-solving process.

PUBLIC HEALTH SOCIAL WORKER

Social workers in the field of public health use their skills with the broad focus of community health. They work primarily in organizations focused on prevention and risk reduction, such as Planned Parenthood, infant and toddler early intervention programs, Head Start programs for prekindergarten children, child and infant mortality teams with the Centers for Disease Control (CDC) and state health departments, and HIV prevention programs with nonprofit human service agencies.

Public health social workers are found in government regional emergency response centers to help educate the community regarding emergency preparedness in times of disasters and epidemics, where everyone in a specified geographic area would be affected by an outbreak of pandemic flu, tuberculosis, or salmonella, or what to do in case of a biohazard threat (e.g., a toxic chemical spill). They will often be trainers of volunteers in the public health system—for example, the Medical Reserve Corps—and help train others to provide PFA in the event of a community emergency or disaster.

Family violence prevention, healthy eating and weight loss, smoking cessation, and substance abuse awareness programs are other public health issues that concern these medical social workers. Public health social workers may even be employed at your workplace through an employee assistance program.

Public health social workers who work for the CDC or state health departments may have specialized knowledge and skills in epidemiology, the study of the origin and spread of disease. Some social workers supplement their BSW or master's degree in social work (MSW) course work with additional courses in epidemiology, attend a dual-degree program in social work and public health, or pursue a doctorate in epidemiology or a related field after completing their MSW.

Social Worker Spotlight
ERICA SOLWAY, MSW, MPH
Doctoral Student in Sociology, University of California, San Francisco

Upon graduation from college, I decided to continue my education and enter a dual master's degree program in social work (MSW) and public health (MPH). Although still a student, I was relatively certain, in light of my previous volunteer, work, and research experiences with older adults, that I wanted to work in the area of aging. Before deciding on the program, I spoke with many people about a career in aging, and I was advised that social work and public health training would provide a strong foundation for understanding the experiences of older adults. It was also suggested that there is a considerable need to study social policy and aging—in particular, aging services. This was extremely valuable advice. While pursuing advanced education in social work and public health, I had the opportunity to work with the local long-term care ombudsman program to plan a conference on the health of older women of color and to work on several research projects that focused on both the health and mental health of older adults and family caregivers. All these opportunities were enlightening and allowed me to contribute in meaningful and diverse ways to improving the lives of older adults.

I am now in a doctoral program in medical sociology. While I am currently focused on a new discipline, it serves to enhance and enrich the many skills and interests I developed as a social work and public health student. Since the beginning of the doctoral program, I have worked with Students for Social Security (SSS) and Concerned Scientists in Aging (CSA), two nonprofit, nonpartisan organizations that work to raise awareness about the important role of social insurance as a foundation of economic and health security through public education. I have worked on organizing campus events, developed a website (www.studentsforsocialsecurity.org) and newsletter, created a documentary film on the importance of Social Security, and am now in the process of editing a book on social insurance with some of my SSS/CSA colleagues, Leah Rogne, Carroll Estes, Brian Grossman, and Brooke Hollister, tentatively titled *Social Insurance, Social Justice, and Social Change*. Furthermore, I am focusing my dissertation research on activities and efforts to help lower the rates of smoking among people with mental illness through a social movement perspective. I became interested in this area of research after I was offered an opportunity to work with an initiative to try and address this important issue thanks to my background in social work and public health. Although I have not worked as a clinical

(continued)

ERICA SOLWAY *(continued)*

social worker as many of my colleagues in this field have, my social work background has opened many doors and has led to enormously fulfilling opportunities in research, advocacy, and social policy in the areas of aging, social insurance, mental health, and smoking cessation.

REHABILITATION SOCIAL WORKER

Rehabilitation social workers are medical social workers who specialize in rehabilitation medicine and are employed in many of the aforementioned settings, in addition to places such as Veterans Affairs (VA) hospitals and clinics.

Rehabilitation social workers provide counseling and psychosocial support as well as direct services to individuals in the process of recovery from various illnesses, accidents, and traumas that resulted in a disabling condition. Persons injured by a medical condition, such as a traumatic brain injury or stroke, as well as those who have survived a car accident or fire or who are coping with the disabling effects of a progressive disease, will most certainly encounter a social worker on their road to recovery.

Social workers in this field may also be employed as *disability experts* who are trained to assist persons in obtaining financial benefits once they have become disabled.

Rehabilitation social workers are in great demand, particularly those who work with American veterans. According to the Defense and Veterans Brain Injury Center (2014), which provides many kinds of rehabilitation for those in active military service and veterans, traumatic brain injury was present in at least 14% to 20% of those surviving combat casualties in previous military engagements. Preliminary information from the current conflict in the Middle East suggests that this number is now much higher. (For more information about working with the military, see Chapter 8.)

PATIENT NAVIGATOR/PATIENT ADVOCATE

Jobs for patient navigators have increased greatly in number since the passage of the Patient Protection and Affordable Care Act. These jobs may also be known as patient advocate jobs depending on the organization. According to the American Medical Association (AMA, 2012),

> The primary role of a patient navigator should be to foster patient autonomy and provide patients with information that enhances their ability to make appropriate

health care choices and/or receive medical care with an enhanced sense of confidence about risks, benefits and responsibilities. Patient navigators can provide patients with guidance in the health insurance marketplace, which is especially critical for patients who have low health literacy skills.

Since the primary role of a patient navigator is to help patients "navigate" the complexity of the U.S. health care system, this has become increasingly important after the creation of the state-based health exchanges. Today, many patients need assistance is figuring out how to access care. The Patient Protection and Affordable Care Act outlines the following responsibilities of patient navigators:

- Provide expertise on eligibility, enrollment, and coverage details for each plan.
- Provide information in a fair, accurate, and impartial manner.
- Facilitate the enrollment process.
- Provide referrals for conflict resolution services for enrollees with complaints or concerns.

Navigators can be employed by nonprofit organizations, hospitals, or insurance companies or may work as independent consultants offering fee-based services. Social workers are ideally suited for these positions, because they are trained to foster patient empowerment and serve as advocates for their clients, particularly those clients who lack the skills, knowledge, or ability to manage complex medical issues on their own.

HEALTH CARE POLICY SPECIALIST

Health is a matter of both economics and social well-being. Social workers in this area of health care are knowledgeable about the larger health care system and have an in-depth understanding of the social, political, and economic factors impacting health. They examine financial expenditures, political reforms, service delivery systems, insurance programs, and community behaviors that either promote health or contribute to illness. Policy social workers in health care are committed to advocating through the political process for policies that will reduce disparities in access to care and improve the quality of life for all.

Social workers in this area are employed with organizations such as the American Cancer Society, American Heart Association, the March of Dimes, and Easter Seals. Social workers in health care policy also work in regional organizations for HIV awareness and prevention, family violence prevention, and local agencies focused on insuring the medically underserved and low-income population, as well as providing accessible transportation for persons with disabilities.

Core Competencies and Skills

- Strong assessment and interviewing skills
- Knowledge of physical health and medicine
- Care coordination and case management skills
- Crisis intervention skills
- CID skills
- Cultural competency with diverse populations
- Ability to use spirituality in social work practice
- Engage in advocacy efforts
- Knowledge of bioethics
- Group work skills
- Planning, administration, program development, and evaluation skills
- Strong counseling skills
- Knowledge of economics and finance
- Knowledge of benefit programs, such as Medicare, Medicaid, CHIP, the VA system, and the new state-based health insurance exchanges

Educational and Licensing Requirements

A BSW is required to be employed in nursing homes and public health clinics where the social worker's primary responsibilities are in case management. Most other areas of medical social work require a master's-level degree. Many positions in health care and medical settings will also require a clinical license (i.e., Licensed Clinical Social Worker).

Many social work programs offer course work and field experience in all aspects of health care. Some MSW programs offer concentrations in health care and/or joint degree programs (e.g., joint MSW/MPH programs). Great educational opportunities exist to do both micro– and macro–social work practice in health-related–field placements.

Best Aspects of This Job

- Working in an exciting and fast-paced environment with the option to specialize (e.g., pediatrics; geriatrics; cancer treatment, etc.)
- The opportunity to support a wide diversity of patients and their families, who often appreciate the help of a social worker who operates from a strengths-based perspective
- The ability to multitask and have concrete results
- Opportunities to address inequality in access to care and treatment on an individual and "big picture" level
- Working with interdisciplinary teams with health care professionals such as physicians, nurses, and physical/occupational therapists

- Education opportunities with ongoing training and specialization
- The opportunity to listen to personal narratives of patients
- Networking with many community agencies and organizations
- Promoting wellness, resiliency, and recovery as a "first responder"
- Helping to prevent illness and loss of functioning
- Resolving ethical dilemmas and mediating conflict

Challenging Aspects of This Job

- Maintaining personal health and wellness in the face of great demands may be difficult.
- Limited economic means for indigent groups often make it hard to locate resources and services.
- Availability to work various shifts or be "on call" may not work well for those who like predictability and a set work routine.
- Helping people cope with loss and bereavement on an ongoing basis may be emotionally draining for you if you do not have a balance of activities.
- Working with patients who are very ill and/or in pain can be difficult.
- Working with end-of-life situations can present ethical dilemmas depending on your personal values and ethics.
- Involvement with chronic and long-term care may provoke heightened anxiety or depression for yourself, especially if you have a family member or friend who is in a similar circumstance.
- Change efforts in policy work often take years to achieve.
- Working in a "host setting" with a diverse range of medical professionals with education and training differs from social work education and training and can be challenging.

Compensation and Employment Outlook

The employment of health care social workers is projected to grow 27% between 2012 and 2022, much faster than the average for all occupations. This is primarily due to the aging of the baby boomers, who will require the services of health care providers, including social workers. According to the U.S. Department of Labor, Bureau of Labor Statistics (2014), the median annual wage for health care social workers in May 2012 was $49,830. The highest salaries were given to those who worked in hospitals, where the median annual wage was $56,290.

Self-Assessment Checklist: Is This Job Right for Me?

- Are you able to work in an emergency room or medical environment where you cannot control who or what you will see?

- If you have had a family member or friend in the hospital, were you able to visit with them despite the physical environment or their medical condition?
- Do you like working in a fast-paced environment where you are required to multitask?
- Are you flexible when your day does not go as planned?
- Can you communicate well when you speak and write?
- Are you able to "think on your feet"?
- Is it possible for you to care about persons from different cultural and religious backgrounds and advocate for their needs?
- Would visiting patients in their home interest you?
- Do you like looking for community resources and working with health care professionals from diverse disciplines?
- Would you be able to work during a religious or cultural holiday that you typically observe?

If you answered "yes" to seven or more of the preceding questions, you may want to do some more research on social work in health care!

RECOMMENDED READINGS/WEBSITES TO LEARN MORE

Association of Oncology Social Workers: www.aosw.org

American Public Health Association: Social Work specialty group: www.apha.org

Gehlert, S., & Browne, T. (2011). *Handbook of health social work* (2nd ed.). Hoboken, NJ: Wiley.

Kaiser Family Foundation. (2013). *The YouToons get ready for Obamacare* (video): http://kff.org/health-reform/video/youtoons-obamacare-video

Moore, M. (Director). (2007). *Sicko* [motion picture]. *United States: Dog eat dog* [documentary film]. www.michaelmoore.com

National Association of Social Workers, Health Specialty Practice Section: www. socialworkers.org

National Institutes of Health: www.nih.gov

National Library of Medicine: www.nlm.gov

Social Work Section of the American Public Health Association. (2012). *Handbook for public health social work*. New York, NY: Springer Publishing Company.

Society for Social Work Leadership in Health Care: www.sswlhc.org

Wilson, J. (2013, April 6). *Helping patients navigate the health care system*. CNN Health: www.cnn.com/2013/04/06/health/patient-navigation-new-field

Social Work in Health Care Exercise

See whether you can locate a hospital, veterans hospital, or rehabilitation facility in the community in which you live. Call and ask for the director of social work or social services, and request an appointment to meet with him or her or someone on the staff so you can tour the facility and ask questions about the profession.

Another way for you to find out more about social work in health care is to volunteer in a medical setting and begin working with patients and their families. You may want to volunteer as a "reader" to kids receiving treatment for cancer or for persons who have limited sight or are blind. Gaining experience through volunteer work can help you decide what you would enjoy doing most and help you plan your educational goals.

REFERENCES

American Medical Association. (2012). *Improving the health insurance marketplace patient navigators*. Retrieved from www.ama-assn.org/resources/doc/market-reforms/patient-navigators.pdf

Code of Ethics of the National Association of Social Workers. (2008). Approved by the 1996 NASW Delegate Assembly and revised by the 2008 NASW Delegate Assembly. Retrieved from www .socialworkers.org/pubs/code/code.asp

Darnell, J. S. (2007). Patient navigation: A call to action. *Social Work, 52*(1), 81–84.

Defense and Veterans Brain Injury Center. (2014). Retrieved from http://dvbic.dcoe.mil/ tbi-awareness-prevention/article/what-are-risks-and-costs-traumatic-brain-injury-tbi-military

Fort Cowles, L. A. (2003). *Social work in the health field: A care perspective* (2nd ed.). Binghamton, NY: Haworth Press.

National Association of Social Workers. (2005). *Standards for social work practice in health care settings*. Washington, DC: Author.

Remen, R. N. (1996). *Kitchen table wisdom*. New York, NY: Berkley.

U.S. Census Bureau. (2013). *Income, poverty and health insurance coverage in the United States: 2012*. Retrieved from www.census.gov/newsroom/releases/archives/income_wealth/cb13-165. html

U.S. Department of Labor, Bureau of Labor Statistics. (2014). *Occupational outlook handbook, 2014–15: Social workers*. Retrieved from www.bls.gov/ooh/community-and-social-service/ social-workers.htm

8 ■ SOCIAL WORK IN MENTAL HEALTH AND ADDICTION

You may be surprised to learn that the largest group of mental health providers in the United States are clinical social workers, not psychologists or psychiatrists. Social work practice in mental health has certainly come a long way, especially over the past 50 years. It was not too long ago when someone who was diagnosed with a mental illness was institutionalized for an indeterminate period of time, whether or not he or she consented to the confinement. The history of mental illness is the history of "insanity." Centuries ago, anyone who did not conform to societal norms was viewed as insane. Individuals deemed "insane" were often incarcerated in prisons and left to languish until their death. During the mid-1750s, physicians in England began to lobby Parliament to build hospitals to cure the condition of "lunacy." Asylums were built in the early 1800s across England, Ireland, Canada, and the United States to more humanely house and treat persons with "insanity" out of the penal system. Often, those who had developmental disabilities or "mental retardation" could not be distinguished from other "lunatics," and they, too, were committed to asylums (Torrey & Miller, 2007).

In 1835, American social activist Dorothea Dix made a trip to England to recover from a long-term illness caused by tuberculosis. While in England, she became acquainted with the readings of a French physician, Dr. Philippe Pinel, and a British doctor, William Turke, who worked on behalf of prison reform and humane treatment for the mentally ill in the 1700s. In 1837, Dorothea Dix returned to the United States committed to improving the conditions for those affected by mental illness in the United States. With the help of educator Horace Mann, abolitionist Charles Sumner, and Samuel Gridley Howe, head of the famous Perkins Institute for the Blind, Dix lobbied to secure legislation in Massachusetts to fund appropriate care for mental illness conditions. Worcester State Hospital became the first publicly funded hospital for treating mental illness in this country (Bookrags.com, 2008). Other states soon followed.

Mental illnesses were not very well understood for the next 175 years until a research revolution took place in the 1990s, which the National Institute of Mental Health refers to as "the decade of the brain." It was during this time that medical science and technology was developed to literally look inside the brain and give us better information on how to treat mental disorders and addictions."

Prevalence of Mental Illness and Substance Abuse

A recent World Health Organization report, *The Global Burden of Disease*, examines the effects of a wide range of diseases on the loss of years of healthy life. This extensive study found that four out of the top 10 causes of disability in the world are mental illnesses: major depression, bipolar depression, schizophrenia, and obsessive-compulsive disorders. Across all age groups worldwide, depression is expected to produce the second-largest disease burden by 2020 (National Alliance on Mental Illness, 2008). According to the National Institute of Mental Health (2014), in 2012 there were an estimated 43.7 million adults who suffered from a mental disorder in the past year. This represented 18.6% of all U.S. adults. Mental illness is costly to society because of what it takes away in productivity to the economy as well as in people's lives.

The next leading high-cost problem in mental health treatment is the devastation caused by substance abuse and dependency. According to the 2012 National Survey on Drug Use and Health, an estimated 22.2 million people had substance abuse or dependency problems in the previous year. The survey showed that 2.5 million people received substance abuse treatment at specialty facilities in 2012.

The costs of substance abuse are enormous. In 1992, a study funded by the National Institute on Drug Abuse and the National Institute on Alcohol Abuse and Alcoholism found the total economic cost of alcohol and drug abuse to be $245.7 billion for that year, a number that increased to $600 billion in 2012. This estimate encompasses treatment and prevention costs, health care costs, costs related to lost earnings and reduced job productivity, an increase in related crime, and social welfare (National Institute on Drug Abuse, 2012). As with other chronic diseases, many people afflicted with drug addiction require continuous mental health care and support to remain drug free and regain control of their lives. It should be noted that mental disorders and substance abuse issues are often linked, so many clients that are seen by social workers will have co-occurring disorders and will need treatment for multiple mental health issues simultaneously. Clients with a mental disorder as well as a problem with drugs and/or alcohol addiction are referred to as having a "dual diagnosis."

Thanks to improvements in psychopharmacology and psychotherapeutic treatments, individuals with mental disorders and addictions can recover and reclaim their lives. This is largely through access to newer medications that have fewer side effects and proven treatment models of care that can reduce hospital stays, incarceration, and homelessness.

Social Work Mental Health Practice Today

Social workers are the largest professional group of trained mental health providers in the United States today. In our profession, all social workers can provide counseling and psychosocial support to clients, and in any number of settings, social workers may encounter clients with substance abuse or mental disorders. But clinical social workers specialize in the treatment of psychiatric and substance abuse disorders. "Clinical social work has a primary focus on the mental, emotional, and behavioral well-being of individuals, couples, families, and groups. It centers on a holistic approach to psychotherapy and the client's relationship to his or her environment" (NASW, 2005a).

CLINICAL SOCIAL WORKER

Clinical social work is defined as "the application of social work theory and methods to the treatment and prevention of psychological dysfunction, disability, or impairment, including emotional and mental disorders" (Barker, 2003, p. 76). Those who do clinical social work have various job titles such as mental health clinician, psychotherapist, and psychiatric social worker.

Clinical social workers are found across wide and varied practice settings, including nonprofit family counseling centers, public community mental health centers, psychiatric hospitals and medical facilities, and day treatment and residential settings. Social workers can also have their own private practice or work with other mental health providers in a group practice. Clinical social workers are employed to help individuals, families, couples, and small groups identify the issues they are facing and to provide specific strategies to improve their unique situation. In this way, clinical social workers help enhance and maintain the coping skills of the consumers they serve within the context of the person's environment to achieve a better balance in living when confronted by life's challenges.

No one type of treatment works with all people needing help, so clinical social workers must be knowledgeable and skilled in many different therapeutic techniques (e.g., cognitive behavioral therapy, solution-focused interventions, narrative therapy, play therapy). In addition to the therapies mentioned, there is growing interest in expressive therapies that incorporate art, music, drama, and journaling into the therapeutic process (see Chapter 17 for more about integrating the arts into social work).

Clinical social workers may also specialize in particular populations (e.g., children, teens, families, older adults) and within specific mental health areas (e.g., schizophrenia, addictions, anxiety and mood disorders, autism spectrum disorders, sleep and eating disorders, and posttraumatic stress disorder [PTSD]). In order to be a clinical social worker, you have to earn your MSW degree, then work under the supervision of a clinical social worker for approximately 2 years, and then pass the clinical social worker licensing exam.

Social Worker Spotlight
SUE MATORIN, MS, ACSW

Treatment Coordinator, Affective Disorder Team, Payne Whitney Clinic, New York Presbyterian Hospital, New York, New York; Faculty Member, Department of Psychiatry, Weill College of Medicine at Cornell, New York, New York; Adjunct Associate Professor, Columbia School of Social Work, New York, New York

In a long, rich career in health/mental health, I have worn many hats—clinician, program developer, social work department director in an academic medical center, adjunct professor. I serve on boards, have published works in the area of stigma and mental illness, and have proudly received some honors, but at the center of my career have always been my remarkable clients. I am relieved that I have the skill to help those damaged by serious psychiatric and medical illnesses reclaim their lives. I am still haunted by my first field-work cases in an urban welfare center—what did a naive young Massachusetts-born student have to offer to these lives of desperation?

Fast forward—I now save lives, often suicidal ones. At the Payne Whitney Clinic, I work with adults with depression and bipolar disorder after they have been hospitalized, some also struggling with serious medical illnesses or economic problems. In my private practice at Cornell, my clients often function well in their work lives but have a myriad of marital and family problems usually fueled by the psychiatric illness of one family member. I lend out my classical music CDs to clinic clients for stress reduction. I endlessly discuss movies, favorite television shows, makeup, diet, and exercise—anything is grist for the therapy. My best conversations about race are with my minority clients.

Check out my video on the National Association of Social Workers website: "On Any Given Day" (www.socialworkers.org/pressroom/events/anyGiven Day1007/default.asp). My 88-year-old mother disliked how I looked, but my clients loved it, and I was thrilled for the opportunity to describe what I do.

SOCIAL WORK WITH GROUPS

Group therapy is an important skill used frequently by social workers. Knowledge and skill in social work practice with groups require specialized education and the ability to understand when group work is the preferred intervention while working with individuals, families, small groups, organizations, and communities.

Many social workers spend much of their day creating, planning, facilitating, and evaluating groups for many different treatment purposes in a variety of practice settings. The most important function of group work is to help each member become part of a collective of mutual aid and support in which individuals learn from and help each other to be more independent in how they cope with change or adversity.

The role of the social worker as a *facilitator* of the group process requires a high level of training and expertise. In 1998, the Association for the Advancement of Social Work with Groups (AASWG) published the first edition of the *Standards for Social Work Practice with Groups*. The standards outline the values, knowledge, and skills required for professional social work practice with groups, and reflect core principles from the NASW *Code of Ethics* (2008). They are applicable to a wide range of different types of groups, which include treatment groups, support groups, psychoeducational groups, task-centered groups, and community action groups.

Professionally led groups are often found in school settings with children and parents, mental health treatment programs, homeless shelters, drug and alcohol awareness programs, family violence prevention programs, victim services, and health care facilities. Group interventions range from learning new social skills, changing unwanted or unhealthy behaviors, learning trust, gaining insight into personal problems to experiencing mutual support and understanding, achieving stated goals and objectives, or organizing for action.

Social Worker Spotlight
MARY KIERNAN-STERN, MSW, LCSW
Northern Virginia Cancer Center, Alexandria, Virginia

After a number of years working in administration and medical social work in hospitals, I began to work at an outpatient cancer treatment center. My role at the cancer center was to assess patients for various needs and to identify risk factors that may have prevented them from completing their treatment. Cancer care is often very costly, and the treatment can be physically challenging to endure at times. For many, treatment may be ongoing, with no definite end in sight—so part of my intervention with people was to help them learn to cope with a catastrophic diagnosis as if it were a long-term chronic illness. To do this requires collective and consistent support.

Extensive research from the 1980s and 1990s, most notably in the work of Dr. David Spiegel, reported that the life expectancy for cancer survivors was longer for those who participated in a therapeutic support group. There was also research indicating that patients who were in a support group coped better with their treatment and more often completed the course of treatment prescribed. One of my first tasks at the center was to create and facilitate a general support group for any patient in the hospital community with a diagnosis of cancer. This group would meet every other week at the cancer center.

Over time, as our group met, certain members made various requests. A couple of members wanted to have an additional forum to discuss particular books they found helpful for coping with their cancer experience. Other members of the general group requested a support group with a spiritual focus. With assistance and guidance from the members, I developed a Cancer Recovery Book Group and a nondenominational Pastoral Care Support Group.

The hospital chaplain agreed to facilitate the Pastoral Care group on the same day of the week during the weeks in between my facilitation of the general support group. In this way, I was able to have a support group every week at the cancer center for those patients who needed an extra level of psychosocial and spiritual care. The nondenominational support group was a model soon adopted by other area hospitals providing cancer care.

At the same time, I was able to give great thought to the creation of a book group using bibliotherapy as an expressive arts intervention for the framework of this particular group. I was concerned about having the

(continued)

MARY KIERNAN-STERN *(continued)*

hospital as the only focal point of psychosocial support. Patients with long-term illnesses and treatments spend many hours and days at hospitals, and this can be psychologically draining. I wanted to be able to help "patients" return to being part of the wider community.

So I approached the community relations director at a local Borders bookstore and asked whether I could use their space to hold a monthly Cancer Survivors Book Group. Not only did they allow us to have space, but they added us to their book group calendar, gave us 10% discounts on book titles used for the group, and provided us with free coffee. Shortly after we started our book group, a Borders employee was diagnosed with cancer, and she was given time off from her work schedule to come join us for group. I am proud to say that this group went on for 7 years at Borders, and I was able to replicate a similar group at a Barnes and Noble in Washington, DC.

Many people who came to the group after hearing a doctor give them a life expectancy limited to months remained participants in these groups for years and continued to be cancer survivors. This is why, as a clinical social worker, I love group work—because of the collective dynamic in the power to heal mind, body, and spirit.

SOCIAL WORK AND SUBSTANCE ABUSE INTERVENTION

Substance abuse intervention is a specialty area in the field of social work, yet it is a specialization in which you may find social workers in almost every practice arena. Substance use disorders (SUDs) know no boundaries. They affect the lives of individuals across the lifespan, families, and every community. In fact, the current aging demographic shift contributes to the increase prevalence of substance abuse among older adults, particularly in urban communities (Angermeyer et al., 2009).

Social workers in this field are employed in hospitals, mental health centers, homeless shelters, nonprofit and for-profit organizations, local government agencies for drug and alcohol services, drug and alcohol treatment centers, court systems and probation offices, schools, and workplaces. As the most numerous providers of mental health services in the United States, social workers routinely confront problems associated with addictions in their work. According to the National Association of Social Workers, "There are many pathways to treatment for people with SUDs; however, the wide range of settings in which social workers practice allows the profession to address the needs of the whole person as he or she seeks to recover from a SUD" (NASW, 2005b, p. 6).

One such pathway is in the field of alcohol, tobacco, and other drugs (ATOD), where treatment interventions are crisis oriented or short term (e.g., smoking cessation program). When working with people with serious drug addictions (e.g., methamphetamines, prescription drugs, cocaine, heroin), newer research has provided evidence that these addictions are chronic and require much longer-term and intensive treatment options for recovery. Social workers are professionally trained to integrate emerging research and translate that knowledge into essential interventions for persons with SUDs.

Social Worker Spotlight
ROBERT KLEKAR, LCSW, LCDC
Social Work and Substance Abuse*

I received my bachelor's degree in social work from Southwest Texas State University (now Texas State University) in San Marcos, Texas, and my master's degree in social work (MSW) from Our Lady of the Lake University in San Antonio, Texas. At the beginning of my university years, I studied art. After about 2 years, I became depressed and sought out counseling. Finding this experience helpful, I opted to change majors and wanted to do something where I could help others (not to suggest that art doesn't affect others in a healing way) on a one-on-one basis. At the time, the only thing I knew about social work was from a leaflet advertising the George Brown School of Social Work stapled to a bulletin board in the Liberal Arts Building. My reaction was, *"What in the world is social work?"* I found an answer to that question after I combed through the university catalogue and read the various degree outlines. Upon reading about social work, I discovered it resonated with me for two reasons: helping others and social action. At the time, I fancied myself a quixotic, social revolutionary, so the latter had great importance. In the 18 years that have elapsed since I completed my MSW, I have worked a couple of administrative roles, but mainly in the area of direct clinical practice. Although I wouldn't describe what I do as radical or revolutionary at a macro level, it does involve helping others. Most of my work has been in the areas of mental health and substance abuse treatment for adolescents and adults. For the past 13 years, my primary focus has been providing substance abuse services to male offenders within a prison setting.

For a social worker considering a career in criminal justice, there may be many questions and concerns. When others talk to me about working in a prison setting, I'm often asked, *"Is it dangerous in there?"* My answer? *"Possibly."* Moving past razor wire each working day is a reminder that I've entered a zone that's potentially hazardous, where some of the inmate histories include the commission of violent crimes. So, it is important to be vigilant and mindful, always keeping personal safety at the forefront of your mind. But the work itself is not all that different from what I've done in other settings. As I see it, risk has always been a part of the change process, regardless of the setting, especially when we work with people who are distressed, in some cases desperate, agitated, or struggling from the change process. I believe that the education and training of social worker students, with its dual emphasis on person and environment, is ideal preparation for social work within drug treatment and prison settings. Sure, the work is challenging, but aside from a paycheck, there are limitless other incentives—to name a few, helping clients make subtle and,

(continued)

ROBERT KLEKAR   (*continued*)

in some cases, dramatic changes in their lives; shaping service delivery; receiving professional training and continuing education; and personal growth.

When people find out that I work in a drug abuse treatment program or prison, the next question I typically encounter is, *"What exactly do you do?"* In general, I retort, *"Ask and answer a lot of questions."* For those inclined to hear me out, I'm likely to give a longer, well-rounded answer. That is, I provide group psychotherapy to clients most of the time. Ironically, I was initially interested in helping people at a one-to-one level, but now I prefer the dynamism of group settings.

During these sessions, clients talk about their drug abuse histories and actions they are taking toward living a drug- and crime-free life. Of course, there are other duties, such as providing drug education classes, performing assessments, treatment planning, individual counseling, copious amounts of documentation, and discharge planning. In some cases, crisis intervention. I also have had the opportunity to receive training and participate on a hostage negotiation team and a crisis support team, both geared toward managing critical incidents that may arise within a prison setting.

Finally, there are those who ask, *"Do you like what you do?"* I answer with a resounding *"Absolutely!"* Sure, there are periods of professional burnout, but I have means to cope with those times. The most interesting and sustaining part of my job are the daily conversations I have with clients. This is where the 'ask and answer' part of my job comes into play. For me, the heart and soul of the change process lies with a social worker's ability to establish rapport with a client and work collaboratively toward problem resolution. This is an exciting, engaging, and often unpredictable endeavor. Someone, and it might be me, is going to change thanks to this process. Although there have been considerable efforts to introduce evidence-based approaches into social work practice, the actual process of direct social work practice reminds me more of the creative arts. Clients have a way of influencing me to tailor interventions to fit their story, rather than the other way around. It never ceases to amaze me that clients, even those with severe deficits, have the means to generate solutions to their problems once they are engaged in a conversation about change. Although these solutions do not solve all the distal factors that come about (e.g., a drug dependency), they are a step toward enhancing client autonomy. After all, two of my favorite axioms from social work practice are "start where the client is at" and "honor the client's right to self-determination."

---

* Opinions expressed in this article are those of the author and do not necessarily represent the opinions of the Federal Bureau of Prisons or the Department of Justice.

Social Worker Spotlight
SHANA SEIDENBERG, MSW, LSW
MISA (Mental Illness Substance Abuse) Coordinator, Kauai Community Mental Health Center, Lihue, Hawaii

After attending Mount Holyoke College in South Hadley, Massachusetts, I had the awesome opportunity to participate in a community service organization called City Year in Boston. My participation in City Year further confirmed my interest in social work as I mentored youth in the public school system. I received my MSW from Simmons College in 2005. Shortly after graduation, I went to Kauai for a vacation. Now I call Kauai home, and I work for the Kauai Community Mental Health Center (CMHC) as their Mental Illness Substance Abuse Coordinator. Community mental health centers provide services that help people with severe and persistent mental illness live out in the community rather than in institutions; being a part of the team at Kauai's CMHC is an exciting and challenging career.

My role is to provide consultation and training to case managers for their clients with co-occurring disorders (also referred to as a dual diagnosis). My favorite part of my job is facilitating groups for clients with co-occurring issues. The group emphasizes psychoeducation, relapse prevention skills, and peer support for clients recovering from mental illness and a substance abuse disorder. The clients have taught me much of what I know, and I am very grateful to everyone I have worked with. Education can teach you a lot, but the experiences of working with people are sometimes more revealing. I really enjoy listening to people's stories and learning about the local culture.

My favorite part of being a social worker is empowering people to make positive choices. People with mental health issues and addiction issues face many difficult choices every day. I am thrilled to be a part of a support network for people in recovery. Social workers need to promote education and awareness of co-occurring issues and battle the ongoing stigma facing this group of people.

EMPLOYEE ASSISTANCE WORKER

The field of employee assistance practice developed with the social work profession during the 1970s in response to employers' and workers' growing social, financial, and emotional needs at the workplace. Today, many large employers, such as Verizon, Apple, and the International Union of Bricklayers & Allied Craftworkers, as well as moderate-sized organizations, such as utility companies or county governments, offer workers the benefits of employee assistance programs (EAPs). Any size business or agency may create an EAP inside their own organization, or they might contract with another outside organization to provide EAP services to their employees. Research has shown that paying and providing such services to workers is a win–win situation for employers in reduced time off from work and improved morale and productivity. The benefits to workers include less lost wages and improved health and mental health. For every dollar invested in an EAP benefit, the financial return is large.

Social workers in EAPs assist both employers and workers with various workplace issues. They provide services in behavioral health and wellness, crisis intervention, work–life balance issues, career transitions, and information and referrals for a great many resources. Employee assistance social workers are trained in critical incident and stress debriefing (CISD) interventions in response to a workplace trauma and often provide psychoeducational workshops and trainings focused on prevention and wellness, in addition to specialty services in substance abuse.

MILITARY SOCIAL WORKER

Military social workers support members of the armed services and their families, both at home and in overseas assignments. They usually provide services ranging from individual counseling and rehabilitation, summer programs for children and teens of military personnel, and victim advocacy to drug and alcohol counseling, family violence prevention programs, and marriage and family counseling. In light of the current shift to a larger proportion of older adults in the U.S. population, better services for older veterans continue to be an issue of much debate and need. The Veterans Administration (VA) Social Work website (U.S. Department of Veterans Affairs, 2014) includes a list that shows the varied range of services provided by military social workers:

- Health care for homeless veterans
- Physical and rehabilitation services
- Substance abuse
- Geriatric and extended care
- Spinal cord injury
- PTSD
- Community re-entry for incarcerated veterans
- Women's health
- Community support/mental health intensive case management
- Community residential care

In addition to the VA, military social workers may be directly employed by a branch of the military (e.g., the Army Medical Command) or may work as independent contractors with a firm hired by the military.

The trauma of participating in or witnessing combat has led to high levels of mental health issues among the military. Various studies show that the incidences of PTSD, depression, suicide, and substance abuse are all high in this population, hence the need for social workers who are educated and trained to treat these conditions.

Another primary focus of military social work is on the family and the multitude of stressors they confront, particularly those related to displacement, relocation, and separation from loved ones who are active military personnel. This role has been growing in importance since the 1990 Persian Gulf War, and the need for military social workers has dramatically increased since 9/11 and the subsequent deployment of U.S. troops in Iraq and Afghanistan.

MENTAL HEALTH ADVOCACY

Some social workers work for advocacy organizations at the local, state, or federal level to advocate for policies and legislation that improve access and services for those with mental disorders. Prominent advocacy organizations at the federal level include the National Alliance on Mental Illness (NAMI) and Mental Health America.

Many social workers practice in the area of policy and advocacy, with respect to mental health or behavioral health issues. Policy practice focuses on areas of need, such as increased federal funding for research on mental illness and universal access to mental health treatment. Important social justice issues abound in the field of mental health. For example, it seems that the United States has gone backward in recent years by sending many with mental illness to jail or prison for treatment, rather than treating them in the community. Some experts have referred to prisons as "the new asylums." Another big policy issue in recent years has been coined "mental health parity." This means that mental health advocates have had to fight for legislation that would force insurance companies to provide the same benefits for mental health treatment as they do for physical health treatment, instead of discriminating against those with mental disorders. Mental disorders are diseases, after all—of the brain.

Whatever direction you take in mental health and substance abuse, social workers are highly skilled and needed professionals.

Core Competencies and Skills

- Be able to interpret social, personal, medical, and mental health information.
- Evaluate and treat mental health conditions appropriately.
- Establish rapport with clients over the short term and long term.
- Facilitate psychological, emotional, and behavioral change.

- Identify appropriate resources.
- Provide culturally and linguistically relevant and age-appropriate services.
- Advocate for client services.
- Collaborate effectively with multidisciplinary professionals.
- Evaluate the outcomes of treatment services.
- Demonstrate in-depth knowledge about multidimensional problems and services.
- Be knowledgeable about psychiatric illnesses, developmental disabilities, and the addiction and recovery processes.

Educational and Licensing Requirements

An accredited MSW is required for all the aforementioned jobs in this chapter. The areas of mental health and addictions are typically regulated by the state, and social workers are required to obtain a clinical license (see Chapter 3) to practice in the state where they are employed. Becoming a licensed clinical social worker is the most time-consuming license to obtain because it involves working under the supervision of an LCSW for a certain number of hours (or about 2 years) after earning the MSW. There is a growing trend in state regulations, and with employers of social workers in the addiction and EAP fields, of requiring additional certifications beyond that of a clinical license. There are national and state organizations that provide certifications in these specialty areas, and some of your graduate-level social work courses and previous employment experiences may be credited toward certification.

Best Aspects of This Job

- Working across cultures and in diverse contexts, across all age groups
- Crisis-oriented
- Offering hope and healing in the recovery process
- Specialization of skills
- In-depth knowledge base of expertise
- Ability to work with clients for a long period of time
- Access to highly specialized training
- Opportunity to work with a variety of medical and mental health professionals
- Helping individuals and families with their personal growth and development (spiritual, emotional, etc.)
- Membership opportunities with peers in the same specialty
- Opportunities for solo or group private practice in counseling services
- Career development opportunities toward consultant/trainer and self-employment

Challenging Aspects of This Job

- It is emotionally difficult to watch a person relapse or come out of remission.
- The work can be emotionally draining, so the need for self-care is high among mental health professionals.
- The road to recovery is very long for some clients.
- Coordination of care can be tedious considering all the professionals and services involved.
- Time and money are needed to meet licensing and certification requirements.
- Coping with suicide or incidents of violence may be emotionally and physically taxing.
- Being "on call" and available for emergencies may make life planning difficult for yourself.
- Traveling to remote locations may be stressful.

Compensation and Employment Outlook

Employment projections from the Bureau of Labor indicate rapid growth in the need for social workers in the area of mental health and substance abuse. In particular, social workers in substance abuse will continue to be in high demand, since substance abusers are increasingly being diverted to treatment programs rather than prison (U.S. Department of Labor, U.S. Bureau of Labor Statistics, 2014). Because of the level of knowledge and training required, including licensure and certification, social workers with these credentials earn substantially better salaries. In 2012, the top 10% of social workers in this field earned more than $72,900.

Self-Assessment Checklist: Is This Job for Me?

- Can you work independently and defend your viewpoint when working with psychiatrists, nurses, and other well-trained professionals?
- Would you be able to compassionately work with a population that is difficult and alienating to others?
- Does it sound appealing to see clients in your office all day as you provide therapeutic services?
- Do you like working primarily with individuals and families?
- Are you willing to spend the time to obtain a license and a credential?
- Can you handle crisis and emergency situations?
- Do you like working with people over a long period of time in an institutional setting?
- Would you be able to manage your own emotions in helping others to cope with grief and loss?

- Are you comfortable providing intensive services to people in their homes and communities?
- Do you see yourself as an "expert" in an area as your career develops?
- Are you someone who is able to prioritize self-care?

If you answered "yes" to seven or more of the preceding questions, then being a social worker in this field may offer opportunities for you to be in a rewarding career.

RECOMMENDED READINGS/WEBSITES TO LEARN MORE

American Psychiatric Association: www.psych.org
Association for the Advancement of Social Work with Groups: www.aaswg.org
Clinical Social Work Association: www.cswf.org
Family secrets: Inside addictions. (2007). ABC News Primetime documentary. (Accessible through www.amazon.com or www.netflix.com.)
Kaysen, S. (1994). *Girl, interrupted.* New York, NY: Vintage.
Mental Health America: www.mha.org
National Alliance on Mental Illness: www.nami.org
National Association of Social Workers: www.socialworkers.org
National Institute on Drug Abuse: www.nida.gov
National Institute of Mental Health: www.nimh.gov
Out of the Shadows (Film showing the effects of mental illness and recovery for person and family): www.outoftheshadows.com
Sheff, D. (2008). *Beautiful boy: A father's journey through his son's meth addiction.* Boston, MA: Houghton-Mifflin.
The New Asylums. (2005). Frontline/PBS. (Documentary depicting the criminalization of those with mental illness): www.pbs.org/wgbh/pages/frontline/shows/asylums
Treatment Advocacy Center: www.psychlaws.org
Veterans Administration Social Work: http://socialwork.va.gov

Mental Health and Addiction Exercise

Case Scenario

Mrs. Reynolds is a 46-year-old married mom of a 15-year-old daughter. She is currently receiving medical treatment for breast cancer at a local community hospital. In visiting her doctor, she learned that her prognosis for a full recovery is good and that she will be finished with her treatments soon. Mrs. Reynolds cries when she hears this news, and tells the doctor she has thought of killing herself recently, since the stress of coping with years of her husband's excessive drinking has now become unbearable. The doctor spends

more time talking with Mrs. Reynolds and obtains her consent to make a refer-
ral to a mental health social worker.

Questions

1. As the clinical social worker for Mrs. Reynolds, what would be your first step in helping her?
2. What kinds of questions would you need to ask to determine a diagnosis for Mrs. Reynolds?
3. What type of treatment intervention would you discuss with this client?
4. Do you know the community resources available to help in her situation?
5. Would you involve the other members of her family in the treatment process?
6. How would you follow up with Mrs. Reynolds after she leaves your office that day?

REFERENCES

Angermeyer, M. C., Bickel, E. M., Bussche, H. V., Cvetanovska-Pllashiniku, G., Eifflaender-Gorfer, S., Haller, F., . . . Zimmerman, T. (2009). At-risk alcohol drinking in primary care patients aged 75 years and older. *International Journal of Geriatric Psychiatry, 24,* 1376–1385.

Barker, R. (2003). *The social work dictionary* (5th ed.). Washington, DC: NASW Press.

Bookrags.com. (2008). *Biography: Dorothea Dix.* Retrieved from http://bookrags.com/biography/dorothea-lynde-dix-woh

Code of Ethics of the National Association of Social Workers. (2008). Approved by the 1996 NASW Delegate Assembly and revised by the 2008 NASW Delegate Assembly. Retrieved from www.socialworkers.org/pubs/code/code.asp

National Alliance on Mental Illness. (2008). *Federal funding of mental health research.* Retrieved from http://nami.org/PrinterTemplate.cfm? Section=Issue_

National Association of Social Workers. (2005a). NASW standards for clinical social work in social work practice. Washington, DC: Author.

National Association of Social Workers. (2005b). *NASW standards for social work practice with clients with substance abuse disorders.* Washington, DC: Author.

National Institute on Drug Abuse. (2012). *NIDA InfoFacts: Costs to society.* Retrieved from www.drugabuse.gov/related-topics/trends-statistics

National Institute of Mental Health. (2014). *Any mental illness among adults.* Retrieved from http://www.nimh.nih.gov/health/statistics/prevalence/any-mental-illness-ami-among-adults.shtml

Torrey, F. E., & Miller, J. (2007). *The invisible plague: The rise of mental illness from 1750 to the present.* New Brunswick, NJ: Rutgers University Press.

U.S. Department of Labor, U.S. Bureau of Labor Statistics. (2014). *Occupational outlook handbook, 2014–2015.* Retrieved from www.bls.gov/ooh

U.S. Department of Veterans Affairs. (2014). *Social work jobs.* Retrieved from www.socialwork.va.gov/index.asp

9 ■ CAREERS IN CRISIS INTERVENTION

Social workers are often called to help in a variety of crisis situations, including terrorist attacks (e.g., the September 11 bombing of the World Trade Center in 2001, the 2013 Boston Marathon bombing), natural disasters (e.g., the 2004 Indian Ocean tsunami, Hurricane Katrina in 2005, Hurricane Sandy in 2012), mass shootings (e.g., the school shooting at Sandy Hook Elementary in 2012, the mass shooting at Virginia Tech in 2007), and random acts of violence (e.g., rapes, assaults, murders, gang violence). Since the beginning of the profession, social workers have responded to the call to offer disaster assistance. When you watch a television show such as *Grey's Anatomy*, news footage of an earthquake or other natural disaster, or a depiction of a violent crime, does your adrenalin start pumping as you visualize yourself intervening to help others in these situations? If so, crisis intervention may be the career path for you! This is an important and valuable skill, as crisis situations require social workers and other helping professionals who can remain calm and composed under pressure in order to aid others in a time of great need.

Social workers can be found working and volunteering in various government and nonprofit organizations, such as the Red Cross, the Salvation Army, the Federal Emergency Management Agency (FEMA), and victim's services programs, which are typically found within police departments. Social workers who work internationally may assist people in the throes of war, displacement, and genocide. They provide a range of services, such as immediate help with food, shelter, and clothing; relocation; information and referral; critical incident debriefing immediately after trauma exposure; short-term crisis counseling; and ongoing treatment for posttraumatic stress disorder (PTSD) and other mental health disorders. See Chapter 8 for more information on working with individuals and groups in a therapeutic context.

However, it is important to understand that crisis intervention is provided in almost every social work setting. No matter where you work, you may come into contact with individuals who find themselves in a crisis situation. You may be working with a client who is suicidal, a family who has just lost their housing, or a child whose parent has passed away. Today, many school social workers are charged with helping schools prepare for crisis events such as school shootings and to assist children and their families after such events occur. Thus it is imperative that all social workers are skilled in crisis intervention.

For some individuals in crisis, their normal coping mechanisms do not work, and they experience a range of emotions such as helplessness, confusion, anxiety, depression, and anger. Crisis intervention work typically involves providing short-term treatment to help people return to their precrisis level of functioning. Individuals suffering from PTSD may emotionally relive the event, experience nightmares and intrusive thoughts, or be in a highly agitated state. Without treatment, these symptoms may last for a significant period of time after the original trauma.

That being said, there are some fields of social work practice in which working with individuals and families in crisis is a primary focus of the job:

■ Child Protective Services caseworkers (Chapter 4)
■ Homeless outreach caseworkers (Chapter 12)
■ Emergency department social workers (Chapter 7)
■ Social workers assisting suicidal patients or those with serious mental illness (Chapter 8)
■ Victim service providers (assisting victims of crime and their families) (Chapter 10)
■ International and global social workers (Chapter 11)

The careers that are profiled in other chapters of this book will not be described again here. This chapter profiles a few careers in which social workers must be highly skilled in crisis intervention: the fields of disaster and emergency management, suicide prevention, family violence, and sexual assault. Careers in policy as related to these areas will also be discussed.

CAREERS IN DISASTER AND EMERGENCY MANAGEMENT

Webster's dictionary defines disaster as "a sudden calamitous event bringing great damage, loss, or destruction." According to the National Association of Social Workers, social workers are "uniquely suited to interpret the disaster context, to advocate for effective services, and to provide leadership in essential collaborations among institutions and organizations" (National Association of Social Workers, 2012).

Disaster relief work is not the most common career path for most social workers. A small number of social workers work for organizations such as the Red Cross, Salvation Army, or FEMA and do this kind of work full time, but many social workers volunteer their time with these various agencies to help out in a time of crisis. Because many social workers are trained in crisis intervention, they are uniquely positioned to aid people in need after an emergency or natural disaster. Even though social workers are concerned about the effects of disasters in general, they are particularly concerned about the effects on vulnerable populations, such as children, people with disabilities, those living in poverty, and older adults. During Hurricane Katrina, for example, Americans watched in horror while many low-income people and residents of hospitals and nursing homes were unable to flee.

One technique that is commonly used by social workers after a disaster is called critical incident stress debriefing (CISD). Responses to trauma can include shock, confusion, depression, anxiety, nightmares or other sleep disturbances, survivor's guilt, and even suicidal ideation. Debriefing allows those involved with the incident to process the event and reflect on its effects. It also allows individuals to vent their emotions and express their thoughts associated with the crisis event. Debriefing is typically provided during the first 24 to 72 hours after the initial impact of the critical event. CISD is provided to individuals to help mitigate the development of posttraumatic stress.

Social Worker Spotlight
BRIAN RIVERS, BSW, LSW
Case Manager/Volunteer Coordinator, East Biloxi Coordination, Relief, and Redevelopment Agency, Biloxi, Mississippi

I am a graduate and licensed social worker (LSW) from the University of Southern Mississippi School of Social Work. My current occupational field is disaster relief, recovery, and redevelopment. The field is just as stated: First comes the disaster, then the initial relief and recovery (also referred to as the crisis intervention stage), then the redevelopment (assisting the community in re-establishing connections and resources). This is a field—I admit—that I never imagined I would be interested in.

I am employed with the East Biloxi Coordination, Relief, and Redevelopment Agency in Biloxi, Mississippi. I also led the committee for the Finish the Job Fund, which I spearheaded before the second anniversary of Hurricane Katrina. My social work education gave me the foresight to see that a crisis was in the making and that the shift of funding and attention would no longer remain with us in Mississippi. At the time of the fund's initiation, many organizations had limited or no correspondence with others who were serving the same arena.

With national attention and funds being diverted to current disasters nationwide, the responsibility has fallen on grassroots organizations and social welfare groups to answer the call of replacing the diminished resources. A significant portion of the state population has an "unmet need" related to Hurricane Katrina. Unmet needs vary from a client who has yet to get himself or herself into a position to provide food for his or her family to a client who resided in an heir property that needs legal assistance before any other form of assistance can be pursued. Throw into the equation a 40% illiteracy rate for the state, and you can begin to grasp the situation here in Mississippi.

The most important aspect of my work is advocacy. The hurricane ravaged people from all economic backgrounds, yet the recovery tools were not available to those who could not afford insurance or those with no funds to go through a court proceeding to have a deed transferred. I consider myself to be in the "trenches," because my position is the first point of contact for clients seeking assistance. This, in itself, adds excitement to the job. The average workday does not exist. I may be fielding client intakes all day on a Monday, Tuesday may require an appearance in court or at a city council meeting, Wednesday may require leading a group of volunteers doing

(continued)

BRIAN RIVERS *(continued)*

manual labor, Thursday may involve presenting at a conference, and Friday might be spent doing crisis intervention or gathering statistics. The following week may consist of none of the above! Grant writing is a daily task that is required, especially to be a successful helping professional in the community in this line of work. As you can see, the skill set for a social worker in this field must be pretty broad.

The question most asked of me is "Why do you do what you do?" My answer is simple. I see jobs in two ways: You can work FOR someone, or you can work WITH someone. This is how I see my role as a social worker—working WITH a client to meet a single goal or a hundred goals. In my current job, working in disaster recovery, I find more personal satisfaction than I ever imagined.

SUICIDE PREVENTION

Working with individuals at risk of suicide is very crisis-driven work, and some social workers are well suited for this work. According to the American Foundation for Suicide Prevention (2014), in 2011, 39,518 suicides were reported, making suicide the 10th leading cause of death for Americans. Though anyone can be at risk for suicide, certain populations are particularly vulnerable including veterans; lesbian, gay, bisexual, and transgender (LGBT) youth; and those experiencing serious mental health disorders. Examples of job settings for those interested in suicide prevention include suicide hotlines, mental health practitioners who work in a range of mental health settings, researchers who study the causes of suicide and evaluate various interventions, and social workers who do community education. Most states have suicide prevention hotlines that people can call when they, or a friend or loved one, is suicidal.

Because of the high risk involved in assisting those with suicidal ideation, social workers are highly trained in assessment and intervention. They need to know the right questions to ask to assess whether someone is actively suicidal and whether someone is at immediate risk of harming himself or herself; in such cases, the individual may need to be voluntarily or involuntarily hospitalized, which requires knowing the laws and procedures that must be followed when these situations arise. This is extremely important, because if these cases are not handled ethically and competently, social workers can be held liable for malpractice. Thus documentation and seeking advice from other experienced professionals (without violating confidentiality) are critical.

FAMILY VIOLENCE COUNSELOR

All men, women, and children should have the right to be free from violence and to be safe in their own home. Unfortunately, domestic violence (DV) is a major social problem in the United States and affects millions of families each year. According to the National Coalition Against Domestic Violence, one in three women and one in four men will experience physical violence by an intimate partner in their lifetime. DV can be defined as a pattern of abusive behavior that is used by one intimate partner to gain or maintain power and control over another intimate partner; this can include physical abuse, sexual abuse, financial exploitation, and emotional and psychological abuse.

There are a number of ways to describe this field of practice when it comes to terminology, and many use these terms interchangeably: DV; family violence; and intimate partner violence. The most common setting for social workers who work in the field of family violence is an emergency shelter where victims of abuse can reside safely until a more permanent living arrangement can be secured. Temporary emergency assistance shelters for women and children can be found in communities around the country, though many would argue that there are not enough of them. The services typically offered to individuals and their children at these shelters range from education and counseling to advocacy and transitional housing. And although women in urban areas may be put on a waiting list because of lack of space in these shelters, rural areas may not have any services at all.

Other social workers may work with perpetrators of family violence to help them understand the root causes of their behavior and hopefully learn alternatives to aggressive behavior. This work may take the form of group counseling, often known as batterer intervention programs.

SEXUAL ASSAULT COUNSELOR

Sexual assault is nonconsensual sexual contact. Women, men, and children can all be victims of sexual assault, although according to experts in the field, the vast majority of victims are female and the vast majority of perpetrators are male. The perpetrator may be a stranger, someone the victim knows, or a relative. It may take years for a victim to recover from the psychological effects caused by the sexual assault. Because DV and sexual assault are linked to the oppression of women and children in the United States and around the world, this social justice issue has particular relevance for the social work profession.

Services for victims of sexual assault are typically provided by a community rape crisis center. In some communities, the women's DV shelter and the local rape crisis center are housed in the same agency. The following services are commonly offered by social workers who work with those who have experienced sexual violence or family violence:

1. **Prevention and community education.** Social workers focus on preventing violence and promoting safe and healthy relationships through community education and school-based programs. Educating the community about DV and sexual assault and giving a voice to survivors who need help and understanding is vital. This can be accomplished through community fairs, media campaigns, community presentations, professional trainings, school-based programs to reach young people, distributing brochures and other informational materials, and public awareness events.
2. **Crisis intervention.** This is perhaps the defining feature of the DV emergency shelter and rape crisis center. Most offer a 24-hour hotline and an emergency shelter for women and their children who need a safe place to stay and have nowhere else to go. Over the phone, hotline counselors listen, counsel, provide information and referral, and do safety planning to help a victim develop a safe plan for leaving her intimate partner. The shelter is a temporary solution until a more permanent living situation can be secured. A range of services are offered to women served by a rape crisis center or staying in an emergency shelter:

   ■ Individual and group counseling; many shelters have special groups and activities specifically for the children in the shelter
   ■ On-call work in health care settings, where social workers will meet sexual assault victims at the emergency room to offer information and support while they undergo a rape exam
   ■ Case management services where clients are connected to needed resources in the community
   ■ Legal advocacy, which includes help obtaining protective or restraining orders, prosecuting offenders, and getting clients connected to attorneys and organizations that offer legal advice
   ■ Helping clients prepare for, and navigate, the legal system (if they choose to pursue legal measures) and deal with the psychological effects of testifying, cross-examination, and other court procedures
   ■ Life-skills training for victims of DV so they will be prepared to live and work on their own
   ■ Many shelters offer transitional housing (typically in an apartment complex) for women and children to live after they leave the shelter, but before they are ready to live on their own

3. **Collaboration.** Meeting the needs of DV and sexual assault survivors often requires collaboration with other community organizations, such as the police department and their victim's services program, Child Protective Services (because children are often at risk when a woman is being abused), the district attorney or county attorney's office, hospitals, housing programs, and programs offering mental health services.

POLICY ADVOCATE

Social workers interested in family violence and sexual assault can work at the micro or macro level. As discussed in the previous section, many social workers choose to work directly with victims or perpetrators of abusive relationships or sexual violence. It can be very gratifying to provide a range of therapeutic interventions that help these clients leave an abusive situation and heal from years of violence.

Other social workers are passionate about decreasing rates of DV and sexual violence. These social workers work to create social change by educating the public about family violence or working in the political arena to pass laws helpful to those who are victims of these crimes. There has been increased attention by state and federal lawmakers to pass legislation to address sexual assault in the military (Military Justice Improvement Act) and on college campuses. For example, the state of California just passed an "affirmative consent" law that will apply to all colleges in that state. Community education can include challenging traditional gender roles that contribute to women being in a subservient role to men as well as educating young people about healthy romantic relationships. Legislative advocacy can involve lobbying legislators at the local, state, and national levels to strengthen laws against family or sexual violence and advocating for increased funding for services. Many states have advocacy organizations that focus their efforts at the state level. There are also a number of prominent organizations, such as the National Coalition Against Domestic Violence and the National Network to End Domestic Violence, that are national in scope.

Social Worker Spotlight
CINDY SOUTHWORTH, MSW
National Network to End Domestic Violence, Washington, DC

I am the founder and director of the Safety Net Project at the National Network to End Domestic Violence (NNEDV), based in Washington, DC. I have been working to end violence against women since before I received my BS in human development and family studies in 1993. As an undergraduate student, I volunteered at a local domestic violence shelter and rape crisis center in State College, Pennsylvania. After volunteering, I moved into a part-time position educating children and parents about child sexual abuse, then on to a full-time job coordinating a transitional housing program. I answered hotline calls, met with survivors every week, trained and supervised volunteers and interns, accompanied victims to court hearings, and saw firsthand the resilience of women who survived horrific abuse. I was, and remain, in awe of their strength.

After several amazing and rewarding years of working with survivors, I decided to get my master's degree in social work (MSW) to give me more tools to change a system that I saw not working as well as it could. After receiving my MSW, I worked in Maine, organizing local domestic violence awareness month activities and improving the law enforcement system's response to domestic violence. I also chaired the state domestic violence coalition's legislative committee.

In 1998, a colleague encouraged me to apply for a national manager position leading an Internet project focusing on violence against women. This technology-focused position led to work supporting another technology project: working with the courts to implement a state-wide restraining order database. Through both of these systems advocacy positions, I realized that front-line victim advocates and the sexual and domestic violence survivors who turn to them did not fully understand the ways that technology could benefit victims and be misused by abusers.

In 2000, two colleagues of mine at the Pennsylvania Coalition Against Domestic Violence and I developed a curriculum on technology, privacy, and victim safety and presented it at a national conference. I quickly realized there was an urgent need for more information to help survivors understand how to strategically use technology to increase their safety. In 2001, I began looking for an organization to house the project that I was creating, and, in 2002, I officially launched Safety Net Project at NNEDV with seed money from the AOL Time Warner Foundation.

(continued)

CINDY SOUTHWORTH *(continued)*

As the director of the Safety Net Project, I, with my team of three trainers, present workshops on technology and stalking, databases and confidentiality, and other technology topics to victim advocates, law enforcement, attorneys, judges, and government officials at state and national conferences. I work with government agencies such as the U.S. Department of Justice, U.S. Department of Health and Human Services, and the Federal Trade Commission to ensure that victims' stories are heard and that technology-related policies do not inadvertently put survivors in more danger. I also provide hands-on assistance when local advocates are trying to help a victim of technology stalking and connect service providers to tech-savvy law enforcement allies I have developed through my work. Recently, I have been working with companies such as AOL and Google on increasing victim privacy and safety. From testifying before the U.S. Senate on victims and stolen phone records to answering a call from a survivor who read a handout we created on spyware use by abusers, every day I feel like I make a difference.

One of the most rewarding parts of this work is knowing how many people are impacted and occasionally making a connection with someone whose life has been touched by this issue. Because studies show that one in three women will be assaulted by an intimate partner in her lifetime, there are survivors everywhere. Sometimes during training, survivors share their own experience; others quietly and intently catch my eye and say, "You do really important work."

Core Competencies and Skills

- Excellent counseling skills (individual and group)
- Strong crisis intervention skills
- Understanding of DV and sexual assault as larger social issues that are linked to the status and oppression of women in society
- Sensitive to the shame that victims often experience and the lengths they will sometimes go to to keep the violence and abuse a secret
- Knowledge of the legal system and laws governing DV and sexual assault
- Ability to assess risk to children and victims
- Knowledge of the dynamics and cycle of intimate partner violence
- Strong advocacy skills
- Ability to collaborate with other systems in the community (particularly the legal and court system) to meet the needs of clients
- Ability to work with diverse populations that experience DV and sexual violence, including LGBT individuals and males

Educational and Licensing Requirements

You will find social workers with bachelor's degrees and master's degrees working in emergency shelters and sexual assault crisis centers. Some social work students will complete their field work in these organizations while completing their undergraduate degree and then obtain a job there after graduation. This is a wonderful learning experience for a new social worker. In most of these settings, you will be provided with in-depth training on the causes and dynamics of sexual violence and intimate partner abuse and many hours of supervised training. Certain jobs at the shelter, such as therapist or administrative positions, may require a master's degree and a specified number of years of previous experience.

Best Aspects of This Job

- Working with a diverse group of individuals and organizations to increase people's awareness and knowledge of DV and sexual assault
- Having the opportunity to be a supportive presence in a victim's life; to be someone who believes the victim and understands
- Having a supportive work environment and working with colleagues who understand the emotional ups and downs of the job
- Seeing victims of DV heal from the abuse they have suffered and take steps toward living a life free from abuse
- Having the opportunity to educate the community and to work on the prevention of problems dealing with family violence
- Helping women and children who find themselves in a serious crisis and providing immediate help and a safe place to live
- Having the opportunity to prevent DV and sexual violence by educating the public about healthy relationships and the effects of violence on men, women, and children

Challenging Aspects of This Job

- Sometimes the system cannot prevent serious or deadly harm to victims.
- You will see firsthand victims who suffer the effects (emotional and physical scars) of DV and sexual violence.
- If you have a history of being a victim of abuse, it can be challenging to do this work unless you have worked through your emotional scars and healed.
- You will work with people who blame the victim instead of the perpetrator (e.g., asking why the victims stay instead of why the perpetrator abuses his loved ones).

- You will work with victims who are not yet ready to leave an abusive situation or who are forced to return to an abuser for financial reasons or lack of support.
- You must balance the need to support and advocate for the victim with the need to make sure that children are safe and protected.
- You must find a line between educating and empowering victims and allowing them to make their own decisions about their life (i.e., self-determination).

Compensation and Employment Outlook

Salaries for social workers working in emergency shelters and crisis centers, most of which are nonprofit organizations, will not be as competitive as other social work jobs, but this work can be incredibly rewarding. Salaries will be higher for those who are in supervisory or administrative positions.

Self-Assessment Checklist: Is This Job for Me?

- Do you enjoy doing work that is crisis driven? Can you stay calm in a crisis?
- Do you have a strong empathy for people who have been traumatized by disaster or violence?
- Would you be able to see physical injuries and hear details of how someone has been sexually assaulted or abused (including physical abuse, sexual abuse, and emotional/psychological abuse)?
- Can you respect someone's self-determination or choice to stay with an abusive partner?
- Do you have a passion for helping people to live free from fear and abuse?
- Would you enjoy educating the public about DV and sexual violence and getting the community to get involved in solving this problem?
- Are you a patient person? (It may take a long time until a victim is ready to leave a dangerous situation.)
- Would you be comfortable working in a shelter environment where women and their children are residing?
- Would you enjoy the legal work involved in this field?
- Do you have strong empathy for those in abusive relationships or who have experienced sexual violence?
- Would you enjoy the challenge of empowering victims of abuse or sexual violence?

If you answered "yes" to seven or more of the preceding questions, then working in crisis intervention might be for you!

RECOMMENDED READINGS/WEBSITES TO LEARN MORE

Crisis Intervention and Trauma

Bussey, M., & Wise, J. B. (Eds.). (2007). *Trauma transformed: An empowerment response*. New York, NY: Columbia University Press.

James, R. K., & Gilliland, B. E. (2012). *Crisis intervention strategies* (7th ed.). Belmont, CA: Brooks/Cole.

Kanel, K. (2011). *A guide to crisis intervention* (4th ed.). Belmont, CA: Brooks/ Cole.

Psychological First Aid: Field Operations Guide: www.ptsd.va.gov/professional/ materials/manuals/psych-first-aid.asp

The National Child Traumatic Stress Network: www.nctsnet.org

Suicide Prevention

American Association of Suicidology: www.suicidology.org/home

American Foundation for Suicide Prevention: www.afsp.org

National Suicide Prevention Hotline: www.suicidepreventionlifeline.org

Society for the Prevention of Teen Suicide: www.sptsusa.org

Veterans Crisis Line: http://veteranscrisisline.net

Family and Sexual Violence

Family Violence Prevention Fund: www.endabuse.org

National Center on Domestic and Sexual Violence: www.ncdsv.org

National Coalition Against Domestic Violence: www.ncadv.org

National Domestic Violence Hotline: www.ndvh.org

National Network to End Domestic Violence: www.nnedv.org

National Sexual Violence Resource Center: www.nsvrc.org

U.S. Department of Justice, Office on Violence Against Women: www.usdoj. gov/ovw

Domestic Violence

Barnett, O. W., Miller-Perrin, C. L., & Perrin, R. D. (2010). *Family violence across the life span: An introduction* (3rd ed.). Thousand Oaks, CA: Sage.

Davies, J. M., & Lyon, E. (2013). *Domestic violence advocacy: Complex lives/ difficult choices* (2nd ed.). Thousand Oaks, CA: Sage.

Morgan Steiner, L. (2013). *Why domestic violence victims don't leave*. Ted.com video. www.ted.com/talks/leslie_morgan_steiner_why_domestic_violence_ victims_don_t_leave.html

Renzetti, C. M., Edleson, J. L., & Bergen R. K. (Eds.). (2010). *Sourcebook on violence against women* (2nd ed.). Thousand Oaks, CA: Sage.

Roberts, A. (2007). *Battered women and their families* (3rd ed.). New York, NY: Springer Publishing Company.

Sexual Violence

Buchwal, E., Fletcher, P., & Roth, M. (2005). *Transforming a rape culture* (2nd ed.). Minneapolis, MN: Milkweed Editions.

Crisis Intervention Exercise Case Study

You were hired a few weeks ago as a social worker in the family violence emergency women's shelter in your area. You are really excited, because of all the jobs you applied for, this was your first choice. You are being trained by your new supervisor and are learning new things every day about women who are abused by their intimate partners. It is difficult to see these women with their physical and psychological wounds.

A new client has been referred to the shelter, and you are finding this to be a challenging case. Sylvia has recently lost custody of her three children (Sophia, Brittney, and Justin) to the state child welfare agency. According to Child Protective Services (CPS), Sylvia was being emotionally and physically abused by her husband, and he had complete control over his family. The children witnessed their father's violence against their mother on many occasions. However, the children were removed due to Sophia's allegations that she was being sexually abused by her father for the past 4 years. She told the CPS investigator that her mother knew this was happening and had even walked in on them on a couple of occasions. The other children report knowing that their sister was being sexually abused. They report living in terror with their father, who was often drunk and who had unpredictable violent outbursts. They are terrified of him.

Their father has been arrested, and the case will be taken to the grand jury. The children have been placed in a foster home together while the caseworker investigates whether there are any relatives who might be able to care for them. Sylvia is extremely distressed that her children have been taken from her. The child welfare agency views her as a mother who did not protect her children from abuse that has been detrimental to their health and safety. Sylvia denies that she knew that her daughter Sophia was being sexually abused, and she downplays the abuse from her husband. In her view, they did not have a perfect marriage, but she believes that through counseling, she and her husband can get back on track. She is extremely upset at CPS for removing her children and feels this is unfair and unjust. Your supervisor disagrees with CPS's

characterization of Sylvia as a nonprotective mother. She sees Sylvia as a bat-
tered woman who needs help and support, not punishment. She attributes
this to CPS's lack of sensitivity and understanding of women who are severely
abused by their husband over a long period. What do you think?

Questions

1. What thoughts and feelings come up for you as you read this case scenario?
2. Do you sympathize with Sylvia, or are you upset with her for not protecting her children?
3. Do you agree with CPS's decision that it was in the children's best interests to take them into custody? Do you think they could be safe with their mother, or do you agree that they need to be in foster care for the time being?
4. What kinds of services would you arrange for Sylvia? What are the short- and long-term goals for Sylvia?
5. What can be done to get social workers from these two agencies to work together so they are not working against each other?
6. Do you think there is any chance of reuniting this family?
7. What do you hope happens in this case?

REFERENCES

American Foundation for Suicide Prevention. (2014). *Suicide deaths: Facts and figures*. Retrieved from www.afsp.org/understanding-suicide/facts-and-figures

National Association of Social Workers. (2012). *Social work speaks: National Association of Social Workers Policy Statements, 2012–2014* (9th ed.). Washington, DC: NASW Press.

10 ■ CAREERS IN CRIMINAL JUSTICE AND THE LEGAL ARENA

If you are passionate about working with offenders or victims of crime and are intrigued by legal dramas such as *Law and Order,* this may be a career option for you. In the early days of the social work profession, social workers provided services primarily in the jails and prisons. Today, social workers are employed throughout the criminal justice system and legal arena in settings that include the courts, police departments, crime victim services programs, and community-based treatment programs. When working in this field, there are opportunities for social workers to work with victims or offenders, and some are very specialized in their work (e.g., by working solely with sexual offenders).

The need for social workers throughout the criminal justice and legal systems is more pronounced today because of the rapid increase in the general incarcerated population, the rapid increase of incarcerated women, including mothers, large increases of incarcerated individuals with undocumented immigrant status, and an ongoing disproportionate increase among incarcerated people of color. The United States is an outlier, by having the highest incarceration rate in the world and using capital punishment in states where it is legal. This raises many social justice and human rights questions, and social workers should weigh in on these debates. Many decades of research has proven a strong correlation between crime and poverty, so social workers are needed to educate policymakers about the need to decrease poverty and find ways to create more educational and economic opportunities for those with low socio-economic status.

Today, the United States is somewhat contradictory when it comes to drug policy and attitudes toward drug usage. On the one hand, the War on Drugs continues, with billions of dollars spent to investigate and incarcerate those who use and sell illicit drugs. On the other hand, states are beginning to liberalize laws regarding the sale and use of marijuana. This area of U.S. policy will continue to evolve in the coming years as Americans are forced to grapple with how much taxpayer money should be used to fight the drug war, whether drugs should be decriminalized, and to what extent these laws disproportionately affect racial/ethnic minorities who live in low-income neighborhoods.

Social workers bring their ethics and values with them when they work in the criminal justice system. They must have the ability to treat individuals with dignity, even when they have committed terrible atrocities, such as violent crimes. Social workers work to ensure that those who are incarcerated are treated humanely. They operate from a strengths-based and person-in-environment perspective and will advocate for treatment for those who need rehabilitation. Because those who get entangled with the criminal justice system are attached to families, friends, and loved ones, many lives are affected. Thus, family members need support as much as the person who has been accused of committing a crime. Victims of crime also need support, and sometimes this includes counseling or therapy.

The association between mental health issues, socioeconomic disparities, criminal activity, and the large percentage of substance abuse–related offenses among offenders is proof that there is an urgent need for social workers in the criminal justice system (Orzech, 2006). Intersected with the aforementioned issues are complex family and personal health problems that inflict those who come in contact with the criminal justice system. Many social workers who work in the criminal justice system provide mental health services, including substance abuse treatment. In fact, some experts have commented that "prisons are the new asylums" in the United States. For many, the only way to get around financial and other barriers and access needed treatment is by being incarcerated. This is an urgent social problem that social workers need to help our policymakers address.

There are a wide variety of options available to social workers who have a strong interest in criminal justice and the law. Social workers can work with people before a crime has been committed (e.g., prevention or diversion programs), work with those who are already involved with the criminal justice system, or work with individuals after they leave the criminal justice system (e.g., reintegration programs). They can choose to work in the juvenile system or the adult system. They can work with female or male offenders. They can work with victims or offenders. They can work for the government or in the community in a community-based program or advocacy organization. There are a growing number of programs that work with the children of incarcerated parents.

Equipped with a dynamic theoretical orientation, professional education, and licensure, social workers in the criminal justice system are well positioned to focus on rehabilitation and prevention rather than punishment. Social workers work with individuals to ameliorate risk factors for involvement in the criminal justice system, while strengthening protective factors for living productive lives. With expertise in policy advocacy, protection of rights, and provision of clinical services, including family services, case management, and crisis intervention, they are able to provide quality services to individuals from diverse backgrounds. Good-quality social work services can not only positively affect treatment of offenders in terms of preventing recidivism, re-entry, and initial contact with the system, but also help prevent victimization of individuals, families, and communities.

The following sections outline some commonly cited job descriptions and educational and licensing requirements for those with social work education, training, and work experience in the criminal justice system and the legal arena.

Social Worker Spotlight
LYN K. SLATER, MA, MSW, PhD
Interdisciplinary Center for Family and Child Advocacy
Fordham University, New York, New York

I have always been interested in the intersection between social work and the law. My first graduate degree was in criminal justice, and my first job was in a residential treatment center for delinquent girls. It was in my first job that I was introduced to the field of social work and began to be more interested in the clinical, rather than correctional, aspects of working with court-placed adolescents. I later became the director of a small residential treatment facility in New York City and decided to obtain a master's degree in social work (MSW).

Throughout my early career, I had frequent interaction with the legal system, both family court and criminal court. In my position as administrator, I became aware of the enormous influence federal laws and state statutes and regulations exerted on my social work practice. There were times that regulations were not in the best interest of my clients, and I had to find unique and creative ways to persuade the judge to make exceptions. When those situations occurred, I worked very closely with the lawyers assigned to my client's cases, and this was when I realized the power and influence I could have as a social worker when I was teamed with a lawyer who shared my client's goals and my professional value of social justice.

For the last 12 years, I have worked side by side with lawyers working on behalf of children and families. First, I worked at Lawyers for Children, one of the first legal organizations in the country to assign interdisciplinary teams of attorneys and social workers to represent children in foster care. I not only worked on individual cases, but also population-based advocacy projects, such as researching and writing a handbook for children in foster care who had been sexually abused and developing testimony for use in class action lawsuits that addressed unsafe and discriminatory practices in the local child welfare system.

Currently, I teach at Fordham University and cosupervise, with a law professor, the Family Advocacy Clinic, in which law and social work students are placed together as interdisciplinary teams and represent parents living in poverty who have children with special needs. The approach is a holistic one in that we may represent a family when they have a housing issue, a special education issue, or a child welfare concern. Evidence-based social work assessment is the cornerstone of our practice and when combined with the processes in the law that allow client's to have a voice and challenge decisions they do not agree with, participation in the clinic is an empowering experience not only for the client, but for the social work and law students as well. It has been an enormous privilege for me to learn, by working with lawyers, how to amplify my client's voice and have their story be told.

PROBATION OFFICER (ADULT OR JUVENILE JUSTICE SYSTEM)

Probation officers with social work backgrounds provide expert knowledge and skills that contribute to innovation in the criminal justice system. As part of a team working with offenders, probation officers are committed to enhancing the social functioning of individuals who are placed on probation rather than incarcerated in prison. Probation officers either work in the juvenile or adult justice system.

Probation officers provide supervision through personal contact with the offenders and their families, home visits, workplace visits, and electronic monitoring. It is their job to ensure that the offender is not a danger to the community and to help aid in his or her rehabilitation. They work together with community entities, such as churches, residents, and neighborhood organizations, to monitor the progress of offenders. Services provided to offenders include individual, group, and family therapy; counseling; substance abuse rehabilitation; and job training. Probation officers primarily work with the courts, investigating offenders' backgrounds, providing presentence reports, recommending sentences, reviewing sentencing recommendations with offenders and their families, testifying in court, and providing ongoing reports on the offenders' rehabilitation and compliance efforts.

PAROLE OFFICER

Parole officers provide many of the same services as probation officers, but they monitor and supervise individuals who have been released from prison. Their goals include setting up various types of services and support to recently released individuals to help them re-enter society and help prevent them from committing new crimes and re-entering the justice system.

CORRECTIONAL OR DETENTION OFFICER

Correctional or detention officers with educational and employment backgrounds in social work are in positions to positively impact the correctional systems. Their job is daunting: They are responsible for monitoring and supervising over a million offenders in the United States awaiting trial or who have been sentenced to serve time in a jail or prison. They ensure security and order and enforce adherence to rules and regulations within the correctional facility to prevent jail or prison riots, assaults, and escapes. They monitor daily activities and work assignments; enforce discipline; conduct regular inmate and cell searches for weapons, drugs, and other contrabands; facility searches; and inspect mail and visitors. The correctional or detention officers' daily report of activities keeps everyone in-check, and the officers enforce regulations primarily through their interpersonal communication skills and through the use of progressive sanctions (e.g., the removal of some privileges). Depending on the offenders' security classification within the institution, correctional officers may have to restrain inmates in handcuffs and leg irons to safely escort them to and from cells, to other areas, and to see authorized visitors. Officers also escort prisoners between the institution and courtrooms, medical facilities, and other destinations outside the institution.

CORRECTIONAL TREATMENT SPECIALIST

Correctional treatment specialists work with those in jail or prison or those who are on probation or parole. They provide expertise in case management and counseling. In jails and prisons, correctional treatment specialists monitor the progress of offenders and help to develop parole and release plans that detail an inmate's history and likelihood of committing another crime. They write treatment plans, which may include education and job training programs, life skills training on coping, anger management, substance abuse treatment, and sexual offender counseling either individually or in groups. Correctional treatment specialists working in parole and probation agencies perform many of the same duties as those who work in correctional institutions.

JUVENILE JUSTICE COUNSELOR

Juvenile justice counselors work in the probation system and residential treatment programs, primarily providing individual or group counseling to juveniles as well as specialty programs, such as substance abuse and sex offender treatment. These counselors also provide counseling to at-risk youth, assisting youth with court appearances and advocating for appropriate services, aiding in educational placements, and linking youth to school officials. Likewise, they work in community corrections as counselors to juvenile offenders who may have served their sentences and have been released to a community-based program that provides less structure and supervision and more autonomy to work toward adjusting to life back in society (Peat, 2004).

GANG PREVENTION COUNSELOR

Social workers who specialize in gang prevention customarily educate children and youth, families, schools, and communities about gangs, risk and protective factors for gang involvement, roles of each party in preventing gang involvement, and consequences of such involvement. Social workers who engage in gang prevention work bring extensive creativity, theoretical orientation, cutting-edge knowledge and research, and advanced skills in the assessment, prevention, and treatment of violent behavior. These social workers may also draw on their expertise in program development, community mobilization, and culturally competent practices with families in the quest to prevent gang involvement among children, youth, and adults.

FAMILY COURT SOCIAL WORKER

Family court social workers may serve as forensic social workers, mediators, and guardians working in drug courts, truancy courts, or mental health courts. Typically, they advocate on behalf of juveniles who must appear in court (although they may also represent adult offenders). These social workers attempt to provide social services in lieu of incarceration, if possible. They use their expertise in assessment and subsequently may recommend services such as counseling, specialized treatment, or residential care. Their recommendations must be approved by a judge and adhered to by the client (who in turn reports to a probation officer). However, if the client is found to be out of compliance with the recommendations, incarceration may result. The same services may also be available to adult offenders, who may have the opportunity to engage in a diversion program in lieu of incarceration.

Social Worker Spotlight
BRANDY MACALUSO, BSW, CVP
Coalition for Independent Living Options, West Palm Beach, Florida

After an internship for my bachelor's degree in social work (BSW), I started work at a Center for Independent Living facility in Florida. The focus of my job was empowering and focusing on strengths as a way to promote independence for people with disabilities. The crime victim practitioner (specializing in people with disabilities) position opened up a few months into my employment as a life skills specialist. I was offered the job and excitedly accepted. I sat for my victim practitioner designation through the Office of the Attorney General, State of Florida.

The job itself exists to assist victims through the legal system that either acquired a disability through an act of violent crime or who were exploited and/or abused due to their disability. I was in charge of assisting in filing compensation claims through various programs within the state, providing counseling, facilitating peer support groups, advocating with various agencies and law enforcement to assist with the victim's needs, providing information and referral services to programs in the area, and providing court accompaniment to victims for restraining order and criminal case hearings.

Being a specialized victim advocate, I sit on various task forces, councils, and coalitions in Palm Beach County to ensure that the specialized needs and accommodations are represented for people with disabilities. I also provide training on how other entities, such as law enforcement, domestic violence shelters, and other victim service agencies, can better assist victims with disabilities.

A crime victim practitioner's job can be outwardly challenging. Victim reprogramming for such things as guilt, helplessness, vulnerability, and extremely low self-esteem can be the most difficult, especially when compounded with a newly acquired or newly exploited disability. The most gripping is when the victim wants to return to the abuser. The biggest component to leave with them is knowledge. There is help if they need it, and I will be here if they need to talk or need information. However, being able to help that person begin a new life without the abuser is the most rewarding. I am able to share in triumphs in court, milestones in counseling, and breakthroughs with empowerment. I turn into that person's biggest cheerleader.

It's those moments that I take home with me. I have learned so much while working at the center. I know I have changed the lives of victims with disabilities by helping them convert such a negative event into a positive new start. There is nothing more rewarding.

LICENSED CLINICAL SOCIAL WORKER (JAILS AND PRISONS)

Social workers who work in prisons or jails generally provide individual and group therapy to inmates. In particular, these social workers provide specialized treatment to substance abusers and sex offenders and those with mental health disorders. Their extensive social work knowledge and skills, particularly in assessments and group work, are beneficial to the inmate population. Although these social workers are integral to the prison/jail system, the high worker:inmate ratio often results in more focused specialized treatments. For more information on social work in mental health and addictions, please see Chapter 8.

VICTIM SERVICES SPECIALIST

Social workers who work for victim services programs are trained to support victims of crime. Most are employed by police departments or nonprofit organizations to provide services to victims of rape, assault, family violence, and other crimes. The services provided might include crisis intervention, advocacy, referrals for counseling for the victim and the victim's family, helping the victim understand his or her options in pressing criminal charges, and helping the victim through the legal process, which can be overwhelming and stressful.

In some cases, workers will need to coordinate with other agencies such as Child Protective Services or Adult Protective Services. Victim services specialists will also provide victims with important information such as their rights as a crime victim; services they are entitled to, such as crime victim compensation; and notification when an inmate is about to be released. These social workers may also provide death notification to families when someone has been killed in a violent crime or traffic accident.

Social workers who specialize in victim assistance may also provide services to police officers and assist in police–community activities. They provide crisis intervention to officers in relation to mental health, substance abuse, or domestic issues. They also assist officers in crime prevention activities, securing social services for those affected by family violence, homelessness, school shootings, deaths, and so forth. These social workers use their expertise to deescalate conflict situations and facilitate the building of police–community cooperation.

Social Worker Spotlight
MARILYN PETERSON ARMOUR, MSW, PhD
Institute for Restorative Justice and Restorative Dialogue, Austin, Texas

I was a family therapist for more than 30 years before being introduced to restorative justice. During that time, I often stood in awe as I witnessed the healing that family members experienced once they could be fully authentic and open to each other—a healing far more powerful and sustaining than anything I could give them as a therapist. The field of restorative justice is not only my home, but also a home that feels familiar because it does the same thing that family therapy does. It attempts to heal the harms caused by crime by bringing together the victim and offender to engage in a dialogue about what happened, the effects of the crime on others, and what can be done to restore the brokenness that others feel.

I am fortunate to live in Austin, Texas, and work in the School of Social Work at the University of Texas at Austin. As a researcher, my primary interest is in evaluating the effectiveness of restorative justice programs in an attempt to mainstream restorative practices. I've worked on several innovative restorative justice programs in Texas. For example, victim–offender mediated dialogue is offered by the Victim Services Division of the Texas Department of Criminal Justice. This program brings together victims and offenders of severely violent crime (e.g., homicide, rape) for a mediated dialogue after a 6-month preparation. Bridges to Life is another in-prison restorative justice program that brings together unrelated crime victims and offenders to meet in small groups over 12 weeks for the purposes of reducing recidivism and advancing the healing of both victims and offenders. Both of these programs are groundbreaking and provide real avenues for victim and offender healing. My interest is in understanding the dynamics of these programs and how the interactions between key people provide experiences of healing and meaningful accountability. Indeed, I believe that if we can discover the mechanisms that make restorative justice work, then we can create interventions to break through denial while addressing the pain and destructive consequences from social injustices and interpersonal conflicts on all sides.

Part of my joy is being able to teach a course in restorative justice to social work and law students together. Their different perspectives enrich their responses to the material I teach and model the learning that comes from exploring each other's worlds. I use numerous panels of victims, offenders, and community members to teach the course. Many of the law students have never heard, firsthand, the experience of a crime victim who

(continued)

MARILYN PETERSON ARMOUR   (*continued*)

was mugged nor one who had a loved one murdered. Many of the social work students have never considered the perspective of anyone other than those who are socially disadvantaged. The course, therefore, stretches students' hearts and minds in unpredictable ways and exposes the assumptions we all make about each other. It also forces students out of their usual dichotomous thinking, because they have to hold onto many differing perspectives at the same time.

I'm proud to be part of a movement that holds such hope and promise and a movement which challenges the cynicism and despair that erodes our connections with each other. Although restorative justice is considered a multidisciplinary field, it is also values-based and, like social work, uses those values to guide practice. Moreover, many of the values overlap making social work a natural and future home for restorative justice.

MEDIATION AND CONFLICT RESOLUTION

Mediation, part of the broader field of conflict resolution, is a growing field within the legal profession, and some have argued that social workers are well suited for this line of work based on their skills and training. Some seek the help of a professional mediator when they would like to settle a legal dispute outside of the courtroom to avoid the stress and high legal costs associated with lawsuits and legal battles. Mediation is commonly used in divorce and custody disputes but can also be used to help resolve a wide range of conflicts between disputing parties (e.g., school-based conflicts, civil offenses). Mediators serve as a neutral party hired to help opposing parties reach a mutually acceptable agreement, so mediators must be skilled listeners, communicators, and negotiators. Formal licensing and certification requirements are evolving and vary by state, however, there are many training programs in the United States that are offered by the private sector or in university settings. Some mediators choose to have their own private practice; others are hired to work for the government, legal service providers, or other private entities.

CAREERS IN RESTORATIVE JUSTICE

One positive movement within the criminal justice system is the promotion of a restorative justice framework in which social workers are not only working with offenders but are also strong advocates for victims' rights and services, whether the victim is an individual, family, or community (Ivanhoff, Smyth, & Dulmus,

2007; Showalter & Hunsinger, 2007). Basically, restorative justice focuses on offender accountability through the provision of opportunities to offer recompense for the harm caused to the victim.

Restorative justice often features face-to-face meetings (mediated by social workers or other mental health professionals) between victims and offenders in which both sides have a chance to discuss the crime and its consequences. Successful restorative justice interventions may help victims feel a sense of empowerment and "closure," and for offenders to understand the full effects of their crime and offer restitution for their actions. Some studies have shown that these interventions may lead to lower recidivism rates among offenders.

Restorative justice has been used between individual offenders and victims, families, communities, and even representatives of warring nations. This framework not only advocates for change in the criminal justice system, but also the resolution of various issues such as child abuse, school bullying, human rights violations, and international conflict (Strang & Braithwaite, 2002).

Core Competencies and Skills

- Embrace a more restorative justice approach to working with individuals, families, and communities.
- Promote policy change, particularly for access to and availability of resources for individuals reentering their communities, research on innovative approaches to issues, and best practices within the criminal justice system.
- Advocate for equality and safe and humane environments for at-risk and incarcerated individuals, protection of the public and community, and provision of culturally relevant services to people of color and other vulnerable populations (e.g., transition planning, substance abuse treatment, mental health services).
- Advocate for policies to combat ethnic minority disproportionality and institutional racial discrimination in the justice system.
- Advocate for availability and accessibility of social work services, high-quality health care, and educational and vocational opportunities in the criminal justice system.
- Advocate for continuous specialized training for social workers in the justice system.
- Advocate for forensic social work practice standards to rehabilitation.
- Provide bilingual services in health, mental health, and rehabilitation.
- Take leadership in educating the justice system regarding cultural competency in services, equal treatment of people, and social work professional values and ethics.

- Advocate for more community-based options that allow some offenders to remain within their communities, thus accessing their families, cultures, and relevant treatment.
- Use excellent assessment, decision making, crisis intervention, case management, program development, mediation, and community organization skills.

Educational and Licensing Requirements

Educational and licensing qualifications for social workers in the criminal justice system vary by state, territory, and facilities. Depending on the state or territory within the United States, officers, specialists, and counselors can be employed in the criminal justice system with a BSW, MSW, or a doctorate in social work (PhD). Likewise, those who hold the title of social worker can be employed with a BSW, MSW, or PhD in social work.

Throughout the United States and its territories, many MSW education programs have concentrations or specializations in criminal justice, which prepare students specifically for a career in the criminal justice system. Some social work students choose to earn a dual degree so that they are more prepared and marketable when they enter the job market (e.g., social work and criminal justice; social work and a law degree), but this is not a requirement. Social workers who provide specialized services, such as substance abuse and sex offender treatment, may also complete certifications or special trainings. Licensure in social work requires an individual to meet the respective state's or territory's standards for licensing and 2-year supervised clinical experience for clinical social workers.

As discussed, social workers in the criminal justice system provide critical services to vulnerable populations, consisting of both offenders and victims, on a variety of levels, including individuals, families, groups, and communities. Consequently, a high degree of knowledge, skills, and training is required to successfully and effectively meet their needs. Social workers are indeed needed in these settings.

Best Aspects of This Job

- Working with both offenders and victims in terms of advocating for self-determination and client-centered approaches to promoting social functioning
- Seeing an offender turn his or her life around after involvement with the criminal justice system
- Working to demystify a system that has been viewed as intimidating, adversarial, punitive, and coercive
- Providing both prevention and intervention as needed by individuals in the justice system

- Working with individuals, families, and communities to mobilize resources and promote the social functioning of all parties involved
- Contributing positively to the lives of offenders and victims
- Expanding knowledge about diverse cultures and developing cultural competency skills
- Opportunity to combat disproportionality of people of color in the criminal justice system
- Opportunity to advocate for equality, protection of rights, self-determination, and humane treatment
- Numerous opportunities for policy advocacy on availability and accessibility of services to offenders and victims
- Expanding knowledge about risk and protective factors (e.g., personal, family, peer, school, community-based) that contribute to risk of involvement in the justice system

Challenging Aspects of This Job

- Safety is sometimes an issue when working in the justice system.
- Working with victims and offenders can be stressful, hazardous, and overwhelming.
- Sometimes one's workday expands beyond the workplace.
- Sometimes it is difficult to build relationships with involuntary clients and ensure client self-determination.
- Working with offenders who do not respond to treatment (e.g., sex offenders) and working with offenders whose actions may be personally objectionable can be tough to deal with.
- Knowing that policies and racial profiling are possible risk factors for disproportionality in the system can be very challenging to confront.
- It is a heavy burden being responsible for appropriate assessments and making decisions that affect children, youth, families, and communities.
- Because demands are extremely high in criminal justice systems, caring for yourself and having a balanced life can be difficult.
- Having a successful program eliminated from the criminal justice system because funding is not available can be frustrating.
- Working with professionals who do not have social work training and backgrounds can be challenging.

Compensation and Employment Outlook

Social workers in the criminal justice system are employed by both public and private agencies, so compensation varies by setting, program, facility, state, and region. In 2012, the median annual income for probation officers and correctional treatment specialists was approximately $48,000; for correctional officers, it was about $39,000 (U.S. Department of Labor, Bureau of Labor Statistics, 2014a, 2014b). The bad news is that the demand for these positions is not expected to grow between 2012 and 2022 owing to limited local and state government funding for corrections, according to the Department of Labor. The picture is a little rosier for those working in mental health, however. In relation to those who hold the title of social worker, in 2012, median annual earnings of mental health and substance abuse social workers was approximately $40,000, and this occupation is projected to grow 23% between 2012 and 2022, much faster than the average for all occupations (U.S. Department of Labor, Bureau of Labor Statistics, 2014c, 2014d).

Self-Assessment Checklist: Is This Job for Me?

- Do you have a passion for working with individuals involved in the justice system, and making sure their educational, personal, social, and mental health needs are met?
- Do you think that you are able to work with people from diverse backgrounds, both culturally and linguistically, and their communities?
- Are you passionate about policy advocacy on behalf of offenders and victims?
- Do you enjoy having a job where your workday is spent working with multiple systems, including individuals, families, schools, communities, and courts, to mobilize resources for the best interest of the individual offender or victim?
- Would you enjoy the challenge of working with a range of individuals from at-risk children to adults with criminal histories?
- Are you comfortable working with involuntary clients?
- Would you enjoy advocating for access to resources and information for those who are incarcerated, as well as their families and communities?
- Would you be comfortable working under stressful and hazardous conditions?
- Do you have an assertive personality? Are you comfortable dealing with conflict?
- Would you be comfortable working for an agency that is bureaucratic and has many rules, regulations, policies, and procedures to follow?
- Are you committed to a restorative justice model for victims and offenders?

If you answered "yes" to seven or more of the preceding questions, then working in a criminal justice setting might be the place for you!

RECOMMENDED READINGS/WEBSITES TO LEARN MORE

American Correctional Association: www.aca.org

American Probation and Parole Association: https://www.appa-net.org/eweb/

Center for Court Innovation: www.courtinnovation.org

Inderbitzen, M., Bates, K., & Gainey, R. (2012). *Deviance and social control: A sociological perspective*. Thousand Oaks, CA: Sage.

Innocence Project: www.innocenceproject.org

National Center for Victims of Crime: www.ncvc.org

Restorative Justice Online: www.restorativejustice.org

Van Wormer, K., & Bartollas, C. (2014). *Women and the criminal justice system* (4th ed.). Boston, MA: Pearson.

The Wire [television series]. HBO. www.hbo.com/the-wire#

Criminal Justice Exercise

Although television shows regarding legal issues are plentiful, many court hearings in local communities are actually open to the public. Research the court services available in your neighborhood, and investigate which sessions are open to the public to attend. You may also want to contact your local legal aid society and ask to visit their offices. Learn the difference between criminal and civil courts. You can make an appointment to "interview" a legal aid attorney and talk to him or her about the types of clients he or she serves and the issues he or she addresses.

Go to the FBI's website (www.fbi.gov) and research the crime statistics nationally and for your state. There is a lot of information you can review, and you may be surprised to learn what has been happening in your own community.

REFERENCES

Ivanhoff, A., Smyth, N., & Dulmus, C. (2007). Preparing social workers for practice in correctional institutions. In A. R. Roberts & D. W. Springer (Eds.), *Social work in juvenile and criminal justice settings* (pp. 341–350). Springfield, IL: Charles C Thomas.

Orzech, D. (2006). Criminal justice social work: New models, new opportunities. *Social Work Today*, 6(6), 34.

Peat, B. (2004). *From college to career: A guide for criminal justice majors*. Boston, MA: Pearson Education.

Showalter, D., & Hunsinger, D. (2007). Social work within a maximum security setting. In A. R. Roberts & D. W. Springer (Eds.), *Social work in juvenile and criminal justice settings* (pp. 366–375). Springfield, IL: Charles C Thomas.

Strang, H., & Braithwaite, J. (Eds.). (2002). *Restorative justice and family violence*. Melbourne, Australia: Cambridge University Press.

U.S. Department of Labor, Bureau of Labor Statistics. (2014a). *Occupational outlook handbook, 2014–15: Correctional officers*. Retrieved from www.bls.gov/ooh/protective-service/correctional-officers.htm

U.S. Department of Labor, Bureau of Labor Statistics. (2014b). *Occupational outlook handbook, 2014–15: Probation officers and correctional treatment specialists*. Retrieved from www.bls.gov/ooh/community-and-social-service/probation-officers-and-correctional-treatment-specialists.htm

U.S. Department of Labor, Bureau of Labor Statistics. (2014c). *Occupational outlook handbook, 2014–15: Social workers job outlook.* Retrieved from http://www.bls.gov/ooh/community-and-social-service/social-workers.htm#tab-6

U.S. Department of Labor, Bureau of Labor Statistics. (2014d). *Occupational outlook handbook, 2014–15: Social workers pay.* Retrieved from http://www.bls.gov/ooh/community-and-social-service/social-workers.htm#tab-5

CAREERS IN FORENSIC SOCIAL WORK

You may be familiar with the term *forensic* if you are an avid fan of the television series *CSI* (Criminal Services Investigation) or if you were a member of your high school or college debate team. *Forensic* comes from the Latin word *forensis*, meaning "before the forum" or the court. You are probably not old enough to remember ancient Rome; however, during that time persons charged with a criminal offense would be given the opportunity to present their case in full view of the public. The person accused of the crime, as well as the accuser, would be given an opportunity to make a speech offering their side of the story. The person who made the most compelling and skillful argument would essentially "win" the case.

Forensics (or forensic science) is the application of several sciences, including social sciences, used to answer questions of interest to the legal system. *Forensic social work* refers to the practice of social work that focuses on the law, legal issues, and litigation in both criminal and civil legal systems (Barker, 2003, p. 166).

As you may have noticed from this chapter, social work and the law have always been related to one another. In fact, the historical connection between the two professions goes back to the late 1800s and the Settlement House movement, with the eventual creation of the first juvenile court.

In today's world, *forensic social work* is a term used more frequently in the profession, and the roles played by social workers in this area are quite diverse, with more roles emerging. Forensic social workers are employed as mediators, victim advocates, family court evaluators, mental health evaluators, expert witnesses, mitigation specialists, and risk assessors.

Forensic social work is a specialized focus of practice that bridges both civil and criminal justice systems. It is the assessment and evaluation expertise of the social worker, as an unbiased party in the legal system, that forms the foundation for this type of social work practice. Many social workers, based on their knowledge, skills, and professional experiences, have been qualified by both civil and criminal courts to be an *expert* in their field. This means they can appear in court and testify in various situations.

Typically, social workers have appeared in court as expert witnesses in the area of adoption, termination of parental rights, child abuse and neglect, substance abuse and various addictions, emotional distress or trauma, and mental illness. Such testimony may be given in person or in a written document, and the testimony is based on the social worker's professional experience and the currently accepted theories of human behavior and social environment in the field (Tyuse & Linhorst, 2005).

CUSTODY EVALUATOR

Sometimes, when families break up, in the wake of a difficult divorce or after the death of a sole parent, the court has to determine who is the best custodian of the minor child (or children). In these cases, social workers may be called upon by a judge in a domestic relations court to prepare an evaluation of the minor child. The purpose of the evaluation is to determine who should have custody of the child. This legal decision is based on the concept of what is considered to be "in the best interest of the child," and the decision may include factors such as the child's level of attachment with each potential custodian, the financial situation of each potential custodian, and the child's social and educational needs.

To make this evaluation, the social worker may interview the child (or children), parent(s), and other family members. After evaluating all the available materials, the social worker prepares a written assessment of what he or she thinks is in the best interests of the child. The social worker may also have to testify in court. The social worker's testimony as an "expert witness" assists the judge in deciding who will have the physical and legal responsibility for the child or children under review.

MENTAL HEALTH EVALUATOR

In some criminal or civil cases, individuals brought before the court may be suffering from mental illness or developmental disabilities that affect their ability to participate in, and understand, the court proceedings. In other words, their level of competency to make appropriate decisions may come under question. Criminal and civil courts require a specific evaluation to determine whether an individual is competent. Social workers are frequently called upon by courts to provide competency evaluations, wherein the social worker helps the courts with these types of decisions. These evaluations often involve interviews with the individual and other family members, mental health assessments, medical and developmental histories, and other materials.

MITIGATION SPECIALIST

A mitigation specialist is a social worker who attempts to present evidence that will justify a more lenient sentence for a person convicted of a crime. The intention is not to excuse the crime, but to provide the judge and jury with a better understanding of why the person committed the act. Mental and physical health issues, substance abuse, family history of abuse and neglect, and community or cultural values all may be presented as mitigating factors.

Mitigation specialist is an emerging area of recognition for social work practice, but the scope of this practice rests on the foundation of basic social work skills—engagement, interviewing, and assessment.

Perhaps the most crucial cases in which mitigation testimony may have an effect are those involving the death penalty. The death penalty is currently used in 38 states. Each state allows for the provision of mitigating factors to be presented to the court on behalf of the defendant. Lawyers working for the defense have been using social workers more often in preparing for the penalty phases of capital punishment trials. Social workers are skilled in interviewing clients and other relevant parties, conducting mental health assessments, presenting the client as a human being in written social histories, and managing conflict between the victim's family and family members of the defendant (National Association of Social Workers [NASW], 2003).

Social Worker Spotlight
ALISON CUSICK, MSW CANDIDATE
George Mason University; Intern, Office of the Public Defender,
Montgomery County, Maryland

I recently completed my field practicum as a graduate social work intern at the Office of the Public Defender (OPD) in Montgomery County, MD. I did this internship as my first-year field practicum requirement in my MSW program at the George Mason University in Arlington, Virginia. At OPD, I was part of the Neighborhood Defense project, a team that consists of three social workers, a civil attorney, an education attorney, several law clerks, and three graduate social work interns. Because my supervisor, Melissa, oversaw all the social workers in the state of Maryland, she was only in our office once a week for supervision. Therefore, I spent a lot of time working directly with the social workers in the office, discussing cases and seeking advice on clients, school, and my own career.

When I began my internship at OPD, I had no idea what to expect. I double-majored in criminal justice and psychology, so I was familiar with the criminal justice system and the role that mental health professionals play in the system. In my first week at OPD, Melissa organized an orientation for all social work interns across the state. We spent a day in Baltimore discussing what our role would be with clients, how the social worker code of ethics applied to our work, and what ethical situations we may encounter working with this particular client base. We also discussed how attorney–client privilege may cause ethical conflicts for social workers, and what to do when an ethical conflict arose.

Back in Montgomery County, I was teamed up with Veronica, an adult social worker, who gave me several client cases to read and learn about. We talked about each client's situation and how the social worker could work with the client, attorney, state's attorney, and the judge together to achieve a final outcome that would satisfy all parties involved. I quickly learned that an intern is given a lot of responsibility, and although we were always under the supervision of a licensed social worker, we were expected to perform the same tasks as a social worker. Over the course of my practicum, I learned that a social worker at OPD doesn't have one specific job to do; we do a little bit of everything. Sometimes we would help a client find housing, apply for Medicaid or food stamps, locate day care for his or her children, or get into a rehab or drug treatment program. We served as a contact person for the client's family, allowing family members to keep up with court dates

(continued)

ALISON CUSICK   (*continued*)

and find out about community resources available to them. Other times, we may have a longer, more in-depth relationship with the client, when we are asked to do a social history, assessment, and make a recommendation to the court. Generally, the goal of the assessment was to figure out why the client did what he or she did and to propose a way to help him or her that did not involve long-term incarceration. To complete the assessment, the social worker or intern would meet with the client several times (usually at the local correctional facility) to get a social, medical, and mental health history; determine the client's current mental health status; determine what needs the client had; gain the client's perspective on his or her criminal case; and determine what programs or treatment approaches might be best for the client. The final report includes information from our client's medical records, conversations with the client's family or friends, and research from journal articles that support our final recommendation.

I found that the biggest challenge in my field practicum at OPD was balancing my work between what the attorney needed for court and what my client needed for his or her own rehabilitation. I had several experiences when I did not feel that what the attorney and court wanted were in the client's best interest. For example, I had one client who was facing serious jail time, and the attorney was able to get him into a drug treatment program as part of his probation. In this specific case, I felt like the program wasn't the best thing for him: The client still didn't believe he had a drug problem, and I believed we were just setting him up to fail.

Before beginning my field practicum in forensic social work, I did not have a definitive career path in mind. I entered the MSW program thinking that perhaps I'd want to work with children in foster care or people struggling with addiction. In my 8 months at OPD, my eyes were opened to many more career paths available to a social worker. I worked with men and women struggling with addiction, severe mental illness, unemployment, and homelessness. Some of them were facing a lifetime in jail or knew that their families or jobs would not be waiting for them upon their release. Going into my second year of the MSW program, I still don't have my career path decided, but my eyes have been opened to the possibility of continuing to work in forensic social work with the incarcerated population. I would recommend this field to someone who is interested in working with many different types of people and who is able to listen to clients talk about their difficult lives and the hard situations in which they have been involved.

FORENSIC SOCIAL WORK IN JUVENILE JUSTICE

Public defender offices in the juvenile justice system have been employing social workers to help them link clients to community-based services (e.g., substance abuse programs) as well as in preparing written psychosocial assessments and testifying in court. In recent years, communities across the United States have instituted specialized criminal courts for juvenile defendants with substance abuse disorders and mental illness. These specialized courts seek to prevent incarceration and facilitate community-based treatment for offenders while at the same time providing for public safety. The purpose of forensic social work in this area is to develop successful sentencing plans in the court system based on the ultimate goal of rehabilitation. For more information on other social work careers in juvenile justice, see job descriptions for probation officer, juvenile justice counselor, and gang prevention counselor earlier in this chapter.

Social Worker Spotlight
JOEL T. ANDRADE, MSW, LICSW, PhD
Boston College Graduate School of Social Work, Chestnut Hill, Massachusetts; Bridgewater State Hospital, Bridgewater, Massachusetts

Going into the MSW program at Boston College Graduate School of Social Work, my career goal was to work with juvenile offenders. My first-year internship was working with adolescents who had been suspended from school over a violent incident. Many of the youth I worked with were somehow involved with the criminal justice system in one form or another—whether by being on probation, having been granted parole, being in youth detention, or having had a family member incarcerated. After this experience, I thought the best way to serve my clients in the future was to gain a better understanding of the criminal justice system, so I elected to do my second-year internship in a correctional setting. Combining my interests in the criminal justice system and mental health, my second-year internship was at Bridgewater State Hospital (BSH) in Massachusetts. BSH is the state's most secure forensic hospital and the staff is charged with evaluating and treating male forensic patients. I loved the forensic work, and when I completed my MSW, I worked for 1 year at a prison in Concord, Massachusetts, before returning to BSH.

Being a clinician in a forensic hospital has many challenges, particularly working with severe character disordered patients. I enjoyed the work and became very interested in the assessment and treatment of psychopathic inmates. In 2001, I decided to go back to the Boston College Graduate School of Social Work for my PhD to pursue this research interest. My dissertation is on the early-life experiences of psychopathic individuals.

While completing the doctoral requirements, I continued to work full time at BSH in numerous capacities, including the director of the seclusion and restraint unit, the admission coordinator, and the clinical risk assessment coordinator. These positions have been extremely rewarding and have continued to fuel my research interests. I became involved in numerous research groups presenting at national conferences in the areas of psychopathy, violence risk assessment, and sexual offending behavior. The combination of my forensic and research interest also led to the upcoming publication of a book I am editing in the area of violence risk assessment, treatment, and risk management for forensic practitioners. The goal of this volume is to provide the forensic practitioner with a hands-on guide to conducting violence risk assessments.

The field of social work, particularly forensic social work, has been an extremely rewarding career choice. Coupling this forensic work with academic pursuits of research has been particularly fulfilling for me. I strongly encourage social work students to consider an internship in a correctional or forensic setting. I considered it—and have never left!

Core Competencies and Skills

- Knowledge of the legal system and terminology
- Strong assessment and interviewing skills
- Ability to work with persons charged with criminal offenses
- Knowledge of the appropriate treatment interventions for mentally ill inmates, substance abusing inmates, juvenile offenders, victims and perpetrators of family abuse and violence, and those returning to the community after incarceration
- Strong mediation skills in high-conflict situations
- Knowledge of risk assessment and prevention
- Ability to advocate for needed community resources
- Demonstrate strong group facilitation skills
- Ability to work successfully as part of a multidisciplinary team

Educational and Licensing Requirements

Forensic social work is an area of specialty practice and requires an MSW. Many aspects of this job also require additional certifications and/or a license in clinical social work.

Working with a BSW in the areas of foster care and adoptions, substance abuse prevention and treatment, juvenile and domestic relations courts, emergency shelters, group homes, case management, child and adult protective services, and disability and rehabilitation services is excellent preparation for gaining experience in this field and preparation for more advanced work in graduate school.

Many universities are beginning to offer specific courses in forensic social work. The National Organization of Forensic Social Workers was created to offer professional continuing education and certification in this growing area of practice.

Best Aspects of This Job

- Working to end disparities in the legal justice system is professionally rewarding.
- Being a valued member of a multidisciplinary team means that you are not working alone in a difficult environment.
- Specializing in a new and growing area and developing expertise is a positive professional challenge.
- Much of this work can be fast paced and crisis oriented, so you are never bored.
- There are many opportunities in this work to have positive outcomes from tragic circumstances.

- Bearing witness to the personal narratives of people whose lives would never be known otherwise offers personal satisfaction.
- The documentation of life stories is a contribution to the historical record so that others may benefit in preventing future tragedies.
- Working on behalf of a typically underserved population (e.g., prisoners) allows you to put social justice into action.

Challenging Aspects of This Job

- Working with difficult clients and families can be emotionally draining, and it is critical that you take care of yourself.
- Working with persons charged with criminal offenses may prove challenging to balancing your personal values and ethics.
- Negotiating with professional colleagues outside of the social work profession who may not respect your contributions can be frustrating at times.
- Working directly with victims and their families may contribute to your own traumatization if you do not provide for your own self-care.

Compensation and Employment Outlook

Most social workers in the area of forensics are working for publicly funded social service agencies, family courts, and state offices of the public defender. Social workers with MSWs working in these places would receive the same salary as other workers in those occupational tiers, but owing to the need for highly experienced social workers in this field, compensation would most likely be higher than that of someone new to the organization with limited professional work.

Many social workers who are self-employed and work as independent licensed clinical social workers contract their services to the aforementioned agencies or are hired on behalf of clients. Social workers in private mental health practices typically earn between $40,000 and $60,000, with approximately 25% earning considerably more (NASW, 2004).

Self-Assessment Checklist: Is This Job for Me?

- Would you be comfortable working with a group of professionals who hold different views and values than those of social workers?
- Can you be objective working on behalf of someone who is guilty of a crime?
- Would the nature of the crime affect your view of the client?
- Are you able to set personal limits and professional boundaries and stick to them?
- Can you deal with conflict or mediate between various parties?

- Can you tolerate your work being interrupted from time to time?
- Are you interested in the law and legal system?
- Would you be comfortable with public speaking and testifying in court?
- Would you be able to manage your own emotions while listening to a victim's story of abuse?
- Can you accept decisions that may be made in opposition to what you would decide?

If you answered "yes" to seven or more of the preceding questions, then you may want to explore this area further!

RECOMMENDED READINGS/WEBSITES TO LEARN MORE

Barsky, A. E., & Gould, J. W. (2012). *Clinicians in court: A guide to subpoenas, depositions, testifying, and everything else you need to know* (2nd ed.). New York, NY: Guilford Press.

Maschi, T., Bradley, C., & Ward, K. (Eds.). (2009). *Forensic social work: Psychosocial and legal issues in diverse practice settings.* New York, NY: Springer Publishing Company.

National Association of Social Workers—Legal Defense Fund: www.social workers.org/ldf

National Organization of Forensic Social Work: www.nofsw.org

Rome, S. H. (2012). *Social work and law: Judicial policy and forensic practice.* Boston, MA: Pearson.

Schroeder, J., Guin, C. C., Pogue, R., & Bordelon, D. (2006). Mitigating circumstances in death penalty decisions: Using evidence-based research to inform social work practice in capital trials. *Social Work, 51*(4), 355–364.

Springer, D. W., & Roberts, A. R. (Eds.). (2007). *Handbook of forensic mental health with victims and offenders: Assessment, treatment, and research.* New York, NY: Springer Publishing Company.

Forensic Social Work Exercise Case Scenario

Shawna Cook is a 23-year-old female who has Down syndrome. Shawna lives in a group home of eight residents—four male and four female. Everyone in the group home is employed in a job that is within easy commuting distance. All the residents are encouraged to lead independent lives and to participate in community activities.

Shawna began dating Paul, a boy she met at her job, about 1 year ago. They are sexually active, and now Shawna has learned that she is 2 months pregnant. The group home administrator notified Shawna's mother, her legal guardian. Mrs. Cook is very upset and has requested that the administrator make arrangements for the pregnancy to be terminated.

Shawna and Paul want to get married and keep the pregnancy. The Family Court Judge has asked the County Social Services to have a social worker evaluate Shawna for a competency hearing to be held in 2 weeks. You are the social worker given this task.

Questions

1. What is the ethical dilemma in this case?
2. As the social worker in this scenario, what will you do first?
3. What kind of information do you need to gather?
4. If Mrs. Cook is Shawna's legal guardian, will you need her permission to interview Shawna?
5. Does the Group Home Administrator have a responsibility in this case? If so, what is it and to whom?
6. What do you think the outcome of this case should be?
7. What are your own personal values or biases as you read this case?

REFERENCES

Barker, R. L. (2003). *The social work dictionary* (5th ed.). Washington, DC: NASW Press.

National Association of Social Workers. (2003). *Social workers as death penalty mitigation specialists.* Retrieved from www.socialworkers.org/ldf/legal_issue/200309.asp

National Association of Social Workers. (2004). *National workforce survey.* Washington, DC: Author.

Tyuse, S. W., & Linhorst, D. M. (2005). Drug courts and mental health courts: Implications for social work. *Health & Social Work, 30,* 233–240.

11 ■ CAREERS IN INTERNATIONAL SOCIAL WORK AND HUMAN RIGHTS

Some social work students dream of doing social work in another country. These adventurous students have a love of travel, a passion for learning about other cultures, and a desire to help underprivileged people around the world. Many of these students will take advantage of taking study abroad courses offered by their university or will apply to volunteer or work in various international organizations, the most famous one being the Peace Corps. Research focused students will apply for a Fulbright scholarship that allows them to carry out research in another country. However, an important thing to consider is that you can do international social work in the United States thanks to the large number of immigrants and refugees living in this country.

In the news, we often see images of the wars in Iraq and Afghanistan and of disasters, such as earthquakes and hurricanes, in various parts of the world. These tragedies leave in their wake individuals, families, and communities who require a variety of types of assistance ranging from basic needs such as food, clothing, and shelter to counseling and mental health services. An emerging issue that has gained increased attention by experts and policymakers in recent years is human trafficking, also referred to as modern-day slavery. Human trafficking is the recruitment, transportation, transfer, harboring, or receipt of persons by improper means (such as force, abduction, fraud, or coercion) for an improper purpose, including forced labor or sexual exploitation. Free the Slaves estimates that 21 to 30 million people are in slavery today. If you are interested in helping in crisis situations around the globe, then international social work may be the career path for you.

Globalization; increased interdependency between cultures, geographic areas, and economies; and increased inequities between the haves and have-nots also warrant social work practice in an international context. The fact that a substantial percentage of people in developing countries live in extreme poverty— on less than $1 a day—is a major concern for the profession of social work. Social workers are called to contribute to knowledge, practice, and advocacy efforts that have global implications for people all over the world. Major organizations that have engaged in these international social work efforts include the United Nations, UNICEF, Save the Children, Amnesty International, the Red Cross, the Peace Corps, Human Rights Watch, the International Association of Schools of Social Work, the International Federation of Social Workers (IFSW), and the International Council on Social Welfare (ICSW). Within these organizations, social workers may be called on to provide leadership on a range of issues, including combating poverty and hunger; social and economic development; assisting immigrants and refugees; providing services to victims of human trafficking; helping those displaced by war, famine, or national disasters; providing health care and mental health services to those suffering from AIDS and other serious illnesses; human rights work; and combating illiteracy.

Social work is essentially an international/global profession. Although, historically, social work accompanied colonization in some countries, social workers today are needed in every country to help alleviate a host of social problems resulting from experiences with colonization and migration (Cox & Pawar, 2012). The emergence of transnationalism among people who claim multiple geographic locations and citizenship is also an important consideration in the work of international social workers especially with children and their families. And even if you do not choose to work internationally, in the aforementioned settings, there remains a high chance that you will serve individuals and families who have migrated from another country. For this reason, some would argue that *all* social work is international social work, even if never done outside the United States.

Social workers who engage in international social work must be culturally competent and well versed in international affairs, global issues and dynamics, theories, and social and economic development. As such, many social work students complete elective courses in international social work or earn a dual or joint degree in international affairs.

This chapter will describe some of the many jobs available for those with social work education, training, and work experience who are interested in working in an international context.

U.S.-BASED IMMIGRANT, REFUGEE, AND ASYLEE RESETTLEMENT WORKER

As the number of immigrants arriving in the United States continues to grow, individuals with social work backgrounds will be needed to serve them. Social workers can contribute their expertise in multicultural practice and crisis intervention to provide services to families and communities in attaining social and economic independence and cultural adjustment. Bilingual social workers are in demand and will be very competitive in the job market. Services provided may include linking families to churches and communities of origin in the United States; helping immigrants locate cash assistance, medical assistance, employment, and housing; and also providing social services, including individual and family therapy, substance abuse treatment, English-language courses and services in their native tongues, educational/vocational training, and other specialized mental health services. The worldwide reach of human trafficking also requires special attention from social workers who are trained to provide mental health services as well as judicial and health services in partnership with other professionals.

Social Worker Spotlight
MARLEINE BASTIEN, BSW, MSW, LCSW
Founder, Fanm Ayisyen nan Miyami/Haitian Women of Miami

I grew up in a small village on the outskirt of Petite Riviere De L'artibonite called Pont Benoit, a town situated north of the capital of Haiti. The tradition of women partaking in all aspects of societal life yet excluded from the decision-making processes of the community is engrained in the village's consciousness. This tradition represents centuries of rigid rules and regulations that no one has ever dared challenging. I vowed, when I was young, to change this state one day, a day that hasn't arrived since I left Haiti after completing secondary school. When the political situation became unbearable in Haiti, I emigrated from Haiti to the United States, in 1981.

Just 2 days after I arrived in Miami, I started volunteering at the Haitian Refugee Center, starting a life of volunteering and strong advocacy on behalf of immigrant women and children. In 1994, I received a Volunteer of the Year award from Miami-Dade County. I obtained an associate in arts degree from Miami Dade Community College and a bachelor's degree in social work (BSW) and a master's degree in social work (MSW) from Florida International University. As a licensed clinical social worker, I worked for 13 years at Jackson Memorial Hospital, where I fought for AIDS, sickle cell, and breast cancer patients of all nationalities. Soon my expertise, compassion, and strong advocacy for patients' rights became well known, as did my expertise in women's challenges, explaining, for example, why a mother failed to bring her child for follow-up care or why an HIV-positive mom would become pregnant again. I was consulted by all the specialty teams, and my opinion in the domain of health access and women's struggle was respected. I was recognized as social worker of the month by Jackson Memorial Hospital in 1996. In 2000, I received the Miami Dade County Social Worker of the Year award.

In 1991, I founded Fanm Ayisyen nan Miyami/Haitian Women of Miami (FANM), an organization whose mission is to empower Haitian women and their families and to facilitate their adjustment to life in South Florida. FANM was a volunteer organization for 9 years. I organized volunteers to keep it going, raising $5,000 a year through selling candies, coordinating yard sales, and selling inexpensive items at flea markets. FANM transitioned to a community-based organization in 2000. Now FANM has a staff of 14 and a budget of $1.7 million, providing an array of services ranging from immigration, mental health, domestic violence, cancer prevention, counseling, crisis intervention, after-school programming for disadvantaged children, a legal clinic, and a citizenship program. FANM was named Best Nonprofit of

(continued)

MARLEINE BASTIEN   (continued)

the Year by the Chamber of Commerce, Best Champion of the Powerless by the *New Times*, and Best Advocate by the *Sun Post*. I received the Human Rights award from Amnesty International in 2000, among many other recognitions and accolades. In May 2005, *Essence Magazine* named me one of the 35 most powerful women in the world.

Besides FANM, I'm also a founding member of the Haitian Coalition on Health (HCH), which (though now defunct) was a pioneer organization playing a vital role in understanding the prevalence of HIV/AIDS in the Haitian American community. I also instituted Miamians Working Together, a collaborative of Haitian and African American women to work together to combat AIDS. Finding too much friction between African Americans and Haitians, I used Miamians Working Together to bring the two groups together, and they learned from each other's histories, traditions, and values through what I called "tea parties" (meetings held at members' houses where they eat, drink, and learn from each other). Once the groups were able to build a strong rapport, they got involved in a joint pilot project called AIDS Education and Prevention. The program was very successful not only in improving relationships between the two groups, but also in fighting against HIV/AIDS.

I have also used the media successfully to shed light on the plight of women with breast cancer. Through sheer resilience and determination, I developed a successful community outreach program that promotes prevention, education, mammograms, and the buddy system to educate the community about breast cancer. I instituted a buddy system, "Fanm men nan men" (women hand in hand), whereby women provide support to others with breast cancer.

Domestic violence is a huge problem not only in the Haitian community, but also in the community at large. When I first implemented a domestic violence community education and intervention program in the early 80s targeting Haitian and Caribbean women, I received death threats. Even women admonished me for "trying to be an American woman who wants women to wear the pants in the families." Now, even men voluntarily come to FANM to seek help and learn how to control their anger. I fought to get domestic violence recognized as a "health issue." I strongly advocated for doctors to assess women who come to the emergency room at Jackson Hospital with serious and often strange injuries for domestic violence. I believe that health access is a human right, not a privilege, and women's health has always been a priority for me.

Since my arrival in the United States, I have advocated at the local, national, and international level on behalf of immigrant women and children.

(continued)

MARLEINE BASTIEN   (*continued*)

I fought to get women and their families out of detention, making a powerful case in their behalf on the streets, in boardrooms around the nation, and in the halls of Washington. Women from all around the world come to this country in search of a safe haven. They have often been traumatized, abused, maimed, jailed, and harassed in their native land. They come here in search of freedom and liberty. The least we can do is afford them the most basic right guaranteed under international laws—the right of due process.

As a social worker, I believe in women's rights. I strive daily to promote women's rights, social and economic justice, human rights, health education/prevention/access services, and treatment. I believe that world peace cannot be achieved without the full and complete emancipation of all women. Our country was built on the cherished principles of justice for all, and through my advocacy work, I wanted to show that women can be strong and compassionate, ambitious and nurturing, forceful but loving and caring.

Social Worker Spotlight
JULIANE RAMIC, MSW
Resettling Refugees

When I took my first job after college, I had no understanding of the field of social work. I was working at a refugee resettlement agency in St. Louis and fell in love with the work. My supervisor told me that there was little opportunity for advancement unless I got my MSW. Within a month, I had submitted my applications to local social work graduate programs. I was accepted at the George Warren Brown School of Social Work at Washington University. During my time there, I did everything I could to gain skills that could be transferred to working with refugees.

When a person is forced to leave his or her home, he or she often finds relative safety in a refugee camp. Then he or she may be deemed eligible for third country resettlement and, if so, be served by a local refugee resettlement agency. Wanting to understand the refugee experience, I sought opportunities to work in refugee camps for national organizations that coordinated domestic refugee resettlement and then at local social service agencies serving newly arriving refugees. After graduate school, I had the honor of working in the Sudanese and Somali refugee camps in Ethiopia. Upon returning, I began working for the U.S. Committee for Refugees and Immigrants, an umbrella organization representing about 30 local refugee resettlement agencies. I loved connecting with the staff of these agencies and providing them with grant support and technical assistance, but I missed working with refugees! In 2004, I had the opportunity to join the Nationalities Service Center in Philadelphia as the director of social services. It's been an incredible experience to gain inspiration from those we serve and use this to mold, modify, and design our programs to best serve the changing needs of refugees. I work with a dedicated team of incredible individuals, and together we try to ensure that our services are innovative, responsive, culturally appropriate, and so forth. Refugees now living in the United States are survivors, amazing advocates, and have so much to give. How can I not love what I do?

IMMIGRATION POLICY ADVOCATE

In addition to providing direct services to immigrants, social workers may help immigrant communities on a macro level by advocating for changes to immigration policies. This is especially true now, as anti-immigration policies in the wake of 9/11 have led to a rise in discriminatory practices against and treatment of many immigrants, both undocumented and documented. Social workers in organizations such as the American Civil Liberties Union (ACLU),

Immigration Equality, the National Immigration Law Center, the National Council of La Raza (a Latino rights organization), and the National Network for Arab American Communities, among many others, are advocating for positive changes in national policies affecting the lives of immigrants, their families, and communities. In addition, there are many opportunities at state and city levels to advocate for local immigrant communities.

DISASTER RELIEF WORKER

Disaster relief workers with social work backgrounds are often employed by organizations such as the Red Cross and other nongovernmental organizations (NGOs) to work in international settings. In these jobs, they contribute their specialized skills in crisis intervention, medicine, public health, and mental health to those recovering from a disaster. These workers also provide food and shelter.

Social Worker Spotlight
SUSAN KOSCHE VALLEM, EdD, LISW
Professor and Chair, Social Work Department, Wartburg College, Waverly, Iowa

Although I teach undergraduate social work at Wartburg College, much of my social work practice was in medical social work. I received my undergraduate education from Wartburg College, my MSW from the University of Iowa, and my doctor of education (EdD) from the University of Northern Iowa. As a practicing social worker, I particularly enjoyed working in the emergency department providing crisis intervention services. From that background, I became an American Red Cross disaster mental health volunteer.

I first became involved with Red Cross disaster mental health after the 9/11 attacks. Since then, the Red Cross has sent me all over the country to work with survivors of all sorts of natural disasters. I discovered how well my social work education and experience had prepared me for crisis intervention.

Two key values of social work are building on strengths and starting where the client is. Crisis intervention is not therapy in the clinical sense, but rather is helping survivors of disasters find their strengths and begin to take control of a life that suddenly went out of control. For example, one of my duties in New York was to take families of victims into the Ground Zero area for some sense of closure. These people did not need therapy, but they did need help dealing with sudden death and grief. Through crisis intervention, I worked with them to help "normalize" an abnormal situation through understanding the grief process. I asked them to tell me about their loved one who had died, to give value to that person's life. And then I thought about what to do next—what little act could they do to begin to take control of their loves and to move forward? The resiliency of people I work with is always amazing.

I believe in practicing what I teach. Working with people from all cultures and walks of life through the Red Cross not only is personally gratifying, but also reinforces that social work education and practice is right on target. I work with many helping professions in the Red Cross, and social workers seem, to me, to be the best suited for crisis intervention. I base this opinion on watching social workers from around the country meet clients where they are at that moment, build on strengths, and use their creativity to develop, always with the client, positive intervention strategies. Volunteering with the American Red Cross fits with social work.

HUMAN RIGHTS WORKER

Human rights workers are advocates for human rights for all people. Those with social work training in policy issues and legislation are able to contribute positively to human rights work. They engage in report writing, monitoring and actively promoting compliance with international standards on human rights, working with intergovernmental organizations and NGOs, and promoting research and legal developments in relation to human rights.

As a component of human rights, fighting against the global span of human trafficking continues to be a critical issue for social work. In addition to policy advocacy against human trafficking around the world, social workers are also needed to provide mental health services to victims as they re-enter their old or new families and communities. Social workers are also able to facilitate the provision of judicial and health services for these victims in collaboration with other relevant professionals.

INTERNATIONAL DEVELOPMENT WORKER

International development workers with social work backgrounds help meet the needs of individuals, families, and communities in developing countries in areas such as health, education, sanitation, businesses, agriculture, and community organization for the betterment of their economic and social conditions. Their work is framed by a collective and global perspective. For instance, Peace Corps workers provide services in education, youth outreach, community development, business development, agriculture and environment, health and HIV/AIDS, and information technology. International development workers engage in a range of activities from counseling an adolescent in Tonga to teaching English in Spain.

CAREERS WITH THE UNITED NATIONS/UNICEF

Social workers who work for the United Nations/UNICEF/UN–Women work in a variety of programs to assist those in need. These workers protect children's rights and women's rights and provide services to victims of war, disasters, exploitation, and poverty. They focus specifically on child survival and development, protection, education and gender equality, and HIV/AIDS prevention.

Social Worker Spotlight
PURNIMA MANE, MSW, PhD
Deputy Executive Director (Program), UNFPA, United Nations Population Fund

My professional life has been fueled by a deep belief in social justice and equity, and this drives me every day. Throughout my career, I have championed sexual and reproductive health, with a particular focus on gender and AIDS. I was, therefore, particularly honored to be appointed deputy executive director for program at UNFPA, the United Nations Population Fund, and assistant secretary-general of the United Nations.

As part of the United Nations, UNFPA promotes the right of every woman, man, and child to enjoy a life of health and equal opportunity. It supports countries in using population data for policies and programs to reduce poverty and promote universal access to reproductive health, gender equality, and women's empowerment.

My position allows me to bring my interests and expertise together to address social causes that are dear to my heart. As deputy executive director, I help shape global policies that directly affect people's lives. I represent UNFPA at the highest level of policy dialogue with government officials, major international partners, and civil society representatives. I participate in many global gatherings and advocate for the goals and values of UNFPA. I also oversee UNFPA's programs and make sure that our activities are strategic and effectively managed, benefiting those who need them most.

What I enjoy most about my work is that it gives me the opportunity to work with inspiring leaders and interact with some of the brightest and most committed people in the world. I am constantly in contact with interesting people and being confronted with complex and challenging situations.

Before joining UNFPA, I served in several international positions in UNAIDS; the Global Fund to Fight AIDS, Tuberculosis, and Malaria; the World Health Organization; and the Population Council. I also worked for over a decade on public health and gender-related issues in my home country, India, and I was honored to teach at the prestigious Tata Institute of Social Sciences in Mumbai, Asia's first school of social work.

To prepare for my career, I completed an MSW, specializing in health, along with a master of philosophy (MPhil) and a doctorate (PhD) in social work, with a specialization in women's studies, from the Tata Institute.

Guided by the principles of human rights and human dignity, I hope that my contribution to the work of the United Nations will make a difference in the lives of the most underprivileged and play a small but meaningful role in building a more humane and equitable world.

Core Competencies and Skills

- Embrace a global/international social and economic development and social welfare policy framework.
- Possess skills in critical analysis and understanding of the interdependency among nations and of inherently complex value and ethical dilemmas, the theories and practices of international social work, and social and economic development.
- Demonstrate cultural and linguistic competencies appropriate for the populations being served.
- Possess understanding of people around the world as transnational beings with relationships and ties in multiple geographic locations and citizenship.
- Demonstrate commitment to the protection of human rights and promotion of equality in an international context.
- Demonstrate sensitivity to the diversity of views on human rights issues.
- Possess skills in political advocacy, crisis intervention, immediate response to emergency situations, and brief therapy.
- Ability to assess needs, make decisions that ensure security and safety, and manage, monitor, and evaluate activities established for the betterment of international communities.
- Possess extensive knowledge and skills in community organizing, networking, teamwork, and relationship building among organizations providing services.
- Excellent verbal and written communication skills for an international audience.
- Skills in strategic planning for long-term development or disaster management.
- Demonstrate skills in research, policy assessment, legislative proposals, and response development appropriate to the respective country.
- Be familiar with the roles of political structures, government, international organizations, and NGOs in international work.
- Possess technological skills that facilitate communication, accessibility, and availability of services to the international community.
- Possess specialized knowledge and skills in working with immigrants, refugees, asylees, and victims of human trafficking.

Educational and Licensing Requirements

Educational and licensing qualifications for social workers working in an international context vary by country. Depending on the country, social workers can be employed in governmental agencies and NGOs including private, nonprofit, and faith-based agencies with a BSW, MSW, or PhD in social work. Throughout the United States and its territories, many MSW programs have concentrations, specializations, emphasis, or certificates in international social work that prepare students specifically for careers in international and global settings. Licensure in social work requires an individual to meet the respective country's standards for licensing, though many developing countries will not have such requirements.

Social workers in international and global settings provide services to vulnerable communities and their members through policy advocacy and practices on the micro, mezzo, and macro levels. As a result, a high degree of knowledge, skills, and training is required to successfully meet the needs of these international communities.

Best Aspects of This Job

- Having the opportunity to live abroad and work with individuals, families, and communities from cultures worldwide
- Gaining a better understanding of the interdependency of countries and contributing positively to strengthening those relationships
- Expanding knowledge and experience with diverse cultures and developing cultural competency skills
- Opportunity to advocate for equality, protection of human rights, and self-determination for all people globally
- Opportunities for political advocacy on behalf of immigrants, refugees, asylees, and victims of human trafficking

Challenging Aspects of This Job

- Policy and practice changes on a global level may be difficult and slow.
- Working with victims of the immigration and refugee experience can be stressful, hazardous, and overwhelming.
- Sometimes domestic/U.S. policies are barriers to providing needed services to immigrants, refugees, and asylees. The current political climate is punishing to undocumented immigrants.
- It is a heavy burden being responsible for appropriate assessment and making decisions that affect children, youth, families, and communities.
- You must learn to be accepting of cultural practices that may be very different from your own.
- You may encounter difficulty dealing with and seeing people who live without the basic necessities of life.

Compensation and Employment Outlook

War and conflict, economic issues, immigration, and refugee circumstances have contributed to the increased amount of international social work, both U.S.-based and U.S.-trained. The need for culturally and linguistically competent service providers in and out of the United States validates social work education and recruitment of social workers from diverse populations. The major shortage of social workers in the United States has led to a good employment outlook.

Salaries for individuals engaged in social work internationally and globally vary by country and organization of employment. For instance, in the United States, the compensation for social workers who engage in U.S.-based international work may range from earning a median income of $38,000 annually (U.S. Department of Labor, Bureau of Labor Statistics, 2008) to receiving only housing and a monthly allowance. In fact, much international humanitarian work is done by volunteers.

Self-Assessment Checklist: Is This Job for Me?

- Do you have an interest in working on social issues that affect people internationally and globally?
- Do you think you are able to work with people from diverse backgrounds, culturally and linguistically, and their communities?
- Are you passionate about political advocacy on behalf of immigrants, refugees, asylees, and victims of human trafficking?
- Do you enjoy having a job where your workday is spent working with groups and organizations (e.g., governmental, NGOs) that embrace equality and protection of human rights?
- Would you be comfortable working under stressful and hazardous conditions?
- Do you have an assertive personality? Are you comfortable dealing with conflict on an international and global level?
- Do you have an interest in living abroad and working with people to mobilize their communities?
- Are you interested in working with people suffering from disasters (e.g., earthquakes, hurricanes)?
- Are you willing to fight for marginalized families?
- Are you interested in the challenge of working with people from diverse backgrounds?

If you answered "yes" to seven or more of the preceding questions, then working in international/global settings might be the place for you!

RECOMMENDED READINGS/WEBSITES TO LEARN MORE

Center for International Social Work: http://socialwork.rutgers.edu/Center-sandPrograms/CISW.aspx

Fulbright U.S. Student Program: http://us.fulbrightonline.org

International Federation of Social Workers: www.ifsw.org/intro.html

International Social Work: www.isw.org
International Social Work journal: http://isw.sagepub.com
Kristof, N., & WuDunn, S. (2009). *Half the sky: Turning oppression into opportunity for women worldwide.* New York, NY: Alfred A. Knopf.
Mapp, S. C. (2014). *Human rights and social justice in a global perspective: An introduction to international social work* (2nd ed.). New York, NY: Oxford University Press.
Planet Social Work: www.planetsocialwork.com
Reichert, E. (2007). *Challenges in human rights: A social work perspective.* New York, NY: Columbia University Press.
Social Work Today magazine: www.socialworktoday.com/archive/swt_0105p14.htm
The New Social Worker online magazine: http://www.socialworker.com/feature-articles/career-jobs/How_to_Snag_a_Job_In_International_Social_Work
United Nations: www.un.org/en

International Social Work and Human Rights Exercise

One of the best ways to experience being a social worker in this setting is to travel. If you have never traveled to a foreign country, planning a trip is an exciting adventure. If the prospect of traveling alone is too intimidating, try going to a travel agency to explore the possibilities of joining a fixed tour to a country where you will be with a group of adventurers like yourself.

Participating in a foreign language immersion program will provide you with the experience of living with a host family while you are learning the language, culture, and history. This is an excellent way to actually be part of a community in a new country.

There are many programs that request help from volunteers to provide services to communities in need around the world. You may want to contact your own religious congregation to see whether it has a program. Many social workers in this field had their own beginnings in volunteering for the Peace Corps (www.peacecorps.gov). If you visit the Peace Corps website, you will see all the wonderful opportunities for international work available with just a click of the mouse.

Happy traveling!

REFERENCES

Cox, D., & Pawar, M. (2012). *International social work: Issues, strategies, and programs.* Thousand Oaks, CA: Sage.
U.S. Department of Labor, Bureau of Labor Statistics. (2008). *Occupational outlook handbook, 2008–09.* Retrieved from www.bls.gov/ooh

12 ■ CAREERS IN POVERTY AND HOMELESSNESS

Americans in need are not strangers, they are citizens—not problems, but priorities.

—Dr. Martin Luther King, Jr.

The social work profession has a special dedication to assisting individuals and families who are living in poverty. This commitment is one of the features of the profession that sets us apart from other related disciplines. Other professions may charge fees for their services that many people cannot afford to pay, but social workers often work in agencies and organizations where the services are free or are offered on a sliding scale according to the client's ability to pay.

Poverty is a serious social problem in the United States. According to data from the U.S. Census Bureau (2013), in 2012, the nation's official poverty rate was 15.0%, representing 46.5 million people living at or below the poverty line. When the United States is compared to other wealthy industrialized nations, it ranks high on levels of poverty (including child poverty) and income inequality.

People who are poor are often stigmatized and stereotyped as being lazy or unmotivated or as having no ambition. Many wrongly believe that poverty comes from a moral or character defect in the individual. However, social workers understand, through research and work experience, that the causes of poverty are complex and multifaceted and that a combination of personal and environmental factors is often at play. Personal factors that contribute to an individual's ability to support himself or herself financially include lack of job skills and education, mental illness, poor health or disability, substance abuse, abuse and battery, single parenthood, ill children, and lack of child care and transportation. Environmental factors can include fluctuations in the health of the larger economy, the failure of the U.S. job market to provide enough jobs, the proliferation of low-paying jobs that pay poverty wages and offer no benefits, lack of affordable housing and child care, substandard education systems, and discrimination. Through research, we know that women, children, and ethnic minorities are overrepresented among those living in poverty.

When we refer to people living in poverty, we are talking about three groups:

1. The working poor (those making minimum wage)
2. The unemployed
3. Those with deficits in human capital (lack of job skills and education)

Social workers who work with those living below the poverty line often work with those who are homeless or are experiencing housing instability as well as those who are receiving government assistance. Social workers believe that the desire to work and contribute is universal. Social workers also believe in the power of government programs, such as Social Security and the Earned Income Tax Credit, to lift millions of people out of poverty. Thus you will find social workers in every state working in various organizations and coalitions at the local, state, and federal levels to address various barriers to self-sufficiency and to create opportunities for people to be able to support themselves and their families.

There are a few new social innovations that are being tested to evaluate their effectiveness in helping people move out of poverty. Asset building programs focus on helping low-income individuals accumulate assets or savings in order to purchase a home, start a business, or save for college. Individuals in these programs establish a savings account (called Individual Development Accounts, or IDAs), which is then matched by public and/or private resources. Microfinance programs allow low-income people to borrow money from a bank to start a small business. This practice was made famous by Nobel Peace Prize winner Professor Muhammed Yunus, who started the Grameen Bank in Bangladesh. The Harlem Children's Zone is another great example of a program trying a different approach to alleviating poverty by providing a holistic array of services to children and their families in a geographic region, Harlem.

No matter the field of practice, social workers will often serve those who are below the poverty level. However, this chapter will highlight some common careers for those interested in addressing poverty specifically on a micro and/ or macro level.

INCOME ASSISTANCE CASEWORKER/EMPLOYMENT COUNSELOR

In 1996, a major change in social welfare policy occurred when the Aid to Families with Dependent Children (AFDC) program ended and was replaced with a program called Temporary Assistance for Needy Families (TANF). Under TANF, welfare assistance is no longer an entitlement program and benefits are time-limited and closely tied to work requirements. Since this new law was passed, a number of government, nonprofit, and faith-based organizations have started new programs and initiatives to focus on helping individuals leave the welfare system. These programs offer a variety of services such as job skills or vocational training; substance abuse treatment; educational programs focused on helping individuals complete high school, get their GED, or get into a community college; affordable housing programs; programs that focus on promoting marriage and preventing out-of-wedlock pregnancies; and programs that offer help with transportation and child care.

Social workers believe that a safety net is important so that when individuals and families fall on hard times, they will at least have their basic needs met. You will find many social workers employed by the government who are charged with distributing cash assistance (e.g., TANF, supplemental security income [SSI]) and in-kind benefits (e.g., SNAP, the U.S. food stamp program; public housing; supplemental food program for women, infants, and children, or WIC; Medicaid; State Children's Health Insurance Program, or S-CHIP) to eligible individuals and families. These social workers have various job titles, such as eligibility caseworkers, income assistance social workers, human services caseworkers, and employment counselors. The following tasks are commonly performed by social workers to help people move out of poverty:

- Helping families in financial crisis receive benefits for which they are eligible
- Case planning and case management
- Teaching clients about financial planning and budgeting
- Providing job skills training, possibly by working with employers to create internship and job preparation opportunities in the private or nonprofit sector
- Providing opportunities for additional education and training required to compete in today's job market (e.g., computer skills training)
- Teaching clients the skills they need to get and keep a job (e.g., résumé writing and cover letters, interviewing skills, dressing for interviews, social skills training)
- Counseling and coaching skills
- Facilitating support groups, mentoring programs, or workshops for participants
- Providing services for children, such as child-care and early education programs (e.g., National Head Start Association and Pre-K)
- Referring clients to other needed community services to address various barriers to employment (e.g., substance abuse treatment, housing assistance, vocational training programs, mental health treatment, battered women's shelter)

Core Competencies and Skills

- Financial planning skills and knowledge of the ever-changing job market
- Knowledge of interviewing techniques to obtain highly personal information
- Understanding, compassionate, and nonjudgmental

- Ability to perform basic arithmetic functions, including using decimals and computing percentages
- Knowledge of the causes of poverty (both personal and environmental)
- Strong administrative and programmatic skills for those who want to run a program or become a program administrator
- Ability to understand complex laws and policies to determine eligibility for various social welfare programs based on income
- Strong coaching skills (need to be very supportive and encouraging)
- Crisis intervention skills
- Knowledgeable about the many governmental and nongovernmental programs serving low-income people

Educational and Licensing Requirements

For most starting positions in government and other settings serving low-income individuals and families, a master's degree is not required. A master's degree would be useful, however, if you would like to move into a supervisory or administrative position in the organization or if you would like to work in public policy to advance sound economic policies that would be beneficial for this vulnerable population (e.g., ensuring that the minimum wage is a livable wage; improving family leave policies).

Best Aspects of This Job

- Being there for a family who is experiencing a crisis of income in their life (e.g., loss of a job, mother fleeing domestic violence, major illness, having a child with a serious illness)
- Having the opportunity to provide or refer families to services that will enable them to gain skills or education so that they can live self-sufficiently
- The satisfaction of serving people who are usually forgotten or marginalized
- Having a job with predictable work hours
- Good benefits (this is typically a government job)
- Having the opportunity to educate others about the causes of poverty and the importance of programs designed to increase opportunities for individuals and families living in poverty

Challenging Aspects of This Job

- Feeling that you are helping clients temporarily but not able to attack the root causes of poverty

- Dealing with the bureaucracy of the job and sorting through the many rules and regulations—lots of paperwork!
- The lack of understanding and compassion for low-income people in our society; "blaming the victim" mentality; feelings that the poor are unworthy of help
- The politics of income: legislators who pass laws that are meant to punish instead of assist people who are poor
- Dealing with burnout
- Clients who are stressed and hopeless seeing you as "the bad guy" or "part of the system" instead of someone who is there to help them
- Seeing the effects of poverty on children and families

Compensation and Employment Outlook

As shown in Table 12.1, there are a wide range of salaries depending on state or region, years of previous experience, and type of degree (undergraduate or graduate degree).

Self-Assessment Checklist: Is This Job for Me?

- Do you have a passion for helping individuals and families move out of poverty?
- Do you strongly believe in the value of economic justice for all people?
- Can you work with people who are living in poverty or receiving government benefits and treat them with dignity and respect?
- Can you serve low-income people without judgment?
- Do you believe that people have the right to basic needs such as food, shelter, and health care?
- Would you enjoy the challenge of helping a family get back on its feet and leave the welfare system?
- Because change often takes some time, do you have the patience to work with this population?
- Are you a strong motivator, mentor, and coach?
- Can you work with people who are low-income and understand the causes of poverty, even if you have not experienced poverty yourself?
- Do you believe that the government has a role to play in combating poverty in our communities?

If you answered "yes" to seven or more of the preceding questions, then working in the field of income assistance might be for you!

TABLE 12.1 Salary Ranges for Eligibility Caseworkers in Selected States, 2014

STATE	QUALIFICATIONS	SALARY RANGE FOR ELIGIBILITY CASEWORKERS (2014)
Texas	Bachelor's degree in human services, business, education, or related field from an accredited 4-year college or university; Computer skills are important; Workforce Development Specialist I, II, III, and IV	$2,144 to 3,238 per month
Oregon	Combination of work experience and college classes; Human Services Specialist I, II, III, and IV	$2,314 to $4,479 per month
Illinois	Requires BA degree in psychology, sociology, anthropology, social welfare or a closely related field, plus 1 year professional casework or crisis intervention experience in a social services agency; Human Services Caseworker	$4,059 to $5,503 per month
Connecticut	Bachelor's or master's degree	1. Connecticut Careers Trainee: $40,512 to $51,535 per year 2. Eligibility Services Worker: $49,149 to $61,628 per year (after 1 year as trainee)

Source: www.twc.state.tx.us/customers/jsemp/job-search.html; www.oregon.gov/jobs/Pages/index.aspx; http://work.illinois.gov; www.ct.gov/dss/lib/dss/jp-cct.esw_all_regions_2012.pdf

RECOMMENDED READINGS/WEBSITES TO LEARN MORE

American Public Human Services Association: www.aphsa.org

Children's Defense Fund: www.childrensdefense.org

Economic Success Clearinghouse: www.financeproject.org/irc/win.asp

Ehrenreich, B. (2001). *Nickel and dimed: On not getting by in America.* London, England: Metropolitan Books.

Institute for Research on Poverty: www.irp.wisc.edu

Joint Center for Poverty Research: www.jcpr.org

Kozol, J. (1995). *Amazing grace: The lives of children and conscience of a nation.* New York, NY: Crown.

National Center on Children in Poverty: www.nccp.org

National Eligibility Workers Association: www.nationalnew.org

Rank, M. R. (2004). *One nation underprivileged: Why American poverty affects us all.* New York, NY: Oxford University Press.

Shipler, D. (2005). *The working poor: Invisible in America.* New York, NY: Vintage.

Income Assistance Caseworker Exercise: Test Your Knowledge

1. True or False

   The United States is the only industrialized country that does not have universal health care.

2. According to the U.S. Census Bureau, about what percentage of the population was living in poverty in 2012?
3. True or False
The poverty rate for children is higher than for any other age group.
4. True or False
A worker making a minimum wage of $7.25 an hour would earn enough to be slightly above the poverty line.
5. Without Social Security, about what percentage of elderly Americans would have incomes below the poverty line?
6. True or False
Most families receiving welfare are large families, and mothers often have more children in order to collect greater benefits.
7. True or False
The United States has the lowest poverty rate of any Western industrialized nation.
8. True or False
Poverty is more likely to befall women than men.
9. True or False
Public assistance benefits provide a disincentive to work.
10. True or False
The SSI program is set up primarily to provide cash assistance to people with disabilities.

Answers: 1. True; 2. 15%; 3. True; 4. False; 5. 50%; 6. False (average size of TANF family is 2.6 persons); 7. False; 8. True; 9. False (because the benefits are too small for a family to live on, the majority of welfare recipients work); 10. True.

SOCIAL WORK CAREERS IN THE FIELD OF HOMELESSNESS

When most of us visualize someone who is homeless, the "bag lady" or disheveled man on the street begging for money usually comes to mind. But the homeless population is extremely diverse and includes families and children. Among the homeless you will find single-parent families, some escaping domestic violence; runaway youth; substance abusers; former foster youth; those with disabilities; the unemployed; individuals recently released from prison; those with mental illness; and veterans. Homelessness is a problem not only in the urban environment, but also in rural areas, where the majority of the homeless are families, single mothers, and children. Because of methodological challenges, there is not good data on the number of homeless individuals in the United States.

According to the National Coalition for the Homeless (2009), two trends are responsible for the rise in homelessness in the past 25 years: an increase in poverty and a growing shortage of affordable rental housing. In recent years, there has been a move away from public housing projects because they are often dilapidated and unsafe. Today, many homeless experts see the benefits of mixed-income communities and are making efforts to help families establish a home in one of these communities (e.g., scattered site apartments). Another model that is gaining a lot of attention is the Housing First model, which provides stable and permanent housing to homeless individuals first, followed by needed services. This varies from other approaches that often require homeless individuals to complete services (e.g., substance abuse; mental health) *before* getting stable housing. The idea is that people are more likely to participate in treatment when they feel safe and secure.

Working with individuals and families who are homeless is very challenging and very rewarding. There are a variety of settings for social workers interested in this field. Perhaps the most common setting is the homeless shelter, where residents can stay temporarily while they are housed, fed, and provided with case management services. All shelters are different in terms of who they serve and the kinds of services they provide. For example, some shelters may serve only women and their children. The services provided on-site may include anything from substance abuse treatment, parenting classes, GED or English as a second language classes, medical care, assistance finding employment, childcare, and a variety of life skills classes. Clients will be referred to other services in the community that are not provided directly by the shelter, and the goal of many shelters is to assist residents in finding permanent housing. You are probably familiar with the domestic violence shelter or the Salvation Army shelter in your community. Another famous organization is Habitat for Humanity, which builds affordable homes for low-income individuals. Families must invest hundreds of hours building their home and the homes of others.

Homeless organizations will employ a variety of employees who have various roles in the organization such as administrative positions (e.g., executive director, program manager) and front-line staff who work directly with the residents. Many shelters and nonprofit organizations serving the homeless also employ outreach workers who go where the clients are (on the streets), build rapport and trust with them, and get to engage them in services.

CAREERS IN RESEARCH

Some social workers with a strong interest in poverty and economic inequality choose to work at the macro level by conducting research. They enjoy doing research so that we can better understand the root causes of poverty and the best way to assist those who are poor or homeless. This is how we ensure that the interventions that we use with clients are "evidence-based." A few of the many questions that can be answered through research include the following: What are the biggest risk factors for living in poverty? How many people are homeless in this country, and what are the demographics of homeless individuals? What are the barriers to people's leaving TANF? What kinds of programs have been most successful in helping people leave poverty? What are the long-term outcomes of individuals who left the welfare rolls under the new welfare reform law? How many people experience hunger in the United States?

Social workers interested in conducting research typically work for universities, the government, nonprofit research organizations, and think tanks. Prominent organizations that conduct research in poverty include the National Poverty Research Center (University of Michigan at Ann Arbor), Institute for Research on Poverty (University of Wisconsin at Madison), University of Kentucky Poverty Research Center, West Coast Poverty Research Center, National Center for Children in Poverty (Columbia University), Economic Policy Institute, Institute for the Study of Homelessness and Poverty, Center of Hunger and Poverty (Brandeis University), Center for the Study of Urban Poverty (University of California, Los Angeles), American Public Human Services Association, Center on Urban Poverty and Social Change (Case Western Reserve University), Institute on Race and Poverty (University of Minnesota), Center on Budget and Policy Priorities, Rural Poverty Research Center, and Urban Institute, as well as Poverty in America (University of Pennsylvania).

POVERTY ADVOCATE

After gaining a number of years of experience at the micro level, some social workers choose to move into an advocacy or policymaking role. Social workers interested in advocacy are charged with educating the public about poverty and homelessness and influencing legislators to pass legislation at the local and national level that would help individuals and families in need. They would advocate for increased funding for community programs that serve those who are low-income or homeless, particularly programs that focus on prevention. They would lobby legislators to strengthen important "safety net" government programs such as Medicaid, SNAP, SSI, WIC, and TANF. Social workers interested in this type of work might work for a legislator or an advocacy organization such as the National Alliance to End Homelessness, End Hunger Network, National Coalition for the Homeless, and the Coalition on Human Needs.

Social Worker Spotlight
KRISTIN NOEL LUDWIG, MSW
Community Action, Hillsboro, Oregon

My bachelor of arts degree in 1971 included concentrated study in French and Spanish. After working with people dealing with poverty in the social services world for 20 years, the urging of another social worker motivated me to combine theory and practice, and I returned to school in 1991. In 1994, I received a master's degree in social work (MSW).

For the past 7 years, I have worked as the McKinney–Vento Student Advocate, a service partnership between Community Action, a nonprofit, and the Hillsboro, Oregon, School District. I spend many of my days in the agency's family shelter (a 100-year-old house). The environment is sometimes chaotic and full of crisis, but it always offers a welcoming place for people to be listened to and accompanied as they reach goals for housing stability and renewed lives of self-sufficiency.

The McKinney–Vento Homeless Education Act is a federal law mandating that all school districts identify and support students who are experiencing homelessness, high mobility, and housing insecurity to ensure school access and achievement. The best interests of children must be considered. In my role as advocate, I inform students, parents, and school staff of rights, expedite enrollment, and arrange transportation to the school of origin. The act addresses best practices, which means dealing with students' emotional and health needs and linking to tutoring and resources for school success. I also find it crucial to dispel stereotypes of people in homeless situations—for example, when they are judged solely by their appearance. Students eligible for McKinney–Vento services are in temporary foster care; staying in family shelters, motels, cars, and unheated garages; students who are doubled up with family and friends due to economic hardship; or students living in substandard housing, including many migrant camps. Some are unaccompanied youth who "sofa surf." Being in tenuous living situations weighs heavily on children and parents. The number of students dealing with the effects of poverty, including housing instability, is growing locally and nationally. Last year, school districts in Oregon counted more than 15,000 students who dealt with homelessness. The high cost of housing is an overarching theme and requires social policy solutions.

In practice, the transformational reality of the social work field acts on many levels.

Examples from my work include the following:

(continued)

KRISTIN NOEL LUDWIG   *(continued)*

- Individual: helping a student gain self-efficacy by making an agreement with himself or herself to attend school regularly and complete homework
- Family: acknowledging a parent's walk toward recovery from substance abuse and the hard work of healing in the family
- Program: witnessing a teacher advocate for a student in foster care to not move schools again but be stable in instruction so that both teacher and student can make strides
- Social policy: organizing with others in my community of Washington County for our 10-Year Plan to End Homelessness, including financial support for emergency housing and more housing options that are sustainable and affordable

What is valuable to me in this work? As social workers, we have a responsibility to effect change. In fact, that is our history, from participating in the tenement worker movement of the 19th century to civil rights legislative action, and in solidarity with those who struggle for family wages, child care access, housing, and beyond. We build community and connections by our common values and actions.

I am inspired by the hope I see reflected in the eyes of students and families.

Core Competencies and Skills

- Knowledge of the housing market and housing options in your city or community
- Understanding and compassionate
- Nonjudgmental
- Knowledge of the causes of poverty (individual and structural)
- Strong administrative and programmatic skills for those who want to run a program or become a program administrator
- Knowledge of the laws and eligibility requirements for various federal housing programs
- Strong coaching skills
- Crisis intervention skills
- Knowledgeable about the many governmental and nongovernmental programs serving low-income people
- Strong advocacy skills

Educational and Licensing Requirements

For most starting positions in a homeless shelter, a bachelor's degree is required. A master's degree would be useful if you would like to move into a supervisory or administrative position in the organization or if you would like to work in public policy to advance sound policies beneficial for this vulnerable population.

Best Aspects of This Job

- Helping a homeless family achieve stable housing that is safe and secure
- Connecting people to available resources in the community to help them address various barriers to self-sufficiency
- Working with individuals and families from diverse backgrounds, ages, and walks of life
- Having the opportunity to advocate on behalf of homeless children and adults in your community and for affordable housing
- The satisfaction of serving a population that is often marginalized and misunderstood
- Being able to work with a wide variety of individuals in the community to solve this problem, including city leaders and faith-based organizations
- Specialization to some degree (e.g., work in a shelter for women and children, work in a program that does outreach work for homeless or runaway teens)

Challenging Aspects of This Job

- Dealing with the myths and stereotypes that many people have about people who are homeless can be frustrating.
- Working to solve this problem can often seem very overwhelming on a large scale.
- You must deal with burnout.
- Trying to serve individuals who do not seem to want your assistance (e.g., those with mental illness) can be challenging.
- Seeing the effects of homelessness on youth and adults can be difficult (e.g., witnessing what people need to do to survive, such as prostitution, going without medical care, or risking victimization by crime and violence).

Compensation and Employment Outlook

Salaries for social workers working in homeless shelters, most of which are non-profit organizations, will vary greatly from agency to agency and by state. Salaries will be higher for those who are in supervisory or administrative positions.

Self-Assessment Checklist: Is This Job for Me?

- Do you have a passion for helping homeless individuals and families find safe and affordable housing?
- Do you strongly believe in the value of economic justice for all people?
- Can you work with people who are living in extreme poverty and treat them with dignity and respect?
- Can you serve people living in poverty without judgment?
- Do you believe that people having adequate food, shelter, and health care are basic human rights?
- Are you comfortable working with individuals who are severely mentally ill or who are substance abusers?
- Because change often takes some time, do you have the patience to work with this population?
- Are you a strong motivator, mentor, and coach?
- Can you work with people who are poor and understand the causes of poverty, even if you have not experienced it yourself?
- Do you believe that the government has a role to play in ensuring safe and affordable housing for low-income people in our communities?

If you answered "yes" to seven or more of the preceding questions, then working with homeless individuals and families might be for you!

RECOMMENDED READINGS/WEBSITES TO LEARN MORE

Homelessness Resource Center: www.nrchmi.samhsa.org

Housing First (a year-long special reporting project from NPR News exploring the housing dilemmas of Americans with special needs): www.npr.org/news/specials/housingfirst

Kozol, J. (2006). *Rachel and her children: Homeless families in America.* New York, NY: Three Rivers Press.

National Alliance to End Homelessness: www.endhomelessness.org

National Association of the Education of Homeless Children and Youth: www.naehcy.org

National Center for Homeless Education: www.nche.org

National Coalition for the Homeless: www.nationalhomeless.org

National Low Income Housing Coalition: www.nlihc.org

Vissing, Y. (2006). *Out of sight, out of mind: Homeless children and families in small town America.* Lexington, KY: University Press of Kentucky.

Homeless Outreach Caseworker Exercise Case Study

You are a social worker who has worked with the homeless for more than 10 years. Over the years, you have learned much about the struggles facing those who are homeless. For the past 2 years, you have been working with city

officials and community leaders to build and develop a new homeless shelter for those with substance abuse problems, a huge issue in your community. Countless hours have been spent designing this new program to be fresh and innovative, meeting the unique needs of this population. The funding is also in place—a combination of grants, government funding, and private donations. However, a major problem arises when the city paper publishes a story about plans for this new shelter and it creates a firestorm of controversy. Many individuals and families who will be living near the new shelter are not happy that they were not consulted. They worry about the safety of their children because the individuals served by this shelter are drug addicts and alcoholics. They have started a petition and have been calling their government representatives, protesting the development of this shelter. You quickly realize that the advocacy skills you learned in your social work program and on the job will be extremely useful, and you get ready to make a plan.

Questions

1. What thoughts and feelings come up for you as you read this case scenario?
2. Do you sympathize with the community members' concerns? Are their feelings valid? Why, or why not?
3. What are your next steps? What can you do to overcome this obstacle at the community level?
4. In retrospect, what could have been done to avoid this problem?
5. One strategy would be to work with other concerned individuals and organizations to devise a media campaign to educate the public on this issue. What would your media campaign look like? What would be most effective? What message would you want to send? Be creative!
6. How could you address the stereotypes and misconceptions that many people have about homeless people and those who suffer from substance abuse?
7. How could you involve your clients in this effort?

REFERENCES

National Coalition for the Homeless. (2009). *Why are people homeless?* Retrieved from www.nationalhomeless.org/factsheets/Why.pdf

U.S. Census Bureau. (2013). *Income, poverty and health insurance coverage in the United States: 2012.* Retrieved from www.census.gov/newsroom/releases/archives/income_wealth/cb13-165.html

13 ■ CAREERS IN THE POLITICAL ARENA

Each time a man stands up for an ideal, or acts to improve the lot of others, he sends forth a tiny ripple of hope, and crossing each other from a million different centers of energy and daring, those ripples build a current that can sweep down the mightiest walls of oppression and resistance.
—Robert F. Kennedy (1925–1968)

All social work is political.
—Haynes and Mickelson, 2009

In Chapter 1, we shared our observation that most people have a fairly limited view of what social workers do. The majority of Americans have no idea that there is a political dimension to social work practice. When many think about social workers, the most common image that comes to mind is that of a professional who is trained to assist individuals and families experiencing a range of problems such as poverty, child abuse, family violence, substance abuse, illness, and other problems of daily living. Even college students who enter social work programs in universities across the country are often surprised (and later delighted) to learn that social work includes macro-level practice and that one of the core values of the social work profession is social justice.

Many are surprised to learn that some social workers work in politics as a way to achieve social justice for many of the populations that social workers serve. In fact, some members of Congress, such as Democratic senators Barbara Mikulsky (Maryland) and Debbie Stabenow (Michigan), have a degree in social work. And many more social workers hold political office at the state and local level or work in advocacy organizations across the United States to effect social and political change. Even though many Americans are disillusioned with the political process, and although trust in our elected leaders is at an all-time low, policy practice is an important tool in a social worker's toolbox when it comes to working toward a more equitable society.

The social work profession has long recognized that to help people, change efforts must be directed at the individual, or micro, level as well as at the macro level. An important part of macro social work is policy practice or political advocacy. Social workers who choose this career path work diligently to pass legislation at the local, state, or national level that benefits the individuals and families we serve and to defeat legislation that would be detrimental or harmful to our clients. Social workers in this field might work for an advocacy organization, a legislator as an aide or staffer, or a research organization, or "think tank," as a policy analyst.

All social work programs accredited by the Council on Social Work Education are required to offer course work in social welfare policy, which is a good place to begin learning about and preparing for this type of work. Social work students may also complete their field work in a political setting as long as they have a social worker to provide them with their required supervision. Students who enter their required policy courses with hesitation often find that learning about the policy world can be quite interesting and invigorating. Some even decide to make a career out of social work policy practice.

Most Americans would be surprised to learn that social workers have a rich history of working in a political context on behalf of various social causes and client populations. Since the profession's beginning, social workers have engaged in political advocacy in efforts to achieve social justice for the poor and disenfranchised in society. Some of the most politically active social workers were the settlement workers during the late 1800s and early 1900s. A large part of the Hull House volunteers' work involved conducting investigations (i.e., survey research) of various social problems and then working to change laws that would improve life for many in the urban slums. The settlement house workers lobbied on behalf of legislation that today is taken for granted, such as granting an 8-hour workday, the minimum wage, worker's compensation, old-age pensions, health insurance, and safe housing, as well as that of outlawing child labor and sweat shops and laws protecting the public's health from industrial hazards such as lead poisoning. They established the world's first juvenile court and improved neighborhood conditions by adding public baths, gyms, and playgrounds and improving sanitation and garbage removal. Their work led to the establishment of clinics to diagnose and treat venereal disease and efforts to provide birth control information to women. Many of the settlement house workers picketed in various labor strikes and marched for women's suffrage and peace. Some were offered important positions in government, including in the U.S. Bureau of Labor and the U.S. Children's Bureau.

During the Great Depression, social workers lobbied elected officials to adopt more humane policies dealing with the millions thrown into poverty. Two key figures in Franklin D. Roosevelt's (FDR) administration were Frances Perkins and Harry Hopkins, both of whom were social workers in their early careers. Hopkins, one of FDR's closest advisors, was hired to oversee the Federal Emergency Relief Administration (FERA), the Civil Works Administration (CWA), and the Works Progress Administration, all of which focused on creating work relief programs for the unemployed. Frances Perkins served as the secretary of labor under FDR, the first woman to hold a U.S. cabinet post. FDR appointed her chair of the Committee on Economic Security, tasked with conducting an investigation of social insurance. Ms. Perkins was one of the chief architects of the Social Security Act and championed the legislation until its passage in 1935. The Social Security Act of 1935 is today considered landmark social welfare legislation that helped create a social safety net. It attempted to protect those most vulnerable in society, including older adults, the unemployed, the poor, the disabled, widows, and children. The act created a combination of social insurance (for those participating in the workforce) and public assistance programs (for nonworking and dependent individuals). The key program would be Social Security, a program that would insure people against poverty in old age.

All of the social upheaval of the 1960s led to many social workers' involvement in social movements, along with a renewed commitment to the need for social change to achieve social and economic justice. The theme of President Lyndon B. Johnson's (LBJ) administration would be the "Great Society," and its focus would be on the elimination of poverty and racial injustice. Johnson would also declare a "War on Poverty" with the goal of eliminating poverty in the United States. This was an interesting time for social workers, because the Great Society programs created by the LBJ administration created thousands of new community-based programs across the country that sought to create a more just society for those who have been left out. Many social workers began to view the community as their client. Social work programs also responded to the changing landscape by offering more courses and concentrations in community practice and community organizing. Important social programs that were created during LBJ's presidency included Medicare and Medicaid, the Food Stamp Program, federal funding for education (Head Start, K–12, and higher education), as well as the VISTA program.

Today, social workers advocate on behalf of various issues in the political arena, including but not limited to improved health care coverage, better services for those in need of mental health treatment, poverty and income inequality, civil rights for gays and lesbians, and more federal funding for vital social services such as child protection. However, despite social work's history of political advocacy, some have argued that this commitment to social justice and political action has waned in recent years. Some social work academics have even argued that social work has abandoned its mission of social justice, and today's social workers are more concerned with being psychotherapists who serve the middle and upper classes. This is an area of vigorous debate within the social work profession.

Evidence of the social work profession's commitment to social change and political action on behalf of the poor and disenfranchised can be seen in the National Association of Social Worker's *Code of Ethics* (2008), which states

> Social workers should engage in social and political action that seeks to ensure that all people have equal access to the resources, employment, services, and opportunities they require to meet their basic human needs and to develop fully. Social workers should be aware of the impact of the political arena on practice and should

advocate for changes in policy and legislation to improve social conditions in order to meet basic human needs and promote social justice. (https://www.socialworkers. org/pubs/code/code.asp)

Many social workers argue that "all social work is political," because our profession is so affected by the laws that are passed at the local, state, and national levels. This chapter will profile a number of careers available to social workers who wish to work specifically in the political arena.

LOBBYIST

Many people have a negative reaction to the word "lobbyist"; immediately the image of a slick, high-powered professional who works for a corrupt corporate entity comes to mind. However, many nonprofit and human services organizations employ lobbyists to advocate for increased funding and other legislation to help children, families, and adults. Other lobbyists are not employed by the organization itself but are contract lobbyists who may have a number of "clients" for whom they lobby. Lobbyists spend their days giving advice to the organization(s) they work for regarding what legislation is "politically feasible" in the current political landscape. Social workers are often very idealistic and usually want big sweeping changes now! However, sometimes lobbyists must explain that smaller, incremental change is necessary, especially when an issue does not have widespread political support or when the bill includes a request for funding.

Lobbyists are experts at knowing how to draft legislation and how to get a bill passed into law. You may be surprised to learn that in Congress each year, approximately 5% to 10% of all bills that are introduced actually become law. As you can imagine, relationship building with legislators and key stakeholders is very important to being successful as a lobbyist. You must be able to engage in coalition building so that you can show legislators that there are a number of important people and organizations that support your bill. Lobbyists tend to be masters of persuasion. In other words, they are very skilled in determining which strategies and tactics will be most successful in getting various legislators to support this bill. Finally, lobbyists help support the organization in designing the overall legislative strategy, which might include letter-writing campaigns, lining up people to testify at a congressional or public hearing, designing a creative media campaign (e.g., website content, informational flyers, radio/television/newspaper ads, billboards), and guiding the grassroots work needed to get a bill passed into law.

CAMPAIGN WORKER

Sometimes social workers are hired (or volunteer) to work on a candidate's political campaign and are then offered a paid position if the candidate wins office (see "Legislative Aide," this chapter). Campaign workers must be okay doing a range of low-level (e.g., making copies and coffee) and high-level tasks. The fun part of working on a campaign includes working with other passionate political types and putting your all into getting your candidate elected. Campaign workers are responsible for making campaign materials, canvassing neighborhoods to talk to community members about your candidate, supervising a phone bank, organizing speaking events and rallies for your candidate, and fund-raising.

Working on a political campaign is exciting work but involves long hours and entry-level pay. However, many young, idealistic individuals are willing to work under these conditions, lured by a better and more prestigious position down the road.

Social Worker Spotlight
GREG SHUFELDT, BSW, MSW
Political Social Worker, Missouri Pro-Vote Coalition, St. Louis, Missouri

I received both my bachelor's degree in social work (BSW) and master's degree in social work (MSW) from St. Louis University (SLU). My time at SLU was rewarding, and I benefited from some nontraditional practicum opportunities that helped shape my practice. It was during my practicum opportunities as an organizer, advocate, and campaign worker that my love for political social work developed.

My first job after earning my MSW was working as a campaign manager for a local state representative campaign in Missouri. After this experience, I managed multiple campaigns for state legislature and helped organize St. Louis's citywide and congressional campaigns. Ultimately, I became the political director for one of my old practicum placements, the Missouri Progressive Vote Coalition (Pro-Vote). Pro-Vote is a coalition of about 40 labor unions and community groups that work together to elect progressive candidates and advocate for progressive public policy solutions at the state and federal levels. I am responsible for recruiting progressive candidates statewide and giving them the tools to run strong, successful campaigns.

People often assume that I have a background in political science, but I see the work that I'm doing as applying some of the central components of social work. I perform assessments on districts, neighborhoods, organizations, and candidates. I design intervention strategies and am constantly evaluating my own practice to improve. I work with consumers to speak up about injustices and am constantly working in coalitions with other community groups and individuals. I work in a small nonprofit setting, so I am grateful for the knowledge base about management, supervision, budgeting, and fund-raising that allows Pro-Vote to thrive. Most important, I am doing political advocacy with the values and knowledge framework of a social worker.

What I really love most about my job is that it is not a job at all. It is a vocation and a passion of mine, and I get excited to go to work every morning to try to bring about change and social justice. My favorite part of my job is that I am a field instructor and get to train more political social workers. My own practicum experiences would have been strengthened by the presence and supervision of a social worker in the political realm. Some of my students have a passing interest in advocacy, whereas others have even thought about running for public office. Being a political social worker has been a great experience for me, and I am excited to share that experience and get more social workers involved in the political process.

LEGISLATIVE AIDE

Many legislators like to hire social workers to work as members of their staff, because they are naturals at responding to constituent problems and concerns, which is very similar to casework. Social workers are also trained to be strong communicators and good listeners, which is important in this line of work. Legislative aides are vital to the work of a legislator. During "session," they work extremely long hours to try to get important legislation passed and bad legislation defeated.

Typically, legislative aides are responsible for legislation in a specific area. For example, someone with a social work degree might be hired to be responsible for tracking, monitoring, and working on any legislation dealing with health and human services. Aides spend their days meeting with individuals and organizations who are trying to influence their boss on a variety of bills or helping these same individuals and organizations draft legislation when their boss has agreed to sponsor a particular bill.

Another important part of the job is called "constituent work." When people who live in your boss's district are having a problem, they sometimes call their legislator for help, and it will be your job to listen to their problem to see how you can assist them. Examples of problems might be an older adult who is being abused and not getting the help she needs from the state, or a family who lives in a housing project and cannot get their landlord to address the rat infestation in the building. Finally, you will be charged with writing speeches and testimony for your boss (who will get all the glory!). This is a fun, fast-paced career for those with a passion for politics and a desire to work at the state capitol or the U.S. Capitol.

FIELD ORGANIZER

Many organizations employ field organizers to assist with building and organizing a grassroots movement around a particular issue (e.g., increasing the minimum wage, passing universal health care, legislation to address climate change). Field organizers must have excellent organizational skills and also be able to recruit and organize staff and volunteers in order to meet stated campaign goals.

Social Worker Spotlight
ELIZABETH ALEX, MSW
Lead Organizer/Manager, CASA de Maryland

I chose to pursue an MSW after serving as a Peace Corps volunteer in Mali, West Africa. I was searching for a profession that would build on the rewarding experience I had encountered as a Peace Corps volunteer, "helping people help themselves and each other" and addressing the systemic barriers faced by vulnerable communities in search of economic and social justice. A friend steered me in the direction of community organizing and suggested the MSW program at the University of Maryland, Baltimore. I graduated in 2002, and 6 years later (and after another Peace Corps stint, this time in Ecuador, South America), I now manage a regional office serving, organizing, and advocating on behalf of low-income Latino and other immigrants. I spend about 40% of my time managing a day labor center where recent immigrants (and some native Baltimoreans) are able to find dignified jobs at fair salaries while also taking advantage of English classes, basic financial literacy, and legal assistance for unpaid wage cases.

But the other 60% of my work is what really motivates me—I coordinate a team of organizers and social work students to develop grassroots leadership, identify campaign priorities, and win real change for our members through advocacy and organizing efforts at the local, state, and national levels. One of my proudest moments has been watching an uneducated mother from Mexico in a lobby visit to Washington, DC—her powerful story, told proudly in broken English, had the entire room (including the congressman's chief of staff) in tears.

In just 1 year, I watched a group of four student leaders grow from innocent, frustrated high school students testifying in the state capitol to gain in-state tuition benefits for themselves and their peers to mature professionals, able to articulate their position in front of U.S. senators and television cameras to rally a crowd of thousands in support of federal legislation to provide a pathway to citizenship for undocumented students. Some campaigns take years to win, but watching these leaders develop, grow, and show their inherent dignity and passion for justice continues to be a tremendously rewarding experience for me. This is what motivates me to continue advocating and organizing for social change. ¡Si se puede!

To learn more about CASA de Maryland, visit www.casademaryland .org/home

POLICY ANALYST/RESEARCHER

Many research organizations and think tanks hire policy analysts to study a specific social problem and evaluate various policy proposals to see which one might best solve the problem. For example, a group of prominent stakeholders in Boston might be interested in reducing chronic homelessness. Thus, a think tank might be asked to evaluate the pros and cons of various policy strategies such as increasing funding for substance abuse services, increasing the number of homeless outreach workers in the city, or providing increased funding for a new "Housing First" model that has shown to be effective in other states.

Policy analysis can also be useful in evaluating the impact of legislation that has already been passed. For example, in 2010, the U.S. Congress passed the Patient Protection and Affordable Care Act, also referred to as "ObamaCare," which overhauled the U.S. health care system. A policy analyst might conduct research several years later to see how the Patient Protection and Affordable Care Act affected those with pre-existing conditions or evaluate whether health insurance costs went up or down after the passage of the law. Social workers interested in this line of work must have strong research and statistical skills and an interest in working with large data sets. Some social workers might obtain a policy analyst position with an MSW, but a doctorate is often preferred.

ADVOCACY ORGANIZATION

Instead of working directly for a legislator, some social workers prefer to work in an advocacy organization, which provides more independence in advocating for an issue that they are truly passionate about. These are nonprofit organizations, so fund-raising will be important to carrying out the organizational mission. Examples of prominent national advocacy organizations include the Children's Defense Fund, Child Welfare League of America, Human Rights Campaign, AARP, National Alliance on Mental Illness (NAMI), Amnesty International, National Alliance to End Homelessness, and National Association of Social Workers (NASW). There are also many advocacy organizations at the state level that are great places to work (e.g., Children First for Oregon). Almost every field of social work practice has advocacy organizations that are working for macro-level change.

Those who work in advocacy organizations are extremely dedicated professionals who work every day to make their issue a priority, to raise people's awareness, and to get legislation enacted that serves the best interests of the population they serve.

Advocacy organizations often include a variety of staff members, including executive director, development staff changed with fund-raising, public relations/marketing staff charged with the organization's "messaging" and responsible for communicating with the media, researchers and data analysts, and policy staff who carry out the policy work of the organization. Most are overseen by a board of directors.

LEGISLATOR OR PUBLIC OFFICIAL

There are a number of examples of social workers with a passion for politics and public service who run for public office at the local, state, or national level. Others get hired or appointed by presidents or governors to serve in important government positions within various state or federal agencies (e.g., health and human service agencies or important boards and commissions). Legislators come from many different walks of life and various educational backgrounds. There are social workers across the country who have won public office with a simple BSW or MSW degree. Others went down this path after getting an additional or joint degree in public policy or law, such as Texas State Representative Elliott Naishtat.

Social Worker Spotlight
REPRESENTATIVE ELLIOTT NAISHTAT, MSSW, JD
Attorney and Texas State Legislator

When I left New York City in 1967 to serve as a Volunteer In Service To America (VISTA) in Eagle Pass, Texas, I had no idea that I would wind up staying in Texas, pursuing graduate degrees in both social work and law at the University of Texas (UT) at Austin and, ultimately, serving as a long-standing member of the Texas House of Representatives. As I look back on my career, I realize that everything I've done is directly related to the community organizing and social work skills I developed fighting poverty in South Texas as a "front-line warrior" in Lyndon B. Johnson's War on Poverty.

Working at the grassroots level, trying to implement the policy of "eliminating the paradox of poverty in the midst of plenty in this nation," was always difficult and challenging. While we obviously didn't eliminate poverty, we did succeed in developing local leadership potential and maximizing the involvement of poor people in decision-making processes that directly affected their lives. Through community action programs, we gave people opportunities related to education, job training, and economic development. We helped people learn to negotiate the system. It was an exciting era in the history of this country, and it put me on a path to public service and advocacy for the needs of low-income families and vulnerable populations.

In the early 1970s, I studied community organizing at the UT School of Social Work, earning my MSW degree. My second-year field placement was with the Legislative Budget Board, which develops the proposed budget for all state agencies in Texas. This internship led to a 4-year stint as a member of the School of Social Work's field faculty, designing and running one of the nation's first legislative training programs for social work graduate students. The students worked on a full-time basis in the offices of state legislators serving on health and human services committees.

In the early 1980s, I attended the UT School of Law and earned my doctor of jurisprudence (JD) degree. Shortly thereafter, I accepted a position as staff counsel for a state senator who had been one of my supervisors when I was a VISTA volunteer. I worked on legislation that enhanced protective services for elderly and disabled people, as well as for abused or neglected children. I drafted the Texas Anti-Hazing Act. I helped the senator become a champion for dropout prevention. I used my skills and training in social work and law to address at the state legislative level many of the same issues we'd focused on during the heyday of the war on poverty.

(continued)

ELLIOTT NAISHTAT   (*continued*)

In 1990, while still working for the senator, I was approached by a group of people who thought I should run for a seat in the Texas House of Representatives against a three-term incumbent from Austin who'd never lost. I told them that as a native New Yorker and ex-VISTA volunteer, I wouldn't have a chance. They convinced me that if I used my community organizing skills to put together an effective campaign, I might be able to win. I decided to give it a shot.

The incumbent had all the money. I had dedicated volunteers and a strong organization. We outworked the incumbent, and I won by 10 percentage points. I took the oath of office in January 1991 and have been reelected eight times. My focus in the Texas House of Representatives has always been on health, human services, housing, domestic violence, discrimination, and social justice. I work on issues that relate to the elderly, people with disabilities, children, minorities, women, and all vulnerable populations.

In nine sessions, I've passed more than 150 bills, including the Braille Literacy Act, the Landlord–Tenant Security Devices Act, the Nursing Home Reform Act, the Newborn Hearing Screening Act, the Medicaid Simplification Act, and the Child Protective Services Reform Act. I've also passed bills that improved child labor law enforcement, enhanced crime victims' rights, and created a statewide guardianship program. In addition, I cosponsored the Texas Anti-Stalking Act and Hate Crimes Act, as well as bills that increased protections for patients in health maintenance organizations and psychiatric, substance abuse, and rehabilitation facilities.

Although I never became a more traditional social worker, I've used my social work and legal training to carve out a career in the political realm. I work part time as an attorney with a small law firm. And every fall semester, I teach social policy and legislative advocacy as an adjunct professor at St. Edward's University. I am proud of what I do, face new challenges every day, and sleep well at night knowing that I'm working in a meaningful way on behalf of people who occasionally need assistance from the government or need laws passed that will protect and enhance their rights.

If you would like to learn more about Representative Naishtat, visit www .house.state.tx.us/members/member-page/?district=49

Core Competencies and Skills

- Strong advocacy skills
- Persuasive speaking skills, including the art of rhetoric, argumentation, and debate (e.g., testifying at a legislative or public hearing)
- Assertiveness and ability to stand your ground and fight for your cause

- Knowledge of the legislative and political process (e.g., how a bill becomes a law)
- Strong writing skills (e.g., policy briefs, op-eds, talking points, written testimony, speeches)
- Knowledge of the research in your substantive area and how this informs the policy process
- Ability to work with and build relationships with individuals and groups, including those with whom you have political differences
- Ability to compromise when necessary
- Skills in building coalitions around a particular issue
- Patience (legislative victories may take many years, and the opposition may be better funded)
- Media skills (e.g., designing media campaigns and websites; writing press releases, brochures, informational handouts)

Educational and Licensing Requirements

As with any job, it helps to have connections, and this job can be fairly competitive, because you will be competing with individuals from other backgrounds, such as law and public policy. However, there are a number of things you can do to get your foot in the door with political work:

1. Get your MSW from a school that has a concentration or specialty in macrosocial or political social work.
2. During your social work program, volunteer or perform field work with an advocacy organization or in a legislator's office.
3. Find an MSW program in which you can get a dual or joint degree, and combine your social work degree with law or public policy.
4. Get political experience on your own time (e.g., volunteer for a political campaign, join a political organization, get involved in your community and network).
5. Do the front-line work before you move into lobbying or advocacy. For example, if you want to work to improve the child welfare system, it helps to begin working at Child Protective Services so that you have the requisite knowledge, experience, and credibility.

All these things can get you a leg up on the competition!

Best Aspects of This Job

- The fast-paced and exciting environment is never boring.
- You will work with smart, ambitious people from a variety of backgrounds, particularly law and public policy.

- The opportunity to work on an issue or for a legislator that you really believe in is very exciting and rewarding.
- You can achieve legislative victories that have the potential to benefit many people.
- You can hone your speaking and writing skills.
- You can move on to other exciting job opportunities in the political arena, such as working for a legislator or national organization or running for office yourself!
- You help give a voice to people who are often marginalized and who have little political power or clout.

Challenging Aspects of This Job

- Long hours and tense work can be stressful, making it difficult to find a good balance between your work and personal life.
- You will work in an environment that is often corrupt or unethical and that does not always operate in the best interests of people.
- You may do the grunt work that is often involved in political or campaign work.
- You will work with others who do not have the same values as social workers.
- You must be careful not to get too caught up in the power and glamour of the political world and lose your commitment to the issues you care about.
- You will have to deal with loss after you have spent many hours fighting for an issue you are passionate about.
- You will earn an entry-level salary, particularly when working in a legislator's office.

Compensation and Employment Outlook

Unfortunately, many jobs in the political arena have a reputation for being demanding and poorly compensated, requiring long hours while being a bit unstable. The common stereotype is of a young person who is smart, ambitious, and accomplished working on Capitol Hill or for a grassroots organization for low wages. To some degree, this is true, but not in all cases. It is true that some of these jobs are not as well compensated as they should be, because working for legislators and nonprofit organizations does not always pay a competitive salary. It is also true that when you have a job working for a political or issue campaign, the job can come to an end when the campaign ends or the legislator you work for leaves office.

However, what these jobs sometimes lack in salary they more than make up for in exciting, invaluable experience. This is one career path in which you often have to work hard and pay your dues until you are rewarded with a more lucrative or prestigious opportunity. Many social workers start out lobbying at the local and state levels before working for a prominent national organization, where the salary (and pressure) is much higher. An entry-level job of $35,000 may lead, in 2 years or so, to a $60,000 to $70,000 salary each year. Many of these jobs will require relocating to Washington, DC. Research or policy analyst positions often require a doctorate, and the salaries that come with them are typically commensurate with the higher level of education required.

Self-Assessment Checklist: Is This Job for Me?

- Would you describe yourself as a "political junkie"?
- Are there important political and social issues, such as poverty, climate change, or health care, that you are passionate about?
- Are you comfortable debating politics and issues with others?
- Do you follow current events closely and watch or listen to political or news shows (e.g., *Meet the Press,* National Public Radio, cable news, *The Daily Show with Jon Stewart*)?
- Are you politically active?
- Do you enjoy advocating for others?
- Are you passionate about legislation and the idea of creating social change on a larger scale?
- Do you believe in the power of government to improve conditions for various groups of people in this country and around the world?
- Do you have a strong and assertive personality?
- Would you be comfortable working in a setting with other professionals who were educated differently and who may have different views and values than those of social workers?

If you answered "yes" to seven or more of the preceding questions, then a career in the political arena may be for you!

RECOMMENDED READINGS/WEBSITES TO LEARN MORE

Children's Defense Fund: www.childrensdefense.org
Child Welfare League of America: www.cwla.org
Coalition on Human Needs: www.chn.org
Congressional Research Institute for Social Work and Policy: http://crispinc.org
Haynes, K. S., & Mickelson, J. S. (2009). *Affecting change: Social workers in the political arena* (7th ed.). Boston, MA: Allyn & Bacon.
Human Rights Campaign: www.hrc.org
Influencing State Policy: www.statepolicy.org
Karger, H. J., Midgley, J., Kindle, P. A., & Brown, C. B. (2007). *Controversial issues in social policy* (3rd ed.). Boston, MA: Allyn & Bacon.

Kush, C. (2004). *The one-hour activist: The 15 most powerful actions you can take to fight for the issues and candidates you care about.* San Francisco, CA: Jossey-Bass.

NASW Pace—Building political power for social workers: www.socialworkers.org/pace/ default.asp

National Alliance on Mental Illness: www.nami.org

National Association for Social Workers. (2012). *Social work speaks: National Association of Social Workers policy statements, 2012–2014* (9th ed.). Washington, DC: NASW Press.

Ritter, J. A. (2013). *Social work policy practice: Changing our community, nation, and the world.* Boston, MA: Pearson.

Social Welfare Action Alliance—A National Organization of Progressive Workers in Social Welfare: www.socialwelfareactionalliance.org

The Daily Show with Jon Stewart: www.thedailyshow.com

The Social Welfare Spot: http://socialwelfarespot.blogspot.com

Careers in Politics Exercise

Test Your Knowledge

1. True or False
   Part of the definition of social welfare policy includes anything a government chooses *not* to do that affects the quality of life of its people.
2. _____ is a framework of commonly held beliefs through which we view the world. How the world works? What has value? What is right?
3. True or False
   Politics is the process by which groups make decisions and can be observed in most organizations and institutions.
4. According to social work professor Diana DiNitto, "deciding what is to be decided" is the most important stage of the policymaking process. She is describing which of the following stages?
   a. Agenda setting
   b. Problem definition
   c. Policy formulation
   d. Legitimizing public policy
   e. Policy implementation
5. Out of the tens of thousands of bills that get introduced in Congress, about what percentage become law?
   a. 75%
   b. 60%
   c. 20%
   d. 5%–10%

6. PACs are important players in the political process. What does PAC stand for?
7. True or False
   You cannot understand a current policy unless you understand the strategies used by policymakers in the past.
8. True or False
   Sometimes policy solutions change and evolve over time because of increasing knowledge about the causes of a social problem.
9. True or False
   Women have made sufficient progress in achieving equality with men in terms of government representation; almost half of U.S. lawmakers in Congress today are women.
10. True or False
   The United States does well compared to other countries when it comes to average voter turnout per year.

How did you do? My score: _____ out of 10 points.

Answers: 1. True; 2. Ideology; 3. True; 4. a; 5. d; 6. political action committee; 7. True; 8. True; 9. False; 10. False.

REFERENCES

Code of Ethics of the National Association of Social Workers. (2008). Approved by the 1996 NASW Delegate Assembly and revised by the 2008 NASW Delegate Assembly. Retrieved from www.socialworkers.org/pubs/code/code.asp

Haynes, K. S., & Mickelson, J. S. (2009). *Affecting change: Social workers in the political arena* (7th ed.). Boston, MA: Allyn & Bacon.

14 ■ CAREERS IN COMMUNITY PRACTICE

When Barack Obama was running for president of the United States, Americans learned that one of his early jobs was as a community organizer. Many wondered aloud what a community organizer is, and some of his critics derided him as a "radical agitator" cast in the mold of famous community organizer, Saul Alinsky. This chapter will profile a number of careers for social workers who prefer to think of the community as their "client."

Although many social workers prefer to work with individuals and families, others choose to work at the community level. They use their social work training to revitalize and strengthen communities so that the individuals and families who reside there can be safe and thrive. Community social workers work to improve the *social capital* of a community. In communities with a substantial stock of social capital, you can see established and strong social networks, high levels of civic engagement, and community members who trust each other and help each other out. Participants' sense of self is less "I" and more "we."

Community work is integral to the social work profession because of its roots in community organization, planning, and development. The early social workers in the settlement house movement were strong community activists who saw firsthand how poverty and unsanitary conditions in urban ghettos affected the individual. Community practice has been an effective mechanism for resource accessibility and availability, particularly by marginalized, underserved, and underrepresented populations. Among indigenous cultures, the community has a personal meaning in that it is a locus of control as well as the hook upon which individual identities hang. Social work promotes and embraces community practice in all its forms, shapes, and sizes as a way to bridge practice to both indigenous and contemporary cultures. It promotes the ideology and value that people are capable of organizing, uniting on a cause, and acting for themselves (Parachini & Covington, 2001). Curriculum in social work programs across the United States includes foundation content, courses, and concentrations in community practice. Indeed, community practice is central to social work education and professional practice.

This chapter will look at a few careers in community practice: planners, developers, organizers, and those who specialize in rural or urban communities.

COMMUNITY PLANNER

Community planners use a systems framework to examine the kinds of needs that exist in a community and devise plans to fill functions that are lacking. Community planners often conduct community needs assessments to determine gaps in services and then balance areas where there is inequity and a lack of resources. Community planners often work in city or county government and nonprofit organizations.

Social Worker Spotlight
ODIS DOLTON, MSSW
Assistant Director for Finance, City of Abilene, Abilene, Texas

My career in social work has covered a variety of fields of practice. I was a clinical social worker at the Abilene State School, a residential care facility for the mentally disabled and dual-diagnosed adult males and females. I worked for Child Protective Services (CPS) as a caseworker, supervisor, and program director. I also worked in day-care licensing and foster care/adoptions during this time. I acquired my master's degree while working for CPS.

I have worked for the city of Abilene for 8 years now. I started as the assistant director for administrative services and now serve as the assistant director for finance.

As a professional, I always found ways to give back to the communities where I lived. I have served on boards and committees for the United Way, the American Red Cross, the Girl Scouts, the Boy Scouts, the National Children's Center for Illustrated Literature (NCCIL), the Juvenile Justice Board, the Fellowship of Christian Athletes, 100 Black Men of America, Inc., and the African American Leadership Committee. I have worked with the social work programs in my area, supervising social work student interns, in efforts to use the community as a learning lab for social work students.

I am one of the founding members, and the current vice chairman, of a local nonprofit organization called Interested Citizens of Abilene North (I-CAN). Our goal is to revitalize communities and help community groups grow, develop, and serve their communities. We meet monthly and plan activities that include community cleanups and health fairs; African American college workshops; tours to historically black colleges and universities; supporting youth groups and Juneteenth celebrations; work with local law enforcement to eradicate drug sales, prostitution, and crime; annually recognize neighborhood heroes and community leaders at luncheons; work with the local school district to solve problems; and much more!

I am also one of the founding directors and chairman of Neighborhoods in Progress (NIP). This is a local nonprofit with a mission to rebuild neighborhoods so low- to moderate-income citizens will have access to safe, decent, and affordable housing; to enhance quality of life for the elderly; to prevent and reduce homelessness; to revitalize neighborhoods; to enhance the physical environment of Abilene; and to enhance the economic well-being of all citizens.

Finally, I am the chairman and founding member of Connecting Caring Communities (CCC), a community nonprofit that replicated the

(continued)

> **ODIS DOLTON** *(continued)*
>
> Shreveport–Bossier City Community Renewal program in Louisiana. Our mission is to systematically rebuild the human relationships needed to sustain community health using a neighborhood-based strategy.
>
> I think I am a good example of a social worker who is committed to community-based social work through empowering communities and local grassroots efforts.

COMMUNITY DEVELOPER

Community developers use entrepreneurial skills to generate funding for needed community resources to enhance the social environment, with a strong focus on urban renewal, asset building, community revitalization, and sustainability. The kinds of projects community developers typically focus on include affordable housing, schools, public transportation, health services, and recreational centers. Community social workers might also help to create a community development corporation (CDC), which is a community-based organization that serves low-income communities. CDCs are usually partnerships between business and government, though they are governed by a community board. There is a strong focus on citizen participation and keeping the profits from the CDC in the community it is serving.

Social Worker Spotlight
AMY KRINGS-BARNES, BSW, MSW
Community Police Partnering Center, Cincinnati, Ohio

I received my bachelor's degree in social work (BSW) from Xavier University in Cincinnati, Ohio. I minored in peace studies and women and minority studies. I was attending Xavier when Cincinnati experienced civil unrest and riots in many communities that were protesting the Cincinnati Police Department.

For my master's degree in social work (MSW), I attended the University of Michigan in Ann Arbor. There, I concentrated in community organization and the management of human services.

After graduation, I returned to Cincinnati with the goal of working to improve race relations—particularly police–community relations. I took a job at a new nonprofit organization called the Community Police Partnering Center. The mission of the Partnering Center is "in partnership with community stakeholders and members of the Cincinnati Police Department, the Community Police Partnering Center will develop and implement effective strategies to reduce crime and disorder while facilitating positive engagement and increased trust between the police and neighborhoods." In other words, community members and police officers are asked to come together as peers to problem solve. Therefore, arrest was no longer the primary tool for police to reduce crime, and it gave citizens greater influence on how their neighborhoods are policed.

My work at the Partnering Center allows me to practice community building, training, and problem solving. I work in many neighborhoods with a broad range of demographics. This excites me. I deeply enjoy spending my time with many types of people as we work together on a common goal such as reducing drug sales, prostitution, domestic violence, or blighted buildings.

In 2006, reducing gun violence in Cincinnati became a priority for the Partnering Center, and therefore my work became more focused in fewer neighborhoods and on this one issue. In partnership with community groups and residents, we launched a campaign called "Cease Fire Cincinnati" in two pilot neighborhoods, and in 2008, we expanded to a third neighborhood. One unique aspect of this model is that it depends on peer mentoring by outreach workers who in many cases either have been shot or have shot someone else. At some point in the outreach worker's life, he or she changed his or her lifestyle and now works to give back to the communities that he or she robbed from. Workers conduct conflict mediation and also have a case load of people at the greatest risk of engaging in gun violence.

My role is to engage the community and faith-based leaders to challenge the norms and expectations of the community as they relate to violence.

(continued)

AMY KRINGS-BARNES (*continued*)

One of the most visible aspects of my job is the organization of "shooting responses" to every shooting that results in injury in my three assigned neighborhoods within 72 hours. I believe in the efforts of this campaign, and the statistics suggest that it is having a positive effect. Still, although lives are being saved, there is still too much violence, and at times this can feel overwhelming. I recognize the need for self-care and the maintenance of a supportive community to stay positive and focused.

My job does not require a social work background, but I believe that my social work education prepared me to do well in micro and macro practice. For example, my social work field internships allowed me to build relationships with many of the people who are involved in community building and police–community relations. I am able to facilitate a meeting or small group. I can listen to individuals and understand their self-interest and their needs. I understand how my daily work affects not just individuals and communities, but also policy and culture on a broader scale. At the same time, I recognize that larger structural issues influence individuals and their choices.

Social work training has also opened doors for my future. This past year, I began adjunct teaching at Xavier University, and I love it. I now have an interest in pursuing a doctoral degree.

I am grateful for my social work degree and I believe that its combination of theory and practice has made me a better change agent, organizer, and leader.

COMMUNITY ORGANIZER

Although community planners and developers use nonconflictual approaches, community organizers tend to embrace a conflict model. Community organizing is based on the philosophy that powerful people and institutions often exploit the community for their own interests, and that those with power never surrender it voluntarily. Community organizers bring together coalitions of people in the community (e.g., citizens, neighborhood associations, churches) to address social problems in their community, assist them in developing their own solutions, and taking on the "powers that be." Examples of issues that can be addressed through community organizing include the following:

- Police brutality
- Rights for immigrants
- Improving substandard schools
- The need for affordable housing

- Preventing a big-box store from coming to town and threatening local businesses
- Challenging predatory lending
- Fighting a powerful developer whose project would harm the environment and the people living there

Social Worker Spotlight
TRINA SCORDO, MSW CANDIDATE
Monmouth University, West Long Branch, NJ, International and Community Development Concentration; Senior Organizer, Change to Win Labor Federation

My current work focuses on developing strategies with low-wage workers to build a worker-controlled union and gain leverage at the collective bargaining table. This includes developing a supportive community movement that holds the employers and developers accountable for environmental issues, workplace health and safety, and issues such as workforce housing and transportation. In addition, many of the low-wage workers are immigrants. Thus working to eliminate the stigma of labels such as "undocumented" and "illegal" is central to this work. Every worker deserves a safe and healthy work environment, as well as a living wage and full health benefits. The formation of a worker organizing committee that builds solidarity among various groups and organizations shifts the balance of power to often marginalized groups.

Through this work, I have had the privilege to work with people from El Salvador, Mexico, and Ethiopia. Through the political struggles in their home countries, these workers taught me how to build solidarity and community. Social work is, in actuality, social justice work. Focusing on a framework of human rights and economic justice is what excites me most. More importantly, the opportunity to work with communities to make change is a revolutionary and transformative process. Communities work collectively to address legislative, policy, and regulatory issues in the areas of workplace health and safety, environment and land use, workforce housing, and transportation.

Through the MSW program at Monmouth University, I was afforded the opportunity to travel to Chile and live in a community called La Pincoya. This experience revolutionized me. I met trade unionists and community activists who had continued to organize during the vicious and violent Pinochet dictatorship. Many of the people whom I met and lived with had family members who had been tortured and disappeared. This experience brought me back to my initial desire in life: to work in a global grassroots movement for social and economic justice.

I did not come to social work through a direct route. In 1996, I graduated from American University in Washington, DC, with a BA in political science. By that time, I had been part of several election campaigns, been a legislative intern on Capitol Hill, and worked in a campaign finance office of a senior Democratic senator. There was always something missing for

(continued)

TRINA SCORDO   (*continued*)

me in this work. I wanted to make change with people, not for people. I was struggling to find a model for change that engaged working-class and poor communities as decision makers, not only recipients of services. Chile and the MSW International and Community Development track at Monmouth University have helped me discover this work.

SOCIAL WORK IN URBAN COMMUNITIES

For many Americans, community means living in an urban area with all the conveniences of modern life with services conveniently located and strong social networks of neighbors helping each other out. Yet many urban cities also have high unemployment rates, substandard public schools, and high rates of poverty, crime, and gang violence. Social workers who work in urban settings may focus on all these areas of practice or work with a particular racial or ethnic group within the community. Also, in light of the recent economic crisis and an increase in the population of urban dwellers, nonprofit organizations and small social service agencies in urban communities have increased in numbers over the years. Social workers are creating jobs for themselves and others through starting an organization focusing on a particular issue or a private practice. Social workers in urban communities are also skilled in creating and working in interdisciplinary teams. Regardless of the social worker's interest, working in urban communities provides opportunities for growth and the sharpening of one's social work knowledge and skills.

Urban Social Worker Spotlight
TRACY HARRIS, BSW, MSW, LGSW
Family Service Case Manager, Roberta's House, Baltimore, Maryland

Tracy Harris is a licensed graduate social worker (LGSW) who earned her BSW from Coppin State University and her MSW from Morgan State University.

Originally, Ms. Harris attended school to become a nurse. As she progressed in her studies, she realized that nursing was not for her, but she knew that she wanted to work with people. Her mother recommended that she look into the profession of social work. Assuming that social workers only worked at the Department of Social Services, Ms. Harris did her research, reading the literature and having conversations with professors of social work. She was pleasantly surprised to learn that social work has an extremely positive effect on people's lives, so she changed her major to social work.

Ms. Harris has worked with multiple populations during her 11 years practicing as a social worker, including children who experienced physical and sexual abuse and neglect; victims of domestic violence; children with autism; adults, teens, and children with mental health issues; individuals currently in the legal system; individuals suffering from multiple sclerosis; and consumers of home care and hospice services. With these populations, she has provided individual and group psychotherapy and has also coordinated and overseen programs for different organizations in Baltimore City and the surrounding areas.

Currently, Ms. Harris works at Roberta's House as a family service case manager. Roberta's House is an urban grief and loss support center located in east Baltimore that specializes in working with families, children, teens, and adults on unresolved grief issues resulting from a significant loss due to death. She coordinates, plans, organizes, and delivers comprehensive family support services for the Family Grief Support Program; assists with the development and organization of parent education, in-service trainings, and family community activities; coordinates and may facilitate family educational opportunities and parent support groups; provides individual support to families and reinforces training components with parents to promote their child's healthy grief experience; provides appropriate community referrals, resources, and information to families; prepares and analyzes the results of parent surveys and participates in program needs assessment activities; provides assistance and resources to families during the in-take process; and plans and organizes special events and community activities. Ms. Harris believes that Roberta's House is an organization that is greatly needed in

(continued)

TRACY HARRIS   (*continued*)

Baltimore city and all urban cities and states by people wounded by the loss of a loved one and the consequences of unexplained grief.

Through years of working and learning, Ms. Harris has learned that being a social worker is not only a profession—it is a passion. A passion for people.

Entrepreneurial Social Worker Spotlight
JOHNNIE FIELDING, MSW
Cofounder, Leading by Example, Baltimore, Maryland

My name is Johnnie Fielding, and I am the cofounder of Leading by Example, a behavioral health company founded in 2009. We provide psychiatric rehabilitation services and therapeutic behavioral services and specialize in serving children and adults who are experiencing difficulties managing their psychiatric symptoms in the home or the community. We have approximately 100 counselors providing services in the community and 14 administrative, clinical, and management staff members. I oversee the administrative and operational systems of the company and provide leadership for management staff members while monitoring the efficiency and effectiveness of our service delivery process. Along with my business partner, I am responsible for the development and management of the company's budget and fiscal planning process.

I entered the social work profession when I was 20 years old. I was in a general studies program attending Baltimore City Community College. Through a friend, I obtained a job as a Direct Care Counselor at a Children's Diagnostic Treatment Facility in Baltimore. Initially, I was just looking for a job. This was my first experience working with children, and I was not sure what to expect. However, I would soon recognize the power, influence, and responsibility that accompanied the role of a helper. I recognized very swiftly how influential I was with young people: They began to mimic my gestures, from the way that I spoke, to the way that I walked. They had a discreet yearning for my validation and regard. These were young people (aged 6 to 14) matriculating through the foster care system with limited involvement from their biological parents and sporadic involvement from extended family members. Many of these young people expressed feeling alone, isolated, and abandoned, existing in a world absent of a natural connection to caregivers. At times their behaviors could have been characterized as extreme, from throwing feces on the walls to self-harm attempts. This experience led me to an epiphany, as it became extremely clear that this was not "just a job" and that I had to lead by example.

With this in mind, I declared social work as my major and fully embraced my role and responsibility to society and the urban community. I believed that deteriorating families was the primary culprit preceding the current conditions of the urban community. I surmised that children should be raised in strong family units, opposed to units in diagnostic treatment centers. I began to assess the urban community, which was resilient and malleable

(continued)

JOHNNIE FIELDING   (*continued*)

but inundated with deteriorating families who were underserved with limited resources. My optics revealed a void of African American men who were whole, healthy, and present in their families, as well as a void of positive African American men in the urban community who were committed to being positive examples for our youth. So I recognized that it was my job to become the very thing I sought out. For this reason, I embarked on becoming tangible hope for my community, electing education as a compass to navigate through the urban maze over the narcotic culture that appeared to be in vogue but that had decimated my neighborhood.

Our vision for Leading by Example was to build an institution around our beliefs and ideas of service. We strategically developed and codified a service delivery and business model that embodied our core principles of integrity, excellence, and professionalism. From our perspective, social workers seemed truant from equitable stake or ownership of the companies in our profession. Through our experience, we understood that business could potentially be intimidating to social workers. However, we embraced the business aspect of our profession by strengthening our business acumen, aligning the fundamentals of corporate law, accounting, and marketing with our core social work principles, values and ethics. Our mission is to improve the lives of children, adults, and families worldwide. Equally important, Leading by Example is our odyssey to redefine and expand the bounds of our profession, once again, serving as tangible hope for social workers while demonstrating a capacity to be exceptional entrepreneurs.

RURAL SOCIAL WORKER

Rural social workers are central to communities in remote areas that struggle with issues of accessibility and availability of services. They commonly work with communities that are in poverty to improve infrastructure and service delivery. These social workers provide primary social services, including case management, referral, prevention and education, crisis intervention, and specialized treatment (e.g., substance abuse), among other things. Because of small populations and proximity of the living arrangements in rural areas, confidentiality may be an issue that rural social workers have to deal with on a continuous basis.

Core Competencies and Skills

- Ability to take risks and recognize the scarcity of resources and resistance of people to change
- Awareness of current trends and their effects on the community
- Value confidentiality and the dynamics of the community, particularly in rural communities
- Strong entrepreneurial skills and knowledge of community development
- Ability to work with people from diverse communities by age, gender, race/ethnicity, sexual orientation, rural versus urban areas, immigrants, and so forth
- Knowledge and skills in conducting a community needs assessment
- Understanding of the power patterns in the community and methods for motivating, empowering, and challenging people to act on their common interests
- Understanding of any special needs or circumstances in rural communities
- Ability to be creative in facilitating change, mediating conflict, and bringing coalitions of people together
- Demonstrate cultural and linguistic competencies appropriate to the populations served, including immigrants and refugees
- Ability to facilitate social action and change behind the scenes and allowing members of the community to be "the leaders"
- Possess technological skills that facilitate communication, accessibility, and availability of services to the community

Educational and Licensing Requirements

Throughout the United States and its territories, many MSWs have concentrations, specializations, emphases, or certificates in community social work practice that prepare students specifically for a career in community settings,

whether rural, urban, or suburban. There are usually no licensing requirements for social workers who work at the community level, though this varies
by state.

Best Aspects of This Job

- Mobilizing an entire community to act on its own behalf to bring about
  social and economic change
- Opportunity to create resources (i.e., jobs) and services for the
  community
- Working with people from urban, suburban, and rural communities
- Expanding knowledge about and experience with diverse cultures and
  developing cultural competency skills
- Opportunity to advocate for equality, accessibility, and availability of
  services to remote communities
- Opportunities for political advocacy for all community members,
  particularly those from underserved and underrepresented
  communities

Challenging Aspects of This Job

- Motivating an entire community to act can be difficult and slow.
- It can be hard to gain the trust of the community if you are an
  "outsider."
- Dealing with the political patterns of the community may be
  difficult.
- Uniting the community to pursue common goals may be a struggle.
- It is a heavy burden being responsible for appropriate assessment
  and making decisions that affect community members.

Compensation and Employment Outlook

Diversity in community membership composition and locations (e.g., rural
areas, inner cities) has contributed to the increased visibility of community
organizers, planners, and developers. The need for culturally and linguistically
competent service providers in communities validates social work education
and recruitment of social workers from diverse populations. The major shortage
of social workers in the United States results in a good employment outlook,
especially in rural settings. Community social workers tend to be employed by
the government and various nonprofit community organizations.

Salaries for community social workers vary according to state and organization. For instance, community organizers may earn a median income of

$35,900 annually (U.S. Department of Labor, Bureau of Labor Statistics, 2014). However, there are also community organizers who are volunteers. Similarly, rural social workers most often make the lowest salaries by comparison.

Self-Assessment Checklist: Is This Job for Me?

- Do you have a strong interest in working on community issues?
- Do you think that you are able to work with people from diverse backgrounds, culturally and linguistically, in the context of their communities?
- Are you passionate about policy advocacy on behalf of communities?
- Do you enjoy having a job where your workday is spent facilitating community action?
- Would you be comfortable working under stressful and hazardous conditions?
- Do you have an assertive personality? Are you comfortable dealing with conflict on a community level?
- Can you be creative in building relationships, developing programs, and making services available and accessible?
- Do you embrace the perspective that people need to live in a strong and healthy community in order to reach their full potential?
- Do you have strong leadership skills?
- Can you train and empower others to be leaders?

If you answered "yes" to seven or more of the preceding questions, then working in a community setting might be for you!

RECOMMENDED READINGS/WEBSITES TO LEARN MORE

A Community Concern: www.acommunityconcern.org
Alinsky, S. (1971). *Rules for radicals.* New York, NY: Random House.
Association for Community Organization and Social Administration: www.acosa.org
COMM-ORG: http://comm-org.wisc.edu
Community Based Social Work: www.scn.org/cmp/modules/adv-sw.htm
Community Development Network: www.cdnportland.org
Community Organizers Guide, Ability Maine: www.abilitymaine.org/rosc/cog.html
Community Organizing Toolbox: www.nfg.org/cotb or www.nfg.org/cotb/07whatisco.htm
Community Practice: A Training Ground for Social Work Students: www.nova.edu/ssss/QR/QR6-1/jennings.html

History Is Undivided Yearning: http://undividedyearning.com

Homan, M. S. (2008). *Promoting community change: Making it happen in the real world* (4th ed.). Belmont, CA: Brooks/Cole.

Media and Process Educational Films & Chicago Video Project (Producer), Baldwin, A. (Narrator). (1999). *The democratic promise: Saul Alinsky and his legacy* [documentary film].

National Public Radio. (2008, March 11). *"Community organizer fights for immigrants."*: www.npr.org/templates/story/story.php?storyID=88083529&sc=emaf

Putnam, R. D. (2001). *Bowling alone: The collapse and revival of American community*. New York, NY: Simon & Schuster.

Salomon, L. R. (Ed.). (1998). *Roots of justice: Stories of organizing in communities of color*. San Francisco, CA: Jossey-Bass.

Sen, R. (2003). *Stir it up: Lessons in community organizing and advocacy*. San Francisco, CA: Jossey-Bass.

Community Practice Exercise

You are a social worker employed as the director of human services for the state of Vermont. There has been a recent influx of immigrants from the countries of Ethiopia and Somalia to several small towns in your state. The immigrants have been arriving by the busload, one to two buses a month for the past several months. The state of Vermont has very little experience with immigration issues and cultural diversity. The mayors of the small towns are very concerned about this rapid and large influx of "outsiders" and the pressures this puts on their local budgets and town services.

They have appealed to the governor for assistance, who asks you for a solution.

Questions

1. What additional information would you need before implementing an intervention plan?
2. With whom would you consult, and why?
3. Briefly describe two possible approaches in addressing this problem: (1) one approach that could be implemented at the local level; and (2) another plan that could be implemented at the state level.
4. The governor has told you to hire one full-time staffer to assist you, but whatever remedy you come up, no additional funding will be available to increase the budget of the local towns. Would this affect any of your recommendations? If so, how?

REFERENCES

Parachini, L., & Covington, S. (2001). *Community organizing toolbox: A funder's guide to community organizing*. Retrieved from www. nfg.org/cotb

U.S. Department of Labor, Bureau of Labor Statistics. (2014). *Occupational outlook handbook 2014–15*. Retrieved from www.bls.gov/ooh

15 ■ LEADERSHIP IN HUMAN SERVICE ORGANIZATIONS

Above all, we need leaders who will not accept that misery and deprivation are inevitable, for failure to act to ease suffering is a choice, and when we have the ability to choose, we have the power to change.

—Intrator and Scribner (2007)

Some social workers are natural leaders and aspire to work in a leadership role, whereas others develop this expertise through experience, education, and training. Social workers perform leadership roles in various ways, such as by sitting on a board of directors, serving as a supervisor or executive director of a government or nonprofit organization, working as a community planner/organizer, being active in a professional organization (e.g., the National Association of Social Workers [NASW] or the Council on Social Work Education [CSWE]), or working in public policy. Being a good leader is hard to define, but we know it when we see it. However, strong leaders help define the mission and vision of an organization or cause, set high standards for strong performance and competence, and inspire others to strive for excellence. They set the tone and provide direction. They are politically savvy and have strong managerial skills. They persevere through good times and bad. With increasing national and global connections and the need for dispersed teams, leaders are required to lead employees from distant locations; hence effective use of technology to maintain productivity has become a needed skill (Allen & Vakalahi, 2013).

The traditional career path for many workers, in general, is that through the course of their experiences in various job settings, they have acquired a knowledge base and developed the skills eventually preparing them to assume a position of leadership within an organization. This path is no different for social workers. Working in various positions within social service delivery systems, over a period of time, is an excellent avenue to building a career path in which you are eventually prepared to assume an administrative position (e.g., supervisor, program coordinator, division chief, executive director).

Many social workers prepare for a leadership role by pursuing a course of study in a master's degree in social work (MSW) program that specializes in administration, management, supervision, or organizational consulting. The MSW program approach to acquiring the knowledge and skills to be an effective leader is a more conscious choice of career goal.

ADMINISTRATOR

Administrators may work in government agencies, private companies, or for-profit or nonprofit social service agencies. Administrators coordinate and direct the many support services that allow organizations to operate effectively, and accordingly they have a wide range of responsibilities. Administrators are responsible for the day-to-day operations of an organization, and their duties may include

- Developing services and programs
- Hiring and supervising employees
- Recruiting, training, and managing volunteers
- Fund-raising
- Communicating with media
- Overseeing community outreach
- Maintaining budgets and payroll
- Managing information and communication systems
- Record keeping
- Procurement of supplies and materials
- Overseeing the secretarial and housekeeping staff
- Security and parking
- Contract negotiation with other service providers

The exact role of an administrator will depend, in a large part, on the size and structure of the organization. In larger agencies (e.g., the department of social services for a city or county), a "first-line" administrator typically would report to a "mid-level" manager, who in turn answers to the executive director of the department or organization.

In larger organizations, some of the aforementioned roles (e.g., overseeing volunteers or fund-raising) may be handled by separate individuals; read on for more about those specific functions.

EXECUTIVE DIRECTOR

In small organizations (e.g., a local nonprofit), executive directors may oversee all day-to-day support and operation services as previously described. Executive directors often report to an organization's board of directors, who are responsible for creating the mission and goals of the organization. Thus executive directors are often concerned with making sure that the organization's programs and services are in keeping with its mission and are responsive to the needs of the community.

Social Worker Spotlight
LAURA ELMORE SMITH, LMSW
Executive Director, Crime Prevention Institute, Austin, Texas

I have known since I was in the 10th grade that I wanted to be a social worker. The therapist my parents sent me to when they got divorced had a degree on her wall that said "MSW." My goal was to be a therapist and work with families in my own private practice. I decided to pursue my MSW, so I went to school and majored in psychology (I wasn't aware at the time that there was such a degree as a bachelor's degree in social work [BSW]) and went from there directly into the MSW program. Through some enlightening course work and field work, and some great relationships with professional and academic mentors, my perspectives, worldview, and goals really shifted during that 2-year program. I entered the MSW program with every intent to graduate as a clinician who would go on to do private psychotherapy, and I graduated wanting nothing more than to dedicate my professional life to making changes in the criminal justice system and those affected by it.

My current position is executive director of the Crime Prevention Institute, a small nonprofit organization whose mission is to break the cycle of crime in those transitioning from incarceration to communities. In short, we provide education, information, support, and job placement assistance to people leaving jail or prison and returning to Austin. Our goal is to help guide them toward law-abiding, productive lives, sometimes for the first time. Our entire agency is located inside a state jail, allowing us to be closer to our clients and to work within the system in which they are incarcerated. I started out doing direct services work—I never saw myself as an executive director, but now that I'm here, I am absolutely in love with it.

I believe so strongly in our mission and in our case management philosophy, part of which states "We believe in the inherent worth and dignity of each individual client, no matter the crime or past behavior." That is not to say that we always like their behavior or even that we find some of our clients easy to be around. But, the successes—while small to some of us—are phenomenal. The client who gets his first job at age 35 because he's been dealing drugs his whole life—that kind of change in a person's life, and the bravery it takes to swim upstream like that, astounds me. The client who gets sober and learns to be a father again once his daughters are grown but can acknowledge that they don't know him any more. That kind of strength and self-honesty takes my breath away. I love working on behalf of those the rest of society has forgotten or would like to forget. Working with these men and women in a direct services capacity was difficult and rewarding

(continued)

LAURA ELMORE SMITH   (*continued*)

and challenging and wonderful. Being the executive director means that it is my job to support those working in that capacity, to bring awareness to this important social issue, and to build effective community relationships that will help solve the complex problem of prisoner reentry in Texas. It also allows me to set the values, tone, and environment for excellence in service and social work ethics. I am so very lucky to have a job I love so much.

PROGRAM MANAGER

The role of a program manager is an example of a "mid-level" management position within an organization. Program managers have oversight responsibility in very discrete areas of social service delivery. They may be responsible for the creation and development of a new program (e.g., initiating a crisis hotline for an agency) or be responsible for improving existing services (e.g., increasing an agency's evening and weekend hours of operation to improve client participation). At times, a program manager may even be the person who conducts the program.

Program managers or coordinators also often use skills in program assessment and evaluation. They examine whether services are being delivered in the most cost-efficient manner, and they evaluate program outcomes to ensure that the goals and objectives of the services are being met. Programs that can prove their effectiveness and positive effects on a community in concrete, measurable terms are more likely to get funding, so program assessment and evaluation is critical to the budget allocation and funding resources of an organization.

Social Worker Spotlight
MARY KIERNAN-STERN, MSW, LCSW
Arlington Hospital, Arlington, Virginia

After graduating with a liberal arts bachelor's degree, I worked as a crisis counselor for 4 years at a community teaching hospital. Over the course of my time on the job, I had been given more responsibilities for supervising the work of the clinic that I always met successfully. I had received excellent training and mentoring in my direct service work and was encouraged by my director, also a social worker, to pursue my MSW. I thought I would like to broaden my knowledge of social work practice and learn new skills in working with people. I specialized in community organization as my major focus and took courses in a minor specializing in employee assistance programs.

This combination of course work prepared me to develop my supervisory and administrative skills giving me a depth of understanding on how organizations operate through various group processes, formal and informal communication structures, and effective and ethical leadership. I was prepared with information regarding grant writing, developing budgets, recruitment and retention of employees, conflict negotiation, mediation techniques, program development, and research and evaluation tools.

When I completed my MSW program, I relocated to another state, and within a short time I interviewed for a director of social work position that became available at a local hospital. Not only did I land that job, but the hospital administration also gave me oversight of another department, the on-site employee day-care center. Based on these additional responsibilities, I was able to negotiate a higher salary. Without a doubt, my previous hospital-based experience, and my specific course work and field experience in my MSW program, certainly prepared me for this new administrative role within a health care organization.

ORGANIZATIONAL CONSULTANT

Many small and large agencies hire or "contract" a professional who has expertise in "growing" organizations. The executive board of an organization may decide in their strategic planning process, for example, that they need to pursue new directions of obtaining funding in order for their organization to continue to provide services to the community or to expand the mission of the agency and offer new or additional services. The executive board then seeks to hire, as a consultant or paid staff member, a person who specializes in fund-raising and grant writing or who may be an effective lobbyist in obtaining government contracts.

Another organization may be experiencing a high rate of staff turnover, which is disrupting the delivery of services to clients. To solve these types of organizational problems of the agency, the executive director will bring in an organizational consultant to assess and analyze the agency's strengths and weaknesses. These job roles are easily filled by social workers who have been trained in working with organizations and in organizational development.

PUBLIC RELATIONS/MEDIA RELATIONS

Social workers who have knowledge of public relations and working with various media outlets can help their organizations in communicating a message for specific agendas related to the organization's functioning. Social workers in public relations require skills in persuasive speech and in communicating a message with only three or four major points to a targeted audience. Media campaigns are coordinated efforts through multiple points of influence to communicate with and persuade people—for example, to use or reuse a service or product or to take action regarding a specific issue or need. Working in public and media relations requires skill in understanding what type of communication activity would give the best result in "getting the message out."

Some of the activities in this area could include writing and sending action alerts regarding an important issue up for vote in Congress or the state legislature; preparing written testimony, or an issue brief, to help educate government representatives on specific issues or funding needs regarding such areas as mental illness or child welfare; or holding a press conference to announce a new program or respond to a particular community concern.

Large health and human service organizations have internal public or community relations departments. Social workers in this role often assist in developing internal media campaigns during times of large-scale transition and change to preserve organizational stability, serve as resources for employees and clients, and serve as marketing tools to promote the organization's services and programs.

Media tools include direct marketing appeals through regular mail, e-advocacy, event sponsorship, television and radio, web pages, word of mouth, and print media. Public relation skills require knowledge of how to work with news organizations and their communication outlets.

Social workers are perfect for this job because they focus on the issues and concerns of people. Social workers understand what people want to know and how to communicate with them because of their professional knowledge of human behavior and the social environment.

VOLUNTEER SERVICES DIRECTOR

This management position is often under the umbrella of an organization with an established administration hierarchy. An administrative role in the recruitment, retention, and professional development of volunteers is an essential and critical position for many organizations that rely on volunteers for a variety of activities, ranging from helping with day-to-day operations to the delivery of direct services to clients and communities. Social workers employed in this area must have skills in general management, budget development, grant writing, and fund-raising.

Meals on Wheels programs are an excellent example of the crucial role of a volunteer services director. The volunteer services director may be paid by the local public social service agency to administer this program, and he or she may be given a budget for the kitchen materials and food supplies. However, without effective leadership in developing and maintaining a pool of high-quality volunteers who prepare the meals and pick up and deliver the meals to those in need, such programs could not exist. Social workers employed in this area must have general management skills as well as skills in budget development, grant writing, and fund-raising.

FUND-RAISER

As you can see from the aforementioned employment opportunities, raising money and writing grants for many different types of organizations is a primary responsibility for administrators in social work management. However, considering that administrators have many tasks to attend to, and that raising money requires specialized skills, this aspect of the job may be carved out for another person or team to manage. Grant writing and fund-raising are, in many cases, the sole responsibility for a social worker who may work independently as a contractor or who may be hired as a salaried member of staff for this function.

There are several aspects to fund-raising. Fund-raisers may oversee annual letter-writing campaigns, charity events, or other programs designed to raise money for the organization. Others may spend most of their time cultivating people or organizations who share the same mission and interests as the organization's leadership and who would be willing to make a financial contribution. This is referred to as *donor development* or *special gifts fund-raising* and is extremely important work in the sustainability of many human services organizations.

Social Worker Spotlight
APRIL KERWIN, LCSW, MSW
Director of Stewardship and Planned Giving, St. David's Episcopal Church, Austin, Texas

I knew I wanted to be a social worker and obtain my MSW within the first 10 minutes of an undergraduate introduction to social work class. The timing was terrible, though: I was on my way to obtaining an anthropology degree and starting a career as a museum curator when that class turned my world upside-down. When the social work professor spoke those hallowed words, "person in the environment," my life changed. I now wanted to be a change agent on a macro level to help those people in need. After obtaining my BA, I enrolled in an MSW program at Our Lady of the Lake University (San Antonio, Texas), a graduate program known for its emphasis in community organization.

In graduate school I narrowed my focus to child welfare and, taking the advice of a mentor who argued the need for direct practice experience, became a child welfare caseworker providing in-home therapeutic services to families where life-threatening child abuse and neglect had occurred. While a caseworker, I obtained my licensed clinical social worker (LCSW) and formed a desire to move from direct practice into administration after witnessing the negative effects on families when the federally funded program that paid my salary was discontinued.

Entering into a human services administration position from direct service felt like slowing down from 65 mph on an interstate to 20 mph in a school zone. Eventually the culture shock of management processes and analysis wore off, and luckily I found my way to the local nonprofit sector, first as the executive director of the Williamson County Children's Advocacy Center, where I grew the staff from 1 to 5 to keep up with the community's explosive growth, then as the director of foundation relations at the Austin Children's Shelter, where my efforts helped the organization move from two side-by-side residential houses to a 13-acre campus.

During this time, I became involved with a professional organization dedicated to promoting professional fund-raisers. Social workers are uniquely positioned to enhancing fund-raising efforts within organizations, because we understand the need to know a client's internal and external driving forces in order to positively affect the client's life. After we know what is important to a client, we can share the client's situation with a prospective funder and explain how the client's life can be improved with program funding.

Since becoming a professional fund-raiser, I've worked as the development director at Mental Health America of Texas, an advocacy organization where we worked closely with legislators on critically needed mental health

(continued)

APRIL KERWIN   (continued)

funding, and at a 167-year-old downtown Episcopal church that has spun off a hospital system, health foundation, and two human service nonprofits. Today, I serve as their director of development and planned giving.

Over my 20 years of experience in the nonprofit and public sector in Central Texas, I've learned that the most important investment for nonprofits is to communicate regularly with people interested in the organization, including volunteers, donors, and special event attendees. These people are constituents to the organization and need access to timely information. Of all the constituents, volunteers are the most likely to stay involved and donate to a nonprofit. Providing volunteers with a positive experience and communicating ongoing needs is paramount to a nonprofit's continued success. Volunteers can serve in leadership, program, and special event capacities.

I like to think of all constituents as communication volunteers. Every constituent can be a volunteer cheerleader and introduce more people to and inform them about the cause through their sphere of influence (e.g., family, friends, professional organizations, civic and religious groups). The most important aspect of my fund-raising work is nourishing these volunteer relationships. I want to know everything I can about a volunteer:

1. How he or she became involved with the organization. (Who provided introductions? What was the first event the volunteer attended? Who does the volunteer maintain friendships with in the organization?)
2. Why does he or she stay involved? (To promote awareness? Advocacy? In memory of a loved one?)
3. What is the volunteer's vision of the organization's future? (How will the mission change over time? How will programs evolve?)

To keep up to date on each volunteer's activities, record keeping of every contact (lunch or coffee date, phone call, e-mail, text, newsletter, thank-you note) with a volunteer is paramount when making sure the volunteer is staying engaged. Replacing a volunteer is much more difficult than retaining one!

Regardless of the many development and fund-raising opportunities available in nonprofit management, the most important skill set for an emerging professional is interpersonal communication. Knowing how to tell a story in multiple settings (e.g., elevator, cold call, cocktail party, event speaker) is key to keeping mission critical programs available to people in need. Social workers are the best storytellers and are ideally suited to inspiring community members to get involved with supporting the vital work of a nonprofit organization.

GRANT WRITER

Oftentimes, a fund-raiser may also be in charge of writing grants. Grant writers must be aware of the many federal, state, and local organizations (e.g., governmental bodies such as the National Institutes of Health, foundations such as the Bill and Melinda Gates Foundation, and many large corporations) known to fund programs in certain areas. They must understand each funder's goals, application requirements, and deadlines. They must be able to write compelling grant applications that will persuade funders that any money granted to the organizations will be well spent. Competition for funding among social service and nonprofit organizations is intense, so grant writers must be able to raise funds in a highly competitive environment. As with fund-raisers, grant writers must understand budgets and organizational needs.

Core Competencies and Skills

- Skilled at creating a vision and leading people there
- Ability to pay attention to details
- Knowledge and skills for effectively managing dispersed teams
- Ability to use technology to enhance staff productivity and manage telework
- Good written and verbal communication skills
- Ability to analyze and quickly solve problems
- Demonstrates openness and flexibility
- Able to be decisive and follow through on a decision
- Able to establish effective relationships with diverse groups of people
- Able to coordinate several tasks at the same time and cope with deadlines
- Strong managerial skills, including managing budgets
- Knowledge of information and management systems
- Knowledge of financial resources

Educational and Licensing Requirements

Education and training requirements, as well as experience, vary widely depending on the size and complexity of the organization. In small social service agencies, experience and a bachelor's degree may be the only requirement for a management position, whereas in larger organizations, education at the graduate level and several years of experience and training may be needed.

Whatever the manager's educational background may be, it must be accompanied by relevant paid work experience reflecting the knowledge base and skills. Some top-level administration positions require additional certification or training beyond a master's degree. As an illustration of this, if your MSW concentrated on direct practice or clinical social work skills, even though you have had work experience as a supervisor of a staff providing social services to clients, you may need evidence of other training or education to demonstrate your knowledge and ability to assume a higher-level management position. This could be done through obtaining a certificate in nonprofit management or advanced training in human service management from a university or professional continuing education program.

Best Aspects of This Job

- Initiating and planning social change
- Independence
- Higher salary
- Mentoring others in professional development
- Creating innovative solutions to traditional problems
- Serving large-scale needs and achieving better outcomes
- Improving the quality of life for workers and clients
- Mediating conflict and growing consensus
- Expanding the delivery of social services to those in need
- Empowering persons in the workplace and in communities to lead the change in their lives

Challenging Aspects of This Job

- Responsibility 24 hours a day, 7 days a week for an organization or department
- Listening to employee problems
- Negotiating with bureaucratic barriers to change
- Managing transitions, change, and resistance
- Operating under tight budgets and searching for funding alternatives
- Firing employees or giving constructive feedback to employees who are not performing well
- Attending to details
- Multitasking often in a fast-paced environment

Compensation and Employment Outlook

Cost-cutting measures to improve profitability, streamline operations, and compete in various marketplaces will continue to be addressed by many public and private agencies during the next decade. This will result in a growing need to outsource or contract with organizational consultants and managers to provide administration, supervision, and the provision of social services outside of the main agency. Job opportunities vary from year to year, because the strength of the economy affects the demand for consulting, planning, and management services. Earnings of administrators greatly depend on the employer, the nature of the "business," and the geographic area. In general, for 2012, the median annual salary for sectors employing the largest numbers of managers was as follows:

Management of companies and enterprises	$88,600
General medical and surgical hospitals	$88,580
State and local government	$81,600
Colleges, universities, and professional schools	$76,800

Source: U.S. Department of Labor, Bureau of Labor Statistics, 2014.

Self-Assessment Checklist: Is This Job for Me?

- Are you politically savvy?
- Can you stick to a course of action after you make a decision?
- Do you enjoy working with different types of people?
- Do you thrive on getting the details "right?"
- Would you be flexible in the amount of time you may need to put into your workday?
- Are you able to handle a number of responsibilities at one time and still move forward?
- Are you okay with making tough decisions that will not always be popular with your staff?
- Do you have the knowledge and skills to mentor and train others?
- Would you enjoy learning about organizations and how they work?
- Are you able to see "the bigger picture" of an issue and communicate this so others may understand?

If you were able to answer "yes" to seven or more questions, get ready to assume a professional leadership role in some area of social work practice as you develop your career goals!

RECOMMENDED READINGS/WEBSITES TO LEARN MORE

Association for Community Organization and Social Administration: www. acosa.org

Bray, I. (2013). *Effective fundraising for nonprofits: Real-world strategies that work* (4th ed.). Berkeley, CA: NOLO.

Intrator, S. M., & Scribner, M. (2007). *Leading from within.* San Francisco, CA: Jossey-Bass.

Kadushin, A., & Harkness, D. (2014). *Supervision in social work* (5th ed.). New York, NY: Columbia University Press.

National Association of Social Workers: www.socialworkers.org
National Center on Nonprofit Enterprise: www.nationalcne.org
National Network of Grantmakers: www.nng.org
Public Administration and Management: www.pamij.com
Reamer, F. G. (2001). *The Social Work Ethics Audit: A risk management tool.* Washington, DC: NASW Press.
The Network for Social Work Management: www.socialworkmanager.org
The Network for Social Work Management, New Jersey Chapter: https://socialworkmanager.org/new-jersey-chapter
Westley, F., Zimmerman, B., & Patton, M. (2006). *Getting to maybe: How the world is changed.* Toronto: Random House Canada.

Leadership in Human Service Organizations Exercise

John Nguyen is the executive director of the only HIV awareness and prevention program in a small county. A significant portion of his agency's budget is received from the federal government, with matching funds from the state. A small amount of revenue is generated from local donations. Mr. Nguyen has learned that in 3 months the federal government will no longer be funding prevention programs. This prevention program targets teens at risk and provides needed testing and counseling. He knows that he will not have the money to pay his staff, his office rent, or his own salary, and fears he may have to close down his agency.

Questions

1. What is the first thing you would do if you were Mr. Nguyen?
2. Should this program continue, and how will you evaluate this?
3. What available community assets or resources could be helpful in the planning process here?

REFERENCES

Allen, S. A., & Vakalahi, H. F. O. (2013). My team members are everywhere! A critical analysis of the emerging literature on dispersed teams. *Administration in Social Work, 37,* 1–8.
Intrator, S. M., & Scribner, M. (2007). *Leading from within.* San Francisco, CA: Jossey-Bass.
U.S. Department of Labor, Bureau of Labor Statistics. (2014). *Occupational outlook handbook, 2014–2015.* Retrieved from www.bls.gov/ooh

16 ■ CAREERS IN RESEARCH AND ACADEMIA

When people think of social workers, they do not often think about "professors" or "researchers." However, there are thousands of social workers across the country who earn a doctorate (PhD) so that they can engage in research and educate the future social work workforce by teaching in university schools of social work. Lifelong learning and continuing education beyond the bachelor's degree in social work (BSW) or master's degree in social work (MSW) is embraced and promoted in social work education. After a number of years of experience, some practicing social workers with an MSW decide to return to graduate school to earn their doctorate and pursue a career in academia or research. An individual may earn a PhD or doctorate in social work (DSW) depending on the degree offered by a particular university. The process of earning a doctorate is a long and challenging road, but the rewards are great. Social work professors are in high demand these days both because of the retirement of current professors at the end of their careers and the steady growth of social work programs in the United States.

The specific requirements for earning a PhD or DSW vary by university. However, a person must have a passion for teaching and the research process. General requirements for earning the degree include earning an MSW, 2 years of post-MSW experience (to teach social work practice courses), obtaining admission to a PhD or DSW program, completing the required course work, passing the comprehensive examinations, and completing a dissertation.

Generally, admission requirements include submission of a university and program application, letters of recommendations, a writing sample, results of the Graduate Record Examination (GRE) or other standardized tests, and other documents requested by the respective university. These admission applications and supporting documents are reviewed and decided on by the PhD admission committee.

Earning the PhD or DSW may take 3 to 10 years, depending on the program and the length of time needed to complete the dissertation stage. The curriculum generally includes advanced courses in policy, research, statistics, and theory. After a student successfully completes these courses, he or she must pass a comprehensive examination related to these courses. After the comprehensive examination, the doctoral student moves to the dissertation stage. In the dissertation stage, students:

1. Select a topic of interest
2. Select a committee with a chair
3. Obtain committee approval of a dissertation proposal
4. Carry out independent research, including data collection and analysis
5. Write the dissertation
6. Defend the dissertation

Upon successful defense of the dissertation, a student earns a doctorate.

Those with a PhD or DSW earn the title "doctor" and have the opportunity and responsibility to engage in service to the community, molding minds, and to contribute to the knowledge base in social work by engaging in innovative and cutting-edge research.

This chapter will highlight some common career tracks for those with a PhD or DSW.

SOCIAL WORK RESEARCHER

Researchers contribute extensively to the practice of social work by devoting their career to furthering knowledge in a given topic of interest. They have important questions that they would like to answer through research. They contribute to the knowledge base by publishing books and articles in peer-reviewed journals. Researchers are employed by governmental bodies, including local, state, and federal governments, as well as by nongovernmental agencies, including private, nonprofit, or for-profit organizations.

Some researchers are employed by universities as research faculty. The University of Hawai'i/Manoa Social Welfare Evaluation, Research, and Training Unit, for example, provides evaluation, research, and training consultation and services to community agencies that provide social welfare services to the people of Hawai'i and the Pacific/Asian region. Likewise, the University of Texas at Austin funds the Center for Social Work Research, which oversees dozens of research projects in any given year. The Institute for the Advancement of Social Work Research (IASWR) and the Society for Social Work and Research (SSWR) are organizations devoted to members whose interests include social work research.

SOCIAL WORK PROFESSOR

Professors are commonly employed by universities at both private and public institutions. An individual begins as an assistant professor, and after 6 to 7 years, he or she may apply for tenure and promotion to associate professor. Tenure gives a professor job security at the granting institution. To be tenured, one must demonstrate excellence in service, teaching, and research. The tenure-earning years can be most stressful for a faculty member thanks to the pressure of what is known as the "publish or perish" effect, but after tenure is earned, job security is increased tremendously. These tenure-earning professors contribute to academia and the profession as a whole through research, teaching, and service. Other faculty positions include practice or clinical faculty, research faculty, and other variations according to terms and contracted responsibilities that are determined by each institution. Non–tenure-eligible, full-time practice faculty, in particular, is becoming an item of further conversation in social work programs as being less expensive in a time of decreasing or scarce resources.

The teaching load for social work university professors varies by university, but is usually somewhere between two and four courses a semester with summers off. If you choose to work for an institution that is research-intensive, the teaching load is lighter due to the increasing demand to engage in research and publication. Those working in universities that emphasize teaching should expect a more demanding teaching schedule. Other than teaching, professors spend their time writing and finding ways to contribute to their community, often by serving on boards of directors or engaging in research and evaluation. Professors are also expected to provide service to their college by serving on various university committees.

Social Worker Spotlight
JESSICA A. RITTER, BSW, MSSW, PhD
Director of BSW Program and Associate Professor, Pacific University, Forest Grove, Oregon

I completed my PhD in social work at the University of Texas at Austin in 2006, and I am a now a tenured social work professor. I have to say, "I *love* my job." Every day, I have the rare opportunity to sit in front of a classroom and talk to undergraduate college students about important social problems in the United States and around the world. My favorite social work classes to teach are macro social work and social policy and social justice, in which my goal is to show social work students that social work at the community level and in the political arena is exciting and interesting and not as scary or intimidating as they often imagine.

Since I have been a social work professor, I have published a number of journal articles, two of which report the results of my dissertation study focused on the political participation of social workers. I have also published two books that are used in social work classes across the country (one of them this one!). However, my true passion is preparing social work students for the wonderfully challenging roles of social workers. Since I have been teaching, my accomplishments as a professor include applying and receiving funds to take students with me to attend Social Work Day at the United Nations in New York City; taking one student with me to Durban, South Africa, to present at an international social work conference; helping students in my macro social work class get a resolution passed by the Portland City Council; organizing a legislative advocacy day for social work students in the greater Portland area; testifying before the Oregon state legislature to promote the rights of undocumented college students to pay in-state college tuition; serving as chair of the Legislative Committee for National Association for Social Workers in Oregon; and serving on the board of directors of the advocacy organization Children First for Oregon.

I am also the director of my small social work program, which has only two social work professors. One of my main tasks is to oversee the curriculum to ensure that we are preparing students to be prepared to practice social work at the micro and macro levels. I also need to make sure that we are meeting the standards set by the Council on Social Work Education.

The best part of my job is teaching and mentoring social work students and serving as advisor of the social work club. Social work students inspire me every day because of their idealism and their desire to make a difference in the lives of individuals, families, and communities. I could not ask for a better job.

ADJUNCT FACULTY/LECTURER

Teaching load and research expectations vary by university. For these reasons, other than the tenure-track positions, social work education programs also employ adjunct professors or lecturers to teach on a part-time, temporary basis in an area of the faculty member's specialty. The continuous growth of social work programs in terms of numbers and curriculum development have resulted in the demand for qualified adjunct professors and lecturers, particularly in social work practice and field education courses. This setting is an excellent choice for social workers who choose to practice social work in the community while also engaging in the education of future social workers. It is not necessary to have a PhD to work as an adjunct faculty member—you just need to have a demonstrated area of expertise as a social work practitioner.

FIELD EDUCATION DIRECTOR/COORDINATOR

Social work is unique among many other academic programs in that, being an applied science, it requires a substantial amount of student field education as a requisite for completing the BSW and MSW. Field education directors are dynamic individuals who have the exciting responsibility of overseeing the field program and coordinating the performance and progress of students, community agencies, and liaisons in the social work program. They establish critical relationships with social service agencies in the community, domestic and international, in which students may be placed to complete the field education requirement. These agencies vary in the services they provide, which could range from casework to individual therapy to political advocacy.

Large social work programs often employ field faculty or clinical faculty whose job is to teach the field seminar and work with students as they progress through the field experience to assess their growth and to assist with any problems that may arise in their field placement. They also train the field instructors who work in the agencies and supervise students in the field to ensure that students have a meaningful learning experience. Field faculty members collaborate with students in planning and implementing their field experience(s) to ensure that they gain skills appropriate for practicing social work upon completion of the degree. The field experience is where the classroom knowledge and experiential learning all come together.

Depending on the academic institution, some field directors are on a tenure-track position and must fulfill the tenure and promotion requirements in order to continue employment, whereas other institutions offer full-time employment with a contract renewal clause. Most field faculty members have their MSW and some have earned a PhD.

DIRECTOR OF SPECIAL PROGRAMS

Often, academic institutions will house interdisciplinary programs that specialize in research, teaching, or clinical work related to their disciplines. For example, the Fordham University Graduate School of Social Service promotes several research centers and institutes: The Bertram M. Beck Institute for Religion and Poverty, the Institute for Women and Girls, and the Ravazzin Center on Aging. Likewise, the various departments and schools of the Western Michigan University College of Health and Human Services provide state-of-the-art clinical programs through its unified clinics to the community. Examples of the estimated dozen unified clinics include the Children's Trauma Assessment Center, Activities of Daily Living Clinic, and Comprehensive Women's Health Clinic. Another example is the Center on Race and Social Problems at the University of Pittsburgh, School of Social Work. Also, an example of a center established by a professional organization is the Council on Social Work Education's (CSWE) Center for Diversity and Social and Economic Justice. Many of these programs are directed or staffed by social work faculty. These settings offer further opportunities to increase the profile of the university and for faculty to continue conducting research and pursuing their professional interests.

PROGRAM DIRECTOR/DEPARTMENT CHAIR/DEAN

Some professors also choose to pursue administrative positions, such as BSW or MSW program director, department chair, dean, or even the provost or president of a university. These administrative positions involve a high level of involvement and leadership in areas such as student admission and registration, curriculum development, financial aid, student life, academic recruitment and retention, faculty life, campus facilities and development, budgeting and finances, and public relations. They are involved not only in overseeing the affairs of the program or university and governing policies and procedures, but also in taking a leadership role in deciding how the program or institution will develop and grow.

Core Competencies and Skills

- Excellent teaching skills to make the classroom an exciting, stimulating, and safe place for students to learn
- Ability to craft and stay committed to a research agenda over the course of a career in academia
- Strong research skills, including ability to engage in data collection and statistical analysis
- Expertise in writing grants and getting external funding for research
- Strong administrative skills and the ability to navigate the politics of academia

- Superior writing skills—a large part of this job involves writing books and research articles
- Good speaking skills, used in teaching and conference presentations
- Ability to link research findings to the practice and theories of social work
- Strong critical thinking skills

Educational and Licensing Requirements

The educational requirements for earning and completing a DSW or PhD were explained in the beginning of this chapter. Earning a doctorate requires a lot of perseverance and determination, because it takes a number of years to complete, and you are being trained to be a scholar in your field. However, it is a wonderful career for anyone who loves teaching and research and wants to have a career with a lot of flexibility and independence. Licensing does not apply to those with a PhD in social work, but many professors and researchers choose to keep up their license as a social worker.

Best Aspects of This Job

- Enjoyment of academic freedom in relation to facilitation of critical thinking and thinking outside the box about social issues among both faculty and students
- Enjoyment of flexible schedules (e.g., faculty are off on weekends, holidays, winter, spring, and summer breaks; faculty have control of their day's plan)
- Opportunity to attend exciting research conferences all over the country and even abroad
- Enjoyment of the opportunity to teach future social workers, conduct research according to your interest, and provide services to your community and university
- Job security and academic freedom protected once academic tenure is earned
- Opportunity to climb the ranks of assistant, associate, and full professor, bringing increase in esteem and salary
- Opportunity to pursue administrative endeavors and learn the politics of the academy

Challenging Aspects of This Job

- Many research and teaching jobs lack the structure and community feel of other jobs, which can feel lonely and isolating for some people.

- The heavy expectations to publish and to gather external funding can be very stressful.
- Balancing the teaching, research, and service expectations of professors can be challenging.
- Professors must be able to adapt to the changing needs of young people and their learning preferences.
- Social work professors must engage in gate-keeping, which involves weeding out students who are not a good fit for the social work profession.
- Social work academics must be careful not to get lost in the ivory tower and need to find ways to stay connected to their practice field.
- The politics of academia can be challenging to deal with.

Compensation and Employment Outlook

Salaries for university professors vary according to state as well as private or public institutions. In 2014, the median expected annual salary for a social work professor in some parts of the United States is about $85,300. Other areas in the United States have a median salary of $56,000 (Salary.com, 2014).

DSW or PhD education has positively affected the employment outlook for social work educators. Current trends indicate that doctoral-level social work faculty is in demand. Across the United States, there are more faculty vacancies than earned doctorates to fill these job vacancies, so when you go out on the job market you will be heavily pursued and have your pick of available faculty positions.

Self-Assessment Checklist: Is This Job for Me?

- Are you extremely self-motivated (since you will be in charge of completing your own projects and meeting self-imposed deadlines)?
- Do you have a love of learning and a thirst for knowledge?
- Do you have a passion for teaching college students?
- Would you enjoy having access to cutting-edge knowledge and working with experts in various fields?
- Can you handle criticism and rejection (e.g., teaching evaluations, submitting articles for publication)?
- Are you someone who often spends time thinking about important questions that you would like to address through research?
- Do you have strong writing skills and the ability to work on a draft and revise over and over again until it is acceptable for publication?
- Would you enjoy a job where you are extremely independent and do not have coworkers or supervisors in the traditional sense?
- Do you enjoy all phases of the research process from coming up with the question to coming up with the appropriate methodology to collecting and analyzing the data?

■ Would you find it fulfilling to train and educate social work students and help them plan their careers?

If you answered "yes" to seven or more of the preceding questions, then getting a DSW or PhD in social work might be for you!

RECOMMENDED READINGS/WEBSITES TO LEARN MORE

Association of Baccalaureate Program Directors: www.bpdonline.org

Council on Social Work Education: www.cswe.org

Group for the Advancement of Doctoral Education in Social Work: www.gadephd.org

Institute for the Advancement of Social Work Research: www.iaswresearch.org

Journal of Social Work Education: www.cswe.org/CSWE/publications/journal

National Institute of Mental Health: www.nimh.nih.gov

Social Work (journal): www.naswpress.org/publications/journals/social work/swintro.html

Society of Social Work and Research: www.sswr.org

Research and Academia Exercise

Take a few minutes to think about and select a social problem that you are very passionate about and then answer the following:

1. What aspect of this problem would you most want to know or understand?
2. What would your research question(s) be?
3. How would you find out whether there has already been research conducted to answer this question? Where would you go to find out?
4. If you were going to devise a research project to answer this question, how would you gather your data (e.g., surveys, interviews, observation, review of existing data set or records)? What are the benefits and disadvantages of these various approaches?
5. Would this be a qualitative or quantitative study? (If you do not know the difference, do an Internet search.)
6. Does your question pass the following test: *So what?*
7. What relevance does this question have for the social work profession?

REFERENCE

Salary.com. (2014). *Professor—Social work salaries.* Retrieved from www1.salary.com/Professor-Social-Work-Salary.html

17 ■ "OUT OF THE BOX" SOCIAL WORK CAREERS

Throughout this book, we have described an impressive array of options that are available for you when you choose a career in social work. Many of these are better known and traditional, such as careers in schools, child welfare offices, or health and mental health care settings. So in this final chapter focusing on careers in social work, we want to encourage you to think outside of the box when it comes to creating a career path that is exciting and tailored to your unique strengths, talents, and interests. Many social workers are blazing new paths and finding social work career paths that are new and exciting such as working in the political arena (see Chapter 13), working in international social work (see Chapter 11), and working as researchers (see Chapter 16). There are countless numbers of social workers in this country, such as Dr. Murali Nair, who have done just that. Dr. Nair has written 10 books, has presented several photography exhibits around the country and overseas, and has been involved in the production of six documentaries. And Elaine Charpentier Philippi is another great example of a social worker who is doing a job that is somewhat untraditional for a social worker—working with the private sector to support young people in gaining vital work skills by offering paid internships to high school and college students in Oregon. Please read their profiles later in the chapter. They are two examples of many in the United States who are thinking outside of the box when it comes to how they can contribute their unique talents as social workers.

DUAL DEGREES

One aspect of the social work profession that is quite special is the opportunity to combine your social work degree with other degrees. Many social workers have multiple passions, and this is a great way to merge those interests. Joint programs have become very popular as universities respond to the appeals of social workers who wish to obtain an array of dual degrees, such as social work and law, social work and public policy, social work and public health, social work and business/nonprofit administration, and so forth.

NOVELIST/JOURNALIST

Social workers are in the unique position of seeing, firsthand, the vast array of social problems experienced by the most vulnerable people in our country—an exciting, yet often daunting, place to be. Because they see and experience life in a way that most people do not, they have a unique perspective to share with the world. Every day they are dealing with fascinating, heartbreaking people and situations: child abuse, poverty and homelessness, drug abuse, mental illness, and sexual assault and violence, to name a few.

Social workers who enjoy writing can choose to use fiction writing or journalism as a way to share their unique viewpoints and outlooks with the world. We can very easily see social workers doing "human interest" stories for newspapers, television shows, and other media outlets. In this new age of reality television, there are ample opportunities for social workers to highlight important social problems in this country and around the world.

Social Worker Spotlight
ANNE DRISCOLL, LCSW
Journalist, Author of the *Girl to Girl* Guidebooks

As a girl I dreamed of becoming a writer, but to the oldest of four children from an Irish Catholic working-class family, that impractical dream seemed well beyond reach. I didn't know any writers, and I didn't know anyone who knew any writers, so when I became the first of my family to pack off to college, I was practical and chose a career I hoped I could actually make a living from. Since I was always interested in what made people tick, I chose to pursue social work at a public college, and the training, education, and internships I received there served me memorably well after I graduated during the 3 years I worked with juvenile delinquent girls. But then it dawned on me—I wasn't really supporting myself all that well as a social worker—so I decided to pursue my dream and become a writer after all. Again, though, it seemed nearly just as impractical and unlikely a career choice as before, since I didn't have any training at all—or so I thought. In the 25 years I've been working as a journalist, there isn't a day that goes by when I'm not thankful for the skills I learned as a social worker: interviewing people from all kinds of circumstances, building a rapport with people from all types of backgrounds, getting them to trust you, open up, and tell you things.

I started out writing for the tiny *North Shore Sunday* and ended up writing for the colossal *New York Times*. It's been an amazing journey. I've been managing editor of *New England Bride Magazine*. I've written for the news wire services, ghostwritten three books on psychic skills and parapsychology, written a series of self-help books for tween-aged girls, and covered a triple murder trial and multiple-alarm fires. I've interviewed both George Clooney on a red carpet for *People* magazine and a woman who is considered a living saint in India. And I now know that it's not only the skills that are the same in both social work and journalism, but it is also the function that is the same, as well. Remarkably, in both roles, you act as a witness for the other person, you validate their experience. That is the basis of the therapeutic social work relationship and it is also the foundation of a journalist's job. The difference is that as a social worker, it's you and that person in an office; as a reporter, it's you and that person and, in the case of *People* magazine, 36 million other readers. My name, Anne, means grace or prayer, and Driscoll means interpreter, intermediary, news bearer. I only hope I live up to my name.

For more information, visit annedriscoll.com or mastermediaspeakers .com.

DOCUMENTARY FILMMAKER

This is a great option for social workers who are attracted to filmmaking and want to tell compelling human interest stories. You have probably seen Michael Moore's *Sicko* and Al Gore's *An Inconvenient Truth*, which were both commercial and critical hits at the box office. Social workers who are trained as filmmakers have the ability to educate the general public and decision makers about the multitude of social problems that social workers confront daily.

Film can be a powerful tool for social change. We live in a media age, and filmmakers have the opportunity to tell important stories, reach millions of people, and educate others about important social justice issues in this country and around the world.

Social Worker Spotlight
MURALI D. NAIR, PhD
Communicating Beyond Print Media

I received my doctorate in social welfare from Columbia University and my master's degree in computer science from New York Institute of Technology. I currently serve as professor of social work at Cleveland State University. Cross-cultural and cross-national understanding of poverty, disaster management, and healing across cultures are some of the interests of mine.

Along with writing 10 social work–related books, I was involved in the production of 6 documentaries, including a 30-minute documentary "Sri Lanka Experience," which documents my interactions with close to 100 poor families in tsunami-affected areas. Photography is a childhood hobby of mine. Over the years, I have had several photo exhibits around the country and overseas.

Enriching our senses is an art. Observing, hearing, tasting, feeling, and smelling needs to be optimized for personal and others consumption. Compared to other senses, visual representation of things seems to stay with us for a long time. There is even a popular saying: "A picture is worth a thousand words."

Though I have been teaching undergraduate and graduate social work students for the past 32 years and have published 10 books, lately I am drawn more and more to producing documentaries. In the past 10 years, I have been involved in six documentaries helping with everything from camera work, editing, scripting, voice-over, and cover design. To me, self-fulfillment in the production of an audiovisual work is much greater than writing a book or an article.

What is involved in making a documentary? Typically, I use video and still cameras in digital format. For a 30-minute video, I may tape up to 100 hours. Before going to the location, I create a mental image of what I intend to obtain on that particular day, then I write a script. Sometimes, I may not be able to collect all the information I need from the field, and at other times, there are new surprises that I should be able to capture spontaneously on my camera.

Subjects for three of my documentaries were from locations where the subjects spoke in local languages. Special attention is needed to make sure voice-over is done properly.

Once all the video, audio, and still clippings are collected from the field, then the real task of editing begins. It can be an emotional issue. I try to save the hundreds of hours of footage rather than discarding it. Every

(continued)

ARTIST

Many social workers who are extremely talented artists in the areas of music, acting, painting, and dance have found creative ways to combine this with a career in social work. Some mental health professionals use art in a therapeutic context with their clients (e.g., music therapy, dance therapy). Others create nonprofit organizations and include art programs as an integral part of their service delivery system. Many organizations have learned that this can be a valuable intervention strategy with at-risk youth, older adults, and a variety of other client populations. For example, youth who have a difficult time expressing themselves by talking may find it safer and more therapeutic to express themselves through writing, music, acting, or painting.

CORPORATE CONSULTANT

Increasingly, social workers are being hired by corporations to fill a variety of important roles, of which consultant may be one. Executives and managers hire consultants in order to help them analyze and improve the operations of the organization. For more on organizational consulting, see Chapter 15.

CAREERS IN HUMAN RESOURCES

Because social workers are highly skilled in communication, group work, mediation, and crisis intervention, many corporations recognize that professional social workers have a unique contribution to make to the "human element" of their operations. Social workers who wish to work in corporate settings can make excellent human resource managers, overseeing recruitment, staff development and training, team building and team development, employee services and perks, organizational work–life balance programs, and much more.

Social Worker Spotlight
ELAINE CHARPENTIER PHILIPPI, BSW, MSW
Program Manager, the Business Education Compact, Beaverton, Oregon

I completed my bachelor's degree in social work (BSW) at Pacific University in 2011. I was a nontraditional student with a breadth of life experience and a long history of working with youth. During my undergraduate social work education, it became apparent to me that macro-level practice had a gravitational pull on me. My search for employment led me to a nonprofit organization, the Business Education Compact, which focuses on student achievement and was doing work at the macro, mezzo, and micro levels. I accepted an entry-level position offering support to two programs: a paid student internship program and a program that focused on professional teacher development. The agency where I am employed is not a typical one for a social worker, but my social work training has prepared me well for this unique position.

Here's an excerpt from the BEC website (www.becpdx.org):

The Business Education Compact (BEC) is a 501(c)(3) nonprofit organization founded in 1984. The BEC's mission to "Make Learning Real" is fulfilled through highly effective programs that prepare students for their future and success in school and work. We do that by

■ Transforming K–12 education through proficiency-based teaching and learning to ensure that every student achieves academic success
■ Providing impactful learning experiences inside and outside the classroom to help students discover and pursue their career dreams and interests.

Highly collaborative partnerships with business and education are key to our work. Together we are improving the quality of education, building inspired connections between learning and working, and helping to prepare a qualified workforce.

As an agent of change, I was able to identify fairly quickly that there were gaps in our delivery of services to our student interns. I advocated for a full-time position for myself in that program, and just 4 months after being hired, I was working exclusively with our student interns. The BEC works with the private sector to place high school and college students into paid

(continued)

ELAINE CHARPENTIER PHILIPPI   (*continued*)

internships so that they can acquire valuable work skills that will help pre-pare them for their future careers.

Because our community/business partners host our students, and our nonprofit carries the role of employer of record, my job was to support the students' professional development as well as carry out any human resources (HR) responsibilities, including professional/personal coaching, performance planning, and termination, when necessary. I worked with our students to build relationships, establish our role as employer, and advocate to help them realize their professional goals. I also established HR processes and coaching of our site supervisors in an effort to minimize the number of terminations we were asked to perform.

I would like to share one success story. One of our site supervisors referred an intern to me for coaching shortly after they had started their internship. The student was high school–aged and had grown up in a home-schooled environment. All of his friends were friends that his parents had selected for him through their church and other home-school groups; he had little con-tact with people outside his family's faith community. He was selected over other student intern candidates because he interviewed with confidence and was very easy to talk to. However, during the internship, it became apparent that he did not have the confidence he demonstrated in the interview pro-cess, and it was showing in his work. He lacked initiative, seemed scattered, had trouble with recall when working on tasks, and struggled to reach out to the work group to follow through with assigned tasks.

I met with the student and offered a collaborative approach to how we might work together to increase his skill sets in a way that would support the work expected of him in his internship. We talked about his strengths and the things that he enjoyed, and then we tackled the performance barriers brought to my attention by his site supervisors. Together, we identified that the skill set gaps he was experiencing were largely informed by the sheltered life he had known. He had always checked in with his parents before making almost any decision, and in their absence he was worried that he could not be successful. We built a performance and professional development plan and met together regularly over the next 2 months until his confidence and performance increased.

This last week, I had the honor of recognizing him at our semiannual intern recognition event. He has grown personally and professionally and was recognized by his site supervisor as the intern who has set the bar for future interns. His integrity, follow-through, and ability to own projects was celebrated.

(*continued*)

ELAINE CHARPENTIER PHILIPPI   (continued)

As I continued to advocate for change within the programs and the overall system of our agency, I began to identify strengths of the individuals and groups that I was working with and worked to build collaborative systems that would enhance the mission of our agency. Our staff and leadership are committed to and passionate about student achievement, which leads to a culture of skilled professionals interested in change, if change is what is required to have the greatest effect on the population that we serve. The wheel is now turning at a steady pace with all staff focused on growth and development of programs and themselves. It is an exciting place to be.

In 2014, 3 years after coming to my organization, I am completing my master's degree in social work (MSW) at Portland State University with a focus on administration and leadership. My role has grown to program manager where I am now overseeing two programs and staff. I am passionate about growth and development at the personal, program, and organizational levels. I work to bring this passion to my supervision meetings with staff, to the development of infrastructure and evaluation informed program change, and to strategic organizational growth.

My degrees in social work have provided me with the tools that I have needed to effect positive change in my organization. It continues to inform and drive me personally and professionally, and I cannot imagine doing it any other way.

CAREERS IN MEDIATION AND CONFLICT RESOLUTION

Mediation is a growing field in social work practice, because social workers are natural mediators and are skilled in helping people resolve disputes. Mediation is part of the larger field of conflict resolution. Mediation involves an impartial person who has the skills to empower others to resolve their conflicts in a constructive way. A mediator understands the "art of compromise." When a mediator has done his or her job well, the parties will reach an agreement, and no one will feel as if he or she "lost." Mediation has been traditionally used in legal settings as a way to help parties reach an agreement in child welfare, child custody, and divorce cases to avoid going to trial (see Chapter 10). However, this practice has been greatly expanded and is now being used in health care, the workplace, labor disputes, in neighborhoods and communities, in landlord/tenant disputes, and in international affairs and peace-keeping efforts. Social work schools are responding to this growing demand by offering special course-work, joint degrees, and certificate programs in mediation and conflict resolution.

OMBUDSMAN

A job related to mediation and conflict resolution is that of an ombudsman. An ombudsman can be found in many government agencies and businesses and is charged with responding to complaints from clients, customers, or members of the public. One example in Oregon is the special ombudsman position that is housed in the Department of Human Services, charged with responding to complaints from youth in state foster care. An ombudsman must have strong investigation skills because his or her work involves trying to gather information to assess what has transpired in a given situation.

SELF-EMPLOYMENT/CONSULTING CAREERS

Being "self-employed" as a social worker used to mean that you were an independently licensed mental health professional in your own private practice or that you worked as a consultant and trainer to organizations. A large number of social workers have learned the business skills required for self-employment on their own and have started their own business, nonprofit organization, or consulting group.

A growing opportunity in this area is the ability for social workers to work in primary care settings, where they consult with physicians, nurses, and other medical staff on mental health issues. These social workers are sometimes referred to as behavioral health consultants. However, social workers who have developed an expertise in a given area or field of practice may be hired by other organizations in the United States or abroad to help with developing a new agency or program.

ANIMAL-ASSISTED SOCIAL WORK

There has been a growing interest by social workers in exploring the therapeutic use of animals to help humans. There are a number of programs that use horses and dogs, for example, with various populations such as older adults, those in prison, and those with disabilities. Some therapists use "therapy dogs" with children. In fact, the University of Denver Graduate School of Social Work has a new program in which social workers can earn a certificate in this area.

Social Worker Spotlight
RICHARD B. JOELSON, DSW, LCSW
Private Practice, New York, New York

My decision to enter the field of social work was, I suppose, somewhat unusual. I became a Peace Corps Volunteer in Liberia, West Africa, immediately after graduation from college in 1965. In addition to my job as an elementary and high school teacher, I worked in a tribal mental hospital alongside a Canadian psychiatrist and several native healers (better known to us as "witch doctors"). The experience dazzled me, and I decided to get trained as a social worker when I returned to the States. The profession seemed just right for me. Fortunately, Columbia University School of Social Work agreed and accepted me with a full-tuition scholarship for the first year of the 2-year master's program.

I have enjoyed a diversified professional life throughout my career, both before and after entering private practice. My first job was the proverbial trial by fire. I was a youth parole social worker with a caseload of 100 troubled adolescent boys living in a Brooklyn ghetto. After that, I worked as a psychiatric social worker and group therapist at a child and family guidance center. My subsequent employment included stints as a director of social work, as an executive director at a mental health clinic in Greenwich Village, and as director of admissions and student affairs at the New York University (NYU) School of Social Work.

My entrance into private practice occurred sooner than I had planned. While at my second job—the child and family guidance center—many families who were on the clinic waiting list requested opportunities to see a staff member privately, rather than wait for weeks and months for service. Senior staff and administrators encouraged me (it didn't take much) to open my own practice so that I could accept referrals from the waiting list. And so my private practice was born!

The private practice of social work and I were a good fit from the start. As someone who always valued autonomy and was comfortable operating independently (perhaps traceable to the loss of my father at an early age), I liked the freedom of being what has been called "an agency of one." With good training and clinical and administrative background, and, I believe, many of the qualities associated with successful autonomous functioning, I enjoyed an active part-time practice for many years prior to making the leap into full-time practice after 5 years as an NYU administrator.

I have been in full-time practice since leaving that job in 1984 and have thoroughly enjoyed my experience and the many opportunities it has afforded

(continued)

RICHARD B. JOELSON   *(continued)*

me. I have taken pride in making full use of the social work principles and values I hold dear. After being in full-time practice for 7 years and feeling the need for a new challenge, I entered the doctoral program at Hunter College School of Social Work in New York and graduated with my doctorate in social work (DSW) 5 years later. I remain pleased that my particular degree indicates that my doctorate is in social work, as opposed to a doctorate (PhD), which is silent on the matter of what subject area was studied.

Beginning in 1991, I taught a course entitled "How to Develop a Private Practice: Essential Steps," which drew many new and seasoned social work practitioners who wanted to begin a private practice or strengthen an already existing one. The course gave me a wonderful opportunity to "preach what I practiced" to others, as well as an additional opportunity to be professionally active out of my office and not just inside; something I have always encouraged other private practitioners to do, as well.

Currently, in addition to a still full schedule of clients in my practice, I have developed a website designed as a resource for people interested in understanding issues and topics in the field of mental health, as well as identifying services available if necessary. I am often contacted by people who read my articles or my monthly newsletter, asking for help in knowing more about existing services and how to access them. This provision gives me a great deal of satisfaction. I have always believed that mental health professionals have an obligation to educate and enlighten the public on matters about which there is still too much mystery, distorted thinking, and negative beliefs. My website is one way that I try to help those unfamiliar with the field of mental health to become open to seeking the help they need.

For more information about Richard B. Joelson, DSW, and his work, visit www.richardbjoelsondsw.com or www.psychotherapy-info.com

SOCIAL ENTREPRENEUR

The concepts behind social innovation and the skills of entrepreneurship have emerged as new areas for the growth of the social work profession. There are now dual and joint degree programs in social work that combine the MSW with a master's degree in business administration, helping social workers understand the technical business knowledge needed to run a successful operation. Entrepreneurship skills take the social work profession a step farther. Creating your own nonprofit agency with innovative service delivery to consumers or developing a business that promotes social and economic benefits for the community is an exciting venture for a "social work entrepreneur." Social work entrepreneurs are able to find new and creative ways to solve some of our most pressing social problems.

ATTORNEY

Many social workers have an interest in law and legal advocacy and go on to work in the following legal arenas: human rights work at the national or international level; children's advocacy, where they may serve as attorneys ad litem for children in the foster care system or those in the middle of a custody dispute; family law; public defender's work, representing those accused of a crime; and the Legal Aid Society, to represent those with limited incomes.

As you can see, there is no "typical" social work career. You don't have to do what is traditional or expected. Don't be scared to create your own unique career as a social worker. Be a rebel. Blaze your own path—the options and opportunities are endless!

RECOMMENDED READINGS/WEBSITES TO LEARN MORE

Art as Healing: www.artashealing.org

Community for Creative Non-Violence: http://users.erols.com/ccnv

Expressive Arts Institute: www.arts4change.com

Linda Grobman, Social Worker/Publisher: www.lindagrobman.com

Pipher, M. (2006). *Writing to change the world.* New York, NY: Riverhead Books.

Schwab Foundation for Social Entrepreneurship: www.schwabfound.org

Small Business Administration: www.sba.gov

Stanford Social Innovation Review: www.ssireview.org/topics/category/social_entrepreneurship

Social Worker and Beyond Exercise

Take a few minutes to brainstorm your hobbies, interests, and passions (separate from social work). Think about what you most enjoy doing when you have some free time and what kinds of activities bring you joy. Write down each one that comes to mind on a piece of paper.

Questions

1. How might you combine these interests with a career in social work?
2. Who might be able to serve as a mentor(s) for you as you work toward creating a unique career of your own?
3. What will your next steps be?

III ■ WHERE DO WE GO FROM HERE?

18 ■ PAYING FOR YOUR SOCIAL WORK EDUCATION

One of the realities of getting a college education is figuring out the best way to pay for this rather expensive investment. Some students are lucky enough to have their education financed by their parents, but many more must rely on a combination of part-time or full-time work, scholarships, and financial aid, which can include grants and loans through the federal government. The theme of this chapter is that you have to be a smart consumer, and you have to take some time to do your research to find out about the vast array of opportunities that are out there to help you pay for your college education.

More and more, students are taking longer than 4 years to complete a 4-year degree. Instead of saving money, many students are actually spending thousands more in tuition payments by extending their time in school when they work more than 15 hours a week. In addition, several studies have shown that there are negative consequences to a student's overall grade point average (GPA) the more hours they work per week while enrolled full time in school (Hawkins, Smith, Hawkins, & Grant, 2005). If your plans include graduate studies later in life, an unsatisfactory undergraduate GPA can be an extremely limiting factor in terms of which programs will admit you. Thus, most experts will discourage students from working full time while going to college because it is simply too challenging to balance work and school.

Working is a necessity for most of us, and a certain amount of part-time work is often helpful in keeping a balanced structure to the day and staying organized with studying and assignments. Looking at paying for college from a financial planning perspective in addition to applying for financial aid may help you reduce the number of hours you feel you must be employed and maximize the time you need to enjoy your education.

THE RISING COSTS OF HIGHER EDUCATION

There are countless news stories that are reporting on the rising costs of higher education (in both public and private universities) in recent years and the hardships this is creating for students who leave college with tens of thousands of dollars in student loan debt. This is particularly concerning for students who are choosing public service careers such as social work with lower starting salaries.

Some state and federal lawmakers are attempting to find ways to bring these costs down, but in the meantime, students need to be creative in finding ways to finance their education to avoid being burdened by debt.

- For students earning your undergraduate degree, you might consider spending the first 2 years at a community college in order to get all your prerequisites completed and then transferring to a 4-year college for your junior and senior year. This will save you a lot of money, but if you take this approach, you will want to be careful when choosing your classes to make sure the classes will transfer to the 4-year college where you plan to transfer. Work closely with your college advisors in the advising office, who often have this information at their fingertips.
- Another great way to earn money while you are in college is to work part time on your campus. Some of these jobs are financed by the Federal Work Study Program (http://studentaid.ed.gov/types/work-study) and you may have a position on or off campus. Some students will work for a professor as a teaching assistant (TA) or research assistant (RA). Holding a job on campus is a convenient option and helps you to build relationships and work experience.
- Apply to several schools and do a cost comparison when considering the cost of tuition and the financial aid package that is offered to you. Some students are scared to consider applying to a private university, but after the aid package is factored in, there may not be as much of a price difference as you would think. Many private universities offer admitted students a significant amount of student aid, and in some cases the final cost can be lower than attending a public university.

THE PUBLIC SERVICE LOAN FORGIVENESS PROGRAM

The Public Service Loan Forgiveness Program is an exciting new federal program that is designed to encourage Americans to enter and continue to work full time in public service jobs. Under this program, borrowers may qualify for forgiveness of the remaining balance of their direct loans after they have made 120 qualifying payments on those loans while employed full time by certain public service employers. This means that any loan money that you owe after 10 years of paying on your student loans will be forgiven by the federal government. There is a process to become eligible for this program, and there are many details, so you will need to do your homework carefully to take advantage of this program. An overview of this program can be found at http://studentaid.ed.gov/repay-loans/forgiveness-cancellation/charts/public-service.

CONDUCTING A SCHOLARSHIP SEARCH

First, let's talk about the free money that's available. The scholarship search begins with learning the best strategy for conducting a search. There are many search engines that can help you navigate the thousands of scholarships available to undergraduate and graduate students.

One of the best free search engines is through the Sallie Mae Corporation at www.collegeanswer.com, where you can register and open an account. You will find very useful information regarding loans, grants, filling out the Free Application for Federal Student Aid (FAFSA) form, and, of course, beginning your search for free scholarship money.

Many social work students become frustrated in their search because only a handful of small dollar amount scholarships are found in the field of social work. However, if you pay attention to certain key words as you fill out your profile for a scholarship search, you will find larger scholarships that almost any student could apply for today.

- It is more helpful to look at your scholarship search as if it is a job, not just a few minutes on Google to see what comes up when you plug in "social work." Dedicate a day every 2 months or so to review your profile and renew your search.
- Scholarship deadlines occur all year long, so you are bound to find something substantial to apply for just about any time you look.
- Fill out your scholarship profile on your Sallie Mae account by looking at every category and filling in what is relevant to you. You can change your profile often, so don't stick with the same information; doing so will keep bringing up the same scholarships.
- For instance, if you look at the ethnicity field at the beginning of the profile and you happen to be of African American, Irish, and Native American heritage, don't select all three at one time—doing so will block out certain key words and "confuse" the system. Try one or two categories at a time. The same is true for the athletics/sports and hobbies categories—try just two or three.
- Read what comes up in your search very carefully. First, look at the scholarships that have at least an 85% match to your profile and then look at the largest dollar amounts. Don't skim through this information—you may miss out on applying for something you actually could be awarded.
- Spend time in crafting your application essay, and make sure it includes the key words that are spelled out in the guidelines. For instance, if you have found a scholarship that is given to a student interested in *leadership* and *social justice* in the *community*, your essay should have these words somewhere in there. Many applications are submitted online and key words play a big part in this format.

- In searching for scholarship money, it is important for social work students to keep in mind these key words: human services, public service, community service, advocacy, social justice, peace, leadership, innovation, communication, marketing, public relations, entrepreneurship, political advocacy, and government service, just to name a few. Many scholarships are focused on the attributes of student applicants and not necessarily what subject they are studying.

OTHER METHODS OF FINANCING YOUR EDUCATION

There are a few more items of information to think about regarding financial planning versus financial aid. Other ways to finance your education include

- Taking out money from your IRA or 401(k), if you have one. A person may pull out up to $10,000 from a retirement account for education purposes without paying a fee in penalty.
- Applying for a home equity line of credit or home equity loan to finance your education. You may also be able to itemize the interest rate on that loan on your income tax forms.
- Looking at the tax benefits and allowable education expenses to deduct online at www.irs.gov by reading IRS Publication 970. Some of your expenses might qualify as education expenses, business expenses, or professional expenses. The IRS offers free help to answer any questions you may have, and it could be worth the time and a little bit of money to pay for expert advice from a tax consultant.
- If you are claimed as a dependent on your parents' tax forms, you may want to talk to them about speaking with a tax consultant. You may qualify for more financial aid if you are not claimed as a dependent.
- Last, many students do not take out enough in financial aid to begin with and do not know what education expenses they should be including in their package. Reviewing IRS Publication 970 should help you determine what your legitimate education expenses are.

SOCIAL WORK SCHOLARSHIPS, FELLOWSHIPS, AND OTHER PROGRAMS

Now you're ready to begin your search. One good place to start is to do an Internet search for "social work scholarships": You'll find a number of websites that list various social work scholarships. The following organizations are also great resources.

Council on Social Work Education

The Council on Social Work Education (CSWE) offers a number of scholarships and fellowships. Please visit www.cswe.org/CentersInitiatives/ScholarshipsandFellowships.aspx for more information.

National Association of Social Workers Foundation

The National Association of Social Workers (NASW) offers scholarships for master's degree in social work (MSW) and doctoral-level students in addition to a research grant to individual NASW state chapters. Click on the "scholarship" link at www.naswfoundation.org.

NASW Press

The journal *Social Work*, published for the NASW by the NASW Press, offers a $500 award for a bachelor's degree in social work (BSW)- or MSW-level student. Submission guidelines may be found at www.naswpress.org.

National Association of Black Social Workers

The National Association of Black Social Workers provides scholarships to qualified applicants every academic year. The scholarship amounts range from $250 to $2,000. Applications must be received by December 17, on the year before the scholarship is due. Any applications received after this date will not be accepted—no exceptions. It is the responsibility of the applicant to ensure that all of his or her materials are received by the required date. Applicants should follow the scholarship criteria and procedure sheet exactly to ensure eligibility of their application. Separate applications must be submitted for each scholarship for which he or she will be considered. For more information, go to www.nabsw.org, click on the "contact us" link, and call the office for scholarship information.

National Association of Puerto Rican and Hispanic Social Workers

The National Association of Puerto Rican and Hispanic Social Workers provides scholarships to full-time graduate social work students who can demonstrate interest in community organization and advocacy that impacts the Puerto Rican and Latino community. Financial need and academic proficiency should also be demonstrated. For more information, visit www.naprhsw.org and click the "Provide Scholarship Monies" link embedded in the second paragraph of the home page.

Jack Kent Cooke Foundation Undergraduate Scholarship Program

The Jack Kent Cooke Foundation Undergraduate Scholarship Program is open to students who currently attend community college or 2-year institutions located in the United States and who plan to transfer to a 4-year college or university. The award will provide funding for tuition, room and board, required fees, and books for the remainder of the recipient's undergraduate degree. Award amounts will vary for each recipient based on the institution he or she attends. Scholarship monies not used during one academic year are not transferable to the next academic year. The scholarship is renewable for each year of the undergraduate study if the scholar continues to meet the program requirements. Application guidelines are found at www.jackkentcookefoundation.org.

National Merit Scholarships

National Merit Finalists in high school who are admitted to college may be eligible for the National Merit Scholarship. Students must apply for admission by January 15 of their senior year. All eligible admission applicants are considered, so no separate application is required. National Merit Finalists are strongly considered for the Presidential Scholarships as well. For more information, go to www.finaid.gmu.edu.

National Science Foundation Graduate Research Fellowship

National Science Foundation Graduate Research Fellowships offer recognition and 3 years of support for *advanced study* to approximately 900 outstanding graduate students in the mathematical, physical, biological, engineering, and behavioral and social sciences, including the history of science and the philosophy of science, as well as to research-based doctorate (PhD) degrees in science education. Approximately 90 awards are in the women in engineering and women in computer and information science components. Awards made in March 2004 carried a stipend for each fellow of $30,000 for a 12-month tenure (prorated for lesser periods) and an annual cost-of-education allowance of $10,500, paid to the fellow's institution in lieu of tuition and fees. Information is available at www.nsf.org.

Scholarships for Cancer Survivors

Some divisions of the American Cancer Society offer college scholarships for pediatric cancer survivors. The Young Cancer Survivor Scholarships are restricted to students within the states served by the division, and details vary from division to division. Several hundred scholarships ranging from $1,000 to $10,000 are awarded each year. Information about these awards and the telephone number for your division can be obtained by calling the American Cancer Society at 1-800-ACS-2345 or by visiting www.cancer.org and entering "scholarships" into the search bar on the top of the home page. Scholarships are also available for nursing studies, including doctoral-level degrees.

Scholarship Information for Gay, Lesbian, Bisexual, Transgender, and Allies

The national association Parents, Families and Friends of Lesbians and Gays (PFLAG) offers several scholarships to high school seniors who self-identify as gay, lesbian, bisexual, transgendered, or allies (students who have an interest in serving this community). For additional information, visit www.pflag.org and click on the link "education and programs" for specific information related to scholarships.

Minority and Corporate Scholarships

There are many scholarships in this category. To see all the listings and application information, please go to www.menominee.edu/newcmn1/FinancialAid/Scholarships.htm.

Scholarships in this category include

■ **Public Relations Society of America (PRSA) National Minority Scholarship Program:** Send your letter of inquiry to the attention of Ms. Elaine Averick, 33 Irving Place, New York, NY 10003-2376. Scholarships are available to minority undergraduate students of junior standing or above. Public Relations Student Society of America member and major/minor in public relations are preferred; minimum GPA is 3.0. Award amount is $1,500.
■ **Coca-Cola 2-Year Colleges Scholarship Program:** For more information, call 1-800-306-2653, or contact Norma Kent at nkent@ aacc.nche.edu. Scholarships are offered for students who are attending 2-year degree-granting institutions throughout the United States, who have offered contributions to community service, and who have shown dedication to education. Scholarship awards must be used for educational expenses at a 2-year degree-granting institution. Please call 1-800-306-2653 for deadline information.

Scholarships for Foster Children and Adoptees

Many scholarships are found at the "scholarship" link of the national organization Onwards and Upwards. For additional information, please visit www .onwardsandupwards.org.

The cost of getting a college education may seem astronomical at first. However, once you have made the decision to pursue that college degree, consider any money you spend on your education as a long-term investment that will pay big dividends. Getting a college degree is like putting money in the bank. Once you land your first professional social work job, you will be earning a good salary to repay any educational loans you may have needed as part of your financial aid package. With a little bit of sweat equity in searching for scholarships, you may not need to take out as much money in loans as you think.

IN SUM

Now, take a deep breath and try not to panic. Your education is an investment, so don't dwell too much on the amount of "debt" you are taking on right now. Student loan debt is the best kind of debt to have in some ways, since it enables you to have your dream career. You will be able to have a good-paying job after you have earned your BSW or MSW, and you will soon be on your way to a sound financial strategy for managing your repayment plan. However, it is important to do your homework and be a smart consumer. Apply to several schools (both public and private) to see what they offer you in terms of a financial aid package. Try to get as much free money as you can in the way of grants and scholarships. And be aware that most students today will work at least part-time to help pay for their college education. Finally, be smart when deciding how much to borrow in student loans—you will be paying back those loans for years to come!

REFERENCE

Hawkins, C. A., Smith, M. L., Hawkins, R. C. II, & Grant, D. (2005). The relationship among hours employed, perceived work interference, and grades as reported by undergraduate social work students. *Journal of Social Work Education, 41*(1), 13–27.

19 ■ JOB HUNTING TIPS

If you are reading this chapter, you are practically on your way to finding that perfect social work job!

Once you discover that you want to be a social worker, one of the most challenging next steps is deciding what you want to do exactly out of the dizzying array of options. Stay abreast of new professional trends to plan your education and career paths accordingly. Many social work students report feeling interested in everything. Initially, you may be drawn to working with a number of client populations as you sit through your courses. Part of this process is discovering where you are most passionate, trying out a number of possibilities, and refining your interests through a process of elimination. All the while, you should keep in mind that the beauty of a social work degree is you can work with one client population for a number of years and then switch to do something different for an exciting new challenge. So you really just need to figure out where you want to begin your career, knowing that you have no idea where this career may end up taking you.

One tip is to take advantage of your field opportunities while you are in school. All social work programs will offer a variety of courses that require spending a certain number of hours in a social service organization, which gives you the opportunity to talk to social workers in a particular field and to see whether this feels like a good fit for you. During your senior year, you will do an intensive field practicum for one or two semesters (depending on the school) during which you will have the opportunity to develop your professional social work skills and understand how the theory and research that you learned in school connect to the practice of social work. Many students who have a wonderful experience in their practicum end up getting hired by the agency—a win for everyone. Others will need to be prepared for all that is involved in going into the job market and landing a job as a social worker.

Take advantage of any professional development workshops (e.g., résumé writing, appearance), seminars (i.e., licensing), and career fairs (i.e., jobs, jobs, jobs) offered by your field education office. Excellent resources regarding résumé preparation, cover letters, thank you letters, followup letters, interviewing, and conducting a job search, as well as linking to employers and job opportunities, may be found through the following resources:

- Careerbuilders.com: www.careerbuilders.com
- *The New Social Worker*: www.socialworkjobs.com
- The Riley Guide: www.rileyguide.com
- ResumeEdge.com: www.resumeedge.com
- Monster: www.monster.com/?re=nv_gh_monsterLogo_%2Fjob-interview%2Fcareers.aspx

BOOKS ON JOB HUNTING

Securing a job requires appropriate preparation of a résumé/curriculum vitae, interview techniques, and presentation. Take the time to create a résumé/curriculum vitae that will impress at first review. Take the time to practice your interviewing skills and responses to questions; doing so will increase your level of comfort and confidence. Whether you are just starting out in your social work career or are a seasoned practitioner looking for a new direction, please read *Social Work Career Development: A Handbook for Job Hunting and Career Planning*, by Carol Nesslein Doelling. This 2005 publication of the NASW Press is well worth its cost. It includes a section on researching potential jobs, networking, résumé writing, and more.

Another excellent resource, particularly for younger graduates, is Nicholas Aretakis's 2006 book *No More Ramen: The 20-Something's Real-World Survival Guide*. This book is very useful in helping you navigate through the minefield of job postings and the online application process. How you format a résumé for an online application often differs from how you would prepare your more formal written résumé. You can also find information from www .NoMoreRamenOnline.com.

One of the best and most affordable guides is *Knock 'em Dead: The Ultimate Job Seeker's Guide*. This book has excellent advice on the interviewing process and negotiating better salaries or benefits, topics with which many of us need assistance when we are first looking for work after graduation.

JOB HUNTING WEBSITES

Many large social work programs have their own job listing area on their website. Specific job listings for social workers are available at the Social Work Job Bank (www.socialworkjobs.com), as well as the national office of the National Association of Social Workers (NASW; www.socialworkers.org) and the NASW state chapter associations.

Check out www.idealist.org for information about internships, fellowships, employment, and volunteer opportunities. Many internships and fellowships are also paid and some provide health benefits. They can be a good short-term solution to keeping you financially afloat and at the same time help you build your experience.

The following websites offer many excellent job opportunities:

■ State employment offices provide information on the application process for state-related jobs in addition to information regarding starting a small business in the state.

■ Federal government: www.usajobs.gov is the official website for federal employment. An additional online resource is www .federaljobsearch.com.

■ U.S. Department of State: There are several career opportunities here, such as foreign service officer, civil service officer, and foreign service specialist, in addition to numerous student internships. More information may be obtained by going to www.state.gov/careers.

■ In the U.S. Department of Health and Human Services (HHS) there is the Emerging Leaders program, which accepts postgraduate students in a 2-year program as part of which they may rotate within the 12 agencies under the umbrella of HHS—see www.hhs.gov/jobs/elp for information on the program as well as for application information.

■ Some students consider applying for a program such as AmeriCorps after graduation, which gives them great experience and the opportunity to get funding for graduate school: www.nationalservice. gov/programs/americorps

■ A 2-year postgraduate fellowship, the Presidential Management Fellows Program (www.pmf.opm.gov), also involves rotational assignments throughout the federal government, including in Congress.

■ Another program in leadership and service, known to be quite competitive, is the White House Fellows Program: www.whitehouse.gov/fellows

■ Other job opportunities for social workers may be found at the Federal Bureau of Investigation (FBI) (www.fbi.gov) and the Centers for Disease Control and Prevention (www.cdc.gov).

Some proactive media through which to share your professional background and interests include the following:

■ LinkedIn (professional profile)
■ Facebook (wide distribution of information through social networking)
■ Institutional or organizational websites
■ Professional listservs

INTERNATIONAL SOCIAL WORK OPPORTUNITIES

If you have always dreamed of traveling or spending time in a foreign country, you may be interested in opportunities for international social work positions. The following organizations offer information as well as job postings:

- Peace Corps: www.peacecorps.gov offers many overseas job opportunities, with a typical 2-year commitment.
- London Qualified Social Workers: www.lqsw.com
- International Federation of Social Work: www.ifsw.org
- International Association of Schools of Social Work: www.iassw-aiets.org
- United Nations: www.UN.org

For a brief article on international social work, go to www.socialworkjobbank .com and follow the "Resources" link to access articles.

ONLINE JOB HUNTING

Because most job searches these days are online, it is important to understand the function of key words in looking for employment opportunities in areas for which social workers are qualified. Start your search by exploring the types of jobs these key words find for you and see how your education and skills match up to the job descriptions. The better the match, the better the chance your résumé will rise to the top of those résumés that employers pull "out of the slush pile" to review. Here are some key words often found in social work jobs:

- executive, director, coordinator, manager, supervisor, administrator, public administrator, development director, fund-raising
- human resources, human services, social services, social work, family services, group services
- social justice, justice, peace and justice, advocacy, lobbying, social policy, policy, policy planning, policy analyst, public administration
- community planning, community development, development planner, regional planner, community organizer, tenant organizer, program planner, community outreach worker
- communications, media, public relations
- counseling, health, mental health, behavioral health, psychology, direct services, case management, community mental health worker
- research, education, support services

CREATING YOUR RÉSUMÉ

As an exercise to get you started in applying for a professional social work job, try formatting your education and experience using the following template:

A. **Name and full contact information, including mobile telephone number and e-mail address:** Create a nice heading and use at least a 14-point font in bold lettering. Employers need to be able to read your contact information to call you for that perfect job. Do not bother to write what your career goals or objectives are: Everyone knows your main goal is to be employed.

B. Education: Put your most recent degree first, giving only the year you received the degree. If you have a master's degree, you no longer need to list high school information. If you have a bachelor's degree, continue to list high school. Make sure to include the name of the school and the city and state where you attended.

C. Certifications and Licenses: Have you received special training or licensing such as Microsoft Office Certification, cardiopulmonary resuscitation (CPR) or Red Cross training, or a social work license of any kind? If so, list it here.

D. Languages: If you have a second-language capability, even at a basic level, enter that information in this section, including any proficiency you may have in American Sign Language.

E. Professional Experience: Include any paid work experience you had while attending college or after graduation. Start with your most recent job first, then work your way back to your undergraduate days. Enter your job title, name of company, city and state, general time frame of employment, and briefly outline what you did in the job. For example:

> Medical social worker, Virginia Hospital, Arlington, Virginia, 2006–present. Responsibilities included conducting intakes and assessments of all emergency room patients, providing information and referral resources, and attending multidisciplinary team meetings.

F. Internships: Use the same format as in the preceding example, and include the number of hours you completed.

G. Service Activities: Typically, this should encompass any volunteer or civic activities you perform. List your role, name of organization, city, state, and time served in that capacity.

H. Awards and Honors: This category includes any achievement you were recognized for in high school, college, or graduate school. You may have won an outstanding athlete award or been inducted into the National Honor Society; these are important items for employers to see if they apply to you. If not, leave this category out of your résumé for the time being.

I. Professional Memberships: Even if you are a student member of an organization such as a fraternity or the NASW, those are professional memberships.

J. Continuing Education Trainings Attended: The section refers to professional formal programs you attended and not casual office trainings. Usually you will receive a certificate of attendance for this type of program. You should keep those for your records.

K. **References:** List three references with their name, title, and *full* contact information, including telephone numbers and e-mail address.

Don't worry about making your résumé look like something Donald Trump would expect to receive. Keep the font clean and simple, in a readable size, and on white or beige paper that is a step above multiuse paper for printers. Plain white linen paper with black or dark blue ink is always a winning combination.

Review your résumé for typing errors and grammatical mistakes. One small error may be enough to put your résumé below many others, and you could miss out on being called to interview for the position you think would be a perfect fit for you.

NETWORKING

Now that you have a professional looking résumé in order, finding your dream job is the next step. One of the most helpful hints all the career development and job hunting resources will give you is to make use of the people you already know and any personal contacts you have through them: In other words, network! This is the number-one source for most people finding a job. Networking in person or through social media is the basic foundation of information sharing, and the more you know about potential openings in different areas, the better prepared you are to submit your résumé and be called for an interview.

Give or e-mail a copy of your résumé to your parents, your friends' parents, college professors, and the family you babysat for in high school. They all have networks and professional contacts, and one of them may be interested in you for that first social work job. With the advancement of technology worldwide, sharing your professional information through a large network is quick and simple.

Best wishes to you as you move closer to having an extraordinary career as a professional social worker.

EPILOGUE

The authors of this book are in various stages of their own social work careers and firmly believe that social work is a career for an extraordinary life. It is challenging, rewarding, exciting, and demanding, all at the same time. It is a career that allows for tremendous professional and personal growth. It is never boring. It requires many skills and personal characteristics, such as compassion; patience; strong ethics; critical thinking; creativity; self-care; strong communication skills; and a passion for helping individuals, families, groups, organizations, and communities. It is a career that will continue to be in demand for years to come, providing job security for many aspiring social workers in this country. The goal of this book has been fourfold:

- To answer the question: What is social work?
- To help readers assess whether they are well suited for a career in social work
- To profile more than 101 career options for social workers and to help readers evaluate which of these might be a good fit for them
- To provide readers with the tools they need to creatively plan their social work career based on their unique skills and interests

As we stated earlier in this book, social work is a wonderful career, but it is not for everyone. There are many misconceptions about social work, so we recommend taking an introductory social work course and talking to social workers in the field. Do some volunteer work where social workers are employed. Get to know yourself very well to assess whether you have the skills and personality needed to be an effective and competent social worker. Are you compassionate and nonjudgmental? Do you get upset by social injustice and inequality? Are you an effective communicator as well as a good listener? Do you have good problem-solving skills? Do you believe that all individuals have dignity and worth? Is appreciating differences among people something you celebrate?

One of the most exciting features of social work is that we get to work with a wide variety of client populations in a vast array of employment settings. Social workers are change agents who work to create positive change with individuals, families, groups, organizations, and communities. We work at the individual level as caseworkers and clinicians, and we also work at the macro level to create needed social and political change at the local, state, national, and international levels. And the best part is you can work in one area of practice for a period of time and then change your career focus to work with a new population, issue, or passion.

The social workers profiled in this book studied social work because it is a profession committed to social justice and helping those in our country who are often forgotten and marginalized. A social work education provides students with the knowledge, values, and skills to intervene with individuals and families in need. But social work students also study and learn to address social problems on a larger scale at the macro level—problems such as poverty and homelessness; violence in our families and communities; the millions of Americans who face barriers to health care; discrimination; child abuse, neglect, and exploitation; human rights violations; inequalities in our public schools; and lack of mental health services. Social workers not only help individuals function better within their environment, but also work on changing the environment so it works better for individuals and families. This is one of the defining features of the social work profession.

If the six core values of the social work profession (service, social justice, competence, the importance of human relationships, integrity, and the dignity and worth of the person) speak to you, then you just might be a social worker!

MORE INFORMATION ABOUT THE SOCIAL WORK PROFESSION

1. National Association of Social Workers: www.socialworkers.org
2. Council on Social Work Education: www.cswe.org
3. Glicken, M. D. (2010). *Social work in the 21st century: An introduction to social welfare, social issues, and the profession* (2nd ed.). Thousand Oaks, CA: Sage.
4. Grobman, L. M. (2011). *Days in the lives of social workers: 58 professionals tell "real-life" stories from social work practice* (4th ed.). Harrisburg, PA: White Hat Communications.
5. Information for Practice: www.nyu.edu/socialwork/ip
6. *Legacies of Social Change: 100 Years of Professional Social Work in the United States*. Video available from NASW Press, www.socialworkers.org

7. Morales, A. T., Sheafor, B. W., & Scott, M. E. (2011). *Social work: A profession of many faces* (12th ed.). Boston, MA: Allyn & Bacon.

8. *The New Social Worker:* www.socialworker.com

9. Segal, E. A., Gerdes, K. E., & Steiner, S. (2012). *An introduction to the profession of social work: Becoming a change agent* (4th ed.). Belmont, CA: Brooks/Cole.

10. Social Workers: Help Starts Here: www.helpstartshere.org

INDEX